THE NEUROSCIENCE OF RELIGIOUS EXPERIENCE

Recent technical advances in the life and medical sciences have revolutionized our understanding of the brain, while the emerging disciplines of social, cognitive, and affective neuroscience continue to reveal the connections of the higher cognitive functions and emotional states associated with religious experience to underlying brain states. At the same time, a host of developing theories in psychology and anthropology posit evolutionary explanations for the ubiquity and persistence of religious beliefs and the reports of religious experiences across human cultures, while gesturing toward physical bases for these behaviors. What is missing from this literature is a strong voice speaking to these behavioral and social scientists – as well as to the intellectually curious in the religious studies community – from the perspective of a brain scientist.

Dr. Patrick McNamara is an Associate Professor of Neurology at Boston University School of Medicine. He has previously edited the three-volume series on religion and the brain entitled *Where God and Science Meet: How Brain and Evolutionary Studies Alter Our Understanding of Religion.* He is the recipient of a VA Merit Review Award for the study of Parkinson's Disease and several National Institutes of Health awards for the study of sleep mechanisms. Dr. McNamara is a member of the American Psychological Association, Division 36, Psychology of Religion; the Society for the Scientific Study of Religion; the International Association for the Cognitive Science of Religion; and the Human Behavior and Evolution Society.

The Neuroscience of Religious Experience

PATRICK McNAMARA

Boston University School of Medicine

CAMBRIDGE
UNIVERSITY PRESS

CAMBRIDGE
UNIVERSITY PRESS

32 Avenue of the Americas, New York NY 10013-2473, USA

Cambridge University Press is part of the University of Cambridge.

It furthers the University's mission by disseminating knowledge in the pursuit of education, learning and research at the highest international levels of excellence.

www.cambridge.org
Information on this title: www.cambridge.org/9781107428010

© Patrick McNamara 2009

First published 2009
First paperback edition 2014

A catalogue record for this publication is available from the British Library

Library of Congress Cataloguing in Publication data

McNamara, Patrick, 1956–
The neuroscience of religious experience / Patrick McNamara.
 p. cm.
Includes bibliographical references and indexes.
ISBN 978-0-521-88958-2 (hardback)
1. Psychology, Religious. 2. Evolutionary psychology. I. Title.
BL53.M355 2009
200.1'9–dc22   2009013025

ISBN 978-0-521-88958-2 Hardback
ISBN 978-1-107-42801-0 Paperback

To:
Ina Livia McNamara
On her first birthday, September 20, 2008

Contents

Preface

Religion is a defining mark of humanity – as emblematic of its bearer as the web for the spider, the dam for the beaver, and the song for the bird. It is, at least partially, created by human beings, and we can learn much about ourselves by studying it as a product of our minds and bodies. Humanity not only creates religion but is also created by it. Religious beliefs and behaviors exert a profound impact on mental and physical health, dietary habits, mating preferences, and economic behavior. They sustain many lethal conflicts and help to heal many others. For billions of people the world over, religious experiences and beliefs influence who they marry, how they rear their children, whom they spend time with, and how they comport themselves in daily life. It may well be that we would not be as we find ourselves in the twenty-first century if our ancestors had not been intensely religious for most of the "life" of our species. It is high time that we have a real science of religion, and thankfully, breakthrough research on religion begun in the last decades of the twentieth century has culminated in the first decade of the twenty-first century in what is arguably the birth of a new science of religion rooted in detailed anthropologic, cognitive, and neuroscientific studies of the manifold features of religious experiences and in evolutionary approaches to religious experiences and behaviors.

This new science of religion has built on work by previous anthropologic, sociologic, psychologic, and "religious studies" investigations conducted throughout the twentieth century by scholars in those fields. Cross-talk between the cognitive neurosciences and the religious studies field needs to increase, however, as most studies of religion by neuroscientists (mine included, I'm afraid) are too focused on the theistic forms of religion common in the West. We need to teach ourselves something about the richness and complexity of religious phenomena before we make any grand claims about its putative functions.

Although cognitive neuroscience has much to offer to the scientific study of religion or religion studies, religion, in turn, has much to teach the cognitive neuroscientists. As far as I can see, none of the extant cognitive or neuroscience models of human nature or of the Mind/brain can adequately account for the range of behavioral and cognitive phenomena associated with religion. The empirical facts with which religion scholars have been grappling for decades, or better, centuries, simply cannot yet be adequately handled by the current models of the Mind/brain in the cognitive neurosciences. I have, therefore, elected in this book to emphasize the empirical data before us in a few selected domains of religious phenomena. I have wherever possible quoted extensively from original sources so that readers and future investigators can get a feel for the kind of behavioral and experimental changes one sees in religious people and in religion-related disorders.

My overall aim in this book is a modest one: I wish to contribute to the emerging cognitive neuroscientific study of religious experiences and practices. Although I attempt to take some account of non-Western, non-theistic, as well as ancient and ancestral forms of religious phenomena, my focus is mainly limited to the theistic forms of religious experience common in the West. My only justification for doing so is my own ignorance of religious traditions other than my own. One has to start somewhere if one is going to make any progress. I have nevertheless attempted to bring into the discussion those aspects of non-Western traditions that I believe can be profitably illuminated by the cognitive and neuroscience perspective that I adopt in this book. I therefore review the available literature on the neurology and neurochemistry of religious experiences of individuals from East and West as well as more traditional forms of religiosity such as shamanism and ancestor worship. Although the range of variance in religious experiences across cultures and time epochs is unknown, I find that changes in religious experiences in the sample of subjects that have been studied with cognitive and neuroscientific techniques are, in fact, reliably associated with a complex circuit of neural structures. This, of course, is a remarkable fact. The fact that a particular circuit of brain regions is consistently associated with religious experiences may tell us something about the nature and functions of religion. Whatever else it is, religion is an integral part of human nature and thus religion is not mere delusion. The functionally integrated religion-related brain circuit involves a widely distributed set of neural regions (depending on particular religious behaviors) but nearly always includes the key nodes of the amygdala, the right anterior temporal cortex, and the right prefrontal cortex. Sometimes the subcortical amygdala is not part of the picture, but the hippocampus is. Sometimes one portion of the prefrontal cortex does not "light up" in association with religious practices, whereas another region of the prefrontal cortex will. Sometimes the parietal lobes are implicated, and so on. Nevertheless, in hundreds of clinical cases and a handful of neuroimaging studies, it is a striking fact that the amygdala, large portions of the prefrontal lobes, and the anterior temporal cortex are repeatedly implicated in expression of religious experiences.

Next, I examine the impact of religious practices on the "Self" and on self-consciousness. I define what I mean by the Self in Chapter 2. Interestingly, there is considerable anatomical overlap between the brain sites implicated in religious experience and the brain sites implicated in the sense of Self and self-consciousness. I then show that religious practices often operate to support transformation of the Self such that the Self becomes more like an "ideal Self" that the individual hopes to become. This hoped-for Self is a more centralized and unified sense of Self. Religious practices also help one to avoid becoming a "feared Self." This combination of a positive "approach" motivational element toward a hoped-for Self and a negative "avoidance" motivational element away from a feared Self makes religion a powerful tool for processes of self-regulation more generally. In short, I argue that religious practices contribute to the creation of a unified self-consciousness and an ideal "executive Self."

Why create an executive Self? The executive Self is better able than a disunified Self to compete, to cooperate, to plan, to think, and to make war. The executive Self can also better process highly complex forms of information; thus it is a better "platform" than is a divided Self for development of various forms of intelligence.

Some might agree with the claim that religions help to construct an executive or centralized form of the Self but add that that is an unfortunate fact. They see the centralized Self as authoritarian, repressive, and intolerant and therefore not desirable. My demonstration that religion helps to create a centralized executive Self, these critics would argue, is just one more reason to dispense with religion altogether.

I do not agree with that assessment. Although some forms of religion undoubtedly do contribute to some form of the Self that might be dubbed "authoritarian," I do not think that most forms of religion and religious practices do so. Instead, when religions are operating normally, they tend to create a healthy, unified, integrated sense of Self. Most religions aim at and are successful in creating mature, autonomous persons, capable of inhibiting their own impulses, planning wisely for the future, and extending service and kindness to others. Religions take as raw material the average man with all of his pettiness, selfishness, blindness, and violence and then create gold out of this unpromising raw material.

Religions accomplish this feat by promoting a cognitive process I call decentering. In this cognitive process, the "Self" (i.e., the Self-construct or the Self-concept) is temporarily taken "off-line" or decoupled from its control over attentional and behavioral goals of the individual while a search is conducted in semantic memory or a suppositional space (or in a "possible worlds" space) for a more ideal or complex Self-concept that can better match the needs and behavioral goals of the individual. When decentering occurs in religious ritual contexts, the ideal Self against which the old Self is compared may constitute a powerful ancestor, a saint, or a god. In these contexts, the old Self is replaced and integrated into a more ideal Self. Story or narrative grammars help to integrate the old into the new Self. New meaning is created, and the individual is enriched by the experience. I show throughout the book that this decentering process shapes many religious phenomena from healing rituals, to religious language, to possession states, and to prayer and religious experiences themselves.

The decentering process, however, can also go terribly wrong. One of the sequential steps in the process (e.g., decoupling, placing the old Self in suppositional space, the search in semantic memory for a more complex ideal Self, or integration into the ideal Self) can be blocked, damaged, or skipped, thus producing aberrant religious phenomena. Fanaticism or dedication to cult leaders, to take just one example, may result from failure to posit an ideal Self or from premature termination of the search process or fusion and integration into a cult leader's personality rather than an ideal Self. Negative spirit possession, to take another example, may involve fusion with a "feared Self" or identity and a failure to find, move toward, or integrate into an ideal identity.

Religious experiences are among the most powerful experiences that human beings can have. They can produce both awe-inspiring saintliness and horror-inspiring maliciousness. They can elicit the most profound pouring out of the Self for others in some people and the most abject self-absorption in others. They are often life changing and are certainly life-sustaining for those who profess them. The extremes produced by religion are all too obvious to require recitation here.

In the process of my work I have developed a fascination and respect for this most powerful of human experiences. I am not interested in debunking religion's supposed pretensions or calling it "nothing but..." Nor am I interested in becoming an ideologically motivated partisan for religion. Rather, I hope to offer readers a serious attempt to understand a wide range of religious phenomena and the powerfully transformative effects of religious experience.

Acknowledgments

I would like to thank Chris Curcio from Cambridge University Press for his advocacy of this project. I would also like to thank Emily Abrams, Donna Alvino, Andrea Avalos, Catherine Beauharnais, Emily Duggan, Patricia Johnson, Deirdre McLaren, and Alexandra Zaitsev for their help with editing and formatting the references for all of the chapters in the book – a thankless task at best, but these assistants did it both conscientiously and carefully. I would especially like to acknowledge Deirdre McLaren and Donna Alvino for obtaining and reviewing all of the case studies that are reported in the book. I thank Drs. Raymon Durso and Sanford Auerbach for many discussions on religion and the brain as well as support and guidance over many years. I thank Dr. Martin Albert for early mentoring and guidance and collegial friendship over many years. I would like to extend a special thanks to Erica Harris, my head Research Coordinator, who helped out on all aspects of this book project – all the while expertly managing a lab and office crew of 10 to 15 people each day. Her conscientious review of dozens of papers on neuroimaging studies of religious experiences is summarized in Tables 5.2 and 5.3a and b. Thanks go to Paul Butler for offering incisive comments on several chapters. My colleagues Wesley Wildman, Robert Neville, and James Burns of the Division of Religious Studies at Boston University tutored me as best they could on psychologic and philosophic issues of religious experience. My work with Wesley Wildman on the nature and functions of religious experience, in particular, has influenced my thought in this area. Robert Neville gave me invaluable feedback on Aquinas's account of free will and the "agent intellect." James Burns helped me to get more precise about claims concerning the interactions of religiousness and executive functions across the life span. My colleague Rich Sosis has inspired me to consider evolutionary aspects of religious behaviors. Joseph Bulbulia provided a detailed critique and offered many excellent suggestions for improvement of the manuscript for which I am very grateful. Finally, I would like to thank my wife, Reka Szent-Imrey, and my mother-in-law, Margit Farkas, for creating the space and the time I needed to write the book you now hold in your hands.

1 God and the Self

> The personal in man is just that in him which he does not have in common
> with others, but in that which is not shared with others is included the
> potentiality of the universal. But personality is not part of the universe,
> the universe is a part of personality, it is its quality. Such is the paradox of
> personalism.
>
> – Nikolai Berdyaev, 1949, p. 22

In the quote above, the Russian philosopher Berdyaev hints at the
"personalist" idea that the Self, while utterly unique, nonetheless contains a universal content that makes the Self an end in itself. The Self is
something that cannot be regarded as a means to some end no matter
how praiseworthy, but rather is an end that is irreplaceable, precious, and
infinitely valuable. Its dignity lies in its rationality, its universal content,
its irreplaceability – a consciousness that can deliberate rationally about
moral ends and choose the good and the true.

This book will examine religion through the eyes of this Self. There
are, of course, many ways to study religion, but I believe an approach to
religion through the lens of the Self will prove especially fruitful because
one of religion's major self-proclaimed aims is the salvation of the individual Self. Despite the Self's great dignity and worth, it is treated by
religion as conflicted and in need of salvation. The sacred texts of both

the theistic and nontheistic forms of religion explicitly claim that they provide a "way" or set of practices that will eventuate in individual salvation. Thus, by studying religion through the eyes of the individual Self, we will be taking religion's own claims about itself seriously.

A second reason for studying religion through the eyes of the Self is that, on the face of it, many religious forms and practices are about transformations of the Self. This focus on transformation of the Self, of course, follows logically from religion's claim that the Self is in need of salvation. Many religious rituals, practices, texts, and institutions are very clearly oriented toward transforming the individual from one state or status into another state or status. For example, many religions in ancestral or traditional societies practiced rites of initiation that would transform an adolescent into an adult. Religions both East and West provide a multitude of individual devotional practices that allow an individual to communicate with and receive guidance from a God and that help to inspire confidence, resilience, and courage. Other ritual practices include healing an individual who has become sick, forgiving an individual who has become lost, and comforting an individual who has become bereft. Many of the prayers, rituals, devotional practices, chants, and hymns found in all the world religions are formulated in the voice of the individual "I." Thus, our focus on the Self when studying religion has face validity. Whatever else it is, religion is very much about transforming the Self and is addressed to the needs of the Self.

A third benefit of looking at religion through the eyes of the Self is that the method will require that we give due regard to the role of the brain in the shaping of religious experiences. There is no human Self that is not embodied. Because no body can function without a brain, there is no human Self without the brain. Consequently, no account of religion's impact on the Self will be complete without an account of how the brain helps to shape expression of both religion and the Self. Obviously, this does not mean that both the Self and religion are only products of the brain. Rather, it means that the brain matters. It counts. To fully understand religious experience, particularly at the individual level, we will need to take into account the brain regions that support religious expression. In the West, the contrary idea that matter and embodiment do not matter was an old Gnostic idea that the Church Fathers fought against and refuted in the first centuries of the Common Era. Despite the ancient roots of the debate, there are still some authors who argue that the body and brain do not matter or at least are of no real importance relative to "things of the spirit," like culture. A careful examination of religion's impact on the Self will demonstrate the crucial importance of the brain in shaping religious experience and that the old Gnostic position on "matter" and embodiment is scientifically untenable.

A fourth benefit of looking at religion through the eyes of the Self is related to this idea of the importance of the brain in understanding religious experience and expression. It is obvious to anyone who has ever reflected on religion's effects on individuals that some of those effects can be quite harmful and even dangerous. Religion produces its share of saints and sinners, as well as visionaries and fanatics. As the events of September 11, 2001, and the international response to those events clearly demonstrate, religion can effectively inspire the most heinous of crimes. Why does religion have this ability to create the most desperate fanaticism and the most sublime saintliness in individuals? I will suggest that part of the answer to that question lies in a detailed understanding of how the brain and cognitive system support the interaction of Self and religious experiences.

A fifth benefit of looking at religion through the eyes of the Self is that we will be obliged to study a whole range of disorders involving changes in religious expression that afflict real people. If we can extend knowledge in this area, it may actually help people with these disorders. We will see in the chapters that follow that there are several disorders of the mind/brain that centrally involve religion in one way or another. Take, for example, schizophrenia with religious delusions. These unfortunate people can experience the most horrific auditory "command" hallucinations involving voices of supernatural agents who demand that the patient harm him- or herself or others. Or take the case of temporal lobe epilepsy (TLE). There have now been dozens of studies that convincingly demonstrate a link between some forms of TLE and heightened religiosity in some TLE patients. During preictal and ictal states, when seizure activity is building up or commences, the religious symptomology may escalate into delusional states during which the patient claims that he or she is God or has seen God face to face. These beliefs may prompt the patient to engage in dangerous or reckless behaviors. Or take a subclass of patients with obsessive-compulsive disorder – namely, the subclass of patients with scrupulosity. These patients may be riddled with anxiety and may spend hundreds of hours each week attempting to say a single prayer "correctly." Or take the case of so-called "demonic possession" states. These patients may become utterly convinced that they are controlled by an evil and alien agent that means them harm. Some patients may be so tortured by the possession experience that the state can be life threatening. Whatever the multifarious causes of these various psychiatric and brain disorders, the patients' religious beliefs are absolutely central to the phenomenology and clinical outcomes of the disorders. Thus, we will need to bring in an understanding of how religion works at the level of the mind/brain to understand and help someone with these sorts of disorders. To the extent that our study of religion's effects on individuals reveals clinical mechanisms of these religion-related disorders, our work may actually benefit some persons with these disorders.

A sixth benefit of looking at religion through the eyes of the Self is that you can test various theories of religion by careful examination of the predictions of those theories for the life of the individual Self. For example, suppose you theorize, as did Durkheim (1954) and many others after him, that religion functions to create within-group cooperation and solidarity. If true, the solidarity theory would predict that religious individuals would develop signaling strategies to identify and cooperate with in-group members. In other words, the solidarity theory predicts specific individual-level effects that can be tested by looking at individual behaviors. Signaling behaviors in particular must rely on the brain to be expressed, so once again, study of the Self's brain can illuminate theoretical constructs in the science of religion, in this case signaling theory. Another way to look at this benefit is to consider this fact: If you think religion promotes within-group cooperation, you can certainly test the theory by comparing religious groups to nonreligious groups on some measure of within-group cooperation. If you found that the religious group evidenced greater within-group cooperation than the nonreligious group, you would certainly have evidence that religion does indeed promote cooperation. What you would not have is an explanation as to how, at the individual level, religion promotes within-group cooperation. To obtain that sort of evidence, you would do well to look at the individual.

For all of these reasons, we will use the Self to probe potential core properties and functions of religion. Conversely, we will also examine the ways in which religion helps to produce and shape the Self. In the process, we will cover a fair amount of ground on both the properties of the Self and of religion. In doing so, we will end up with the materials that will motivate a new theory of both the relation of the Self to religion and the functions of both the Self and religion.

To forecast the main contours of the new theory of religion's effects on the individual, I will propose the following in this book: Insofar as religion is concerned with the Self, it functions to provide a range of techniques that have the effect of transiently "decentering" the agentive or executive Self. Decentering will be explained more fully in Chapter 3. Suffice it to say here that decentering involves a temporary decoupling of the Self from its control over executive cognitive functions and a search for some more effective controlling agency over cognitive resources and mechanisms. The idea is that religious practices create a decentering effect that transiently relaxes central control but that leads ultimately to greater self-control. Depending on the intensity of the decentering mechanism effected by a particular religious practice, operations and consciousness of the central executive Self are transiently suspended, and thus the individual enters a liminal state. That liminal state is filled with potentially positive and negative consequences. On the positive side, decentering puts the individual into a receptive and integrative mode, allowing the individual to perform a lot of off-line maintenance and integrative information-processing tasks. Religious practices and rituals provide the protective cognitive scaffolding to promote integration of all kinds of cognitive and emotional content in such a way as to put that content into the service again of the executive or agentive Self. This Self is enriched, transformed, and transfigured by religious beliefs and practices – depending on the intensity of those beliefs and practices. Another positive benefit of the decentering process is that the individual enters a kind of transient, trance-like state that promotes healing capacities of the organism. On the negative side of the ledger, the decentering process can, depending on context, lead to dangerous, disintegrative psychic states including fanaticism and psychotic and delusional states.

I will show that one can observe the mechanics of the decentering process by examining disorders that include a change in religious expression as part of the clinical picture. One can even see decentering at work in brain-damaged patients who spontaneously express changes in their religious interests. Studies of these same patients, along with studies of healthy research participants, are yielding a picture of the ways in which the brain shapes and mediates both normal and extreme religious experiences. These neuropsychological data also demonstrate considerable overlap between brain regions implicated in the Self-construct with regions implicated in religious experiences.

I claimed earlier in this chapter that the examination of religion from the point of view of the Self would also yield a new theoretical perspective on the nature and functions of the Self. This is what I mean: When we look at how the decentering process works and what its functional effects are, it soon becomes clear that the central executive Self functions to unify a range of capacities possessed by the individual so that the individual can more effectively pursue goals and desires. The Self is a tool that is specialized for accessing and orchestrating skills and processing resources and knowledge domains in service to the individual. Selves can access, create, orchestrate, and realize new human capacities and powers. They should be seen, in part, as tools or perceptual devices created by cultural beliefs and practices and put in service to an individual such that that individual can vastly increase his fitness by enhancing his cognitive and behavioral capacities. Insofar as religion is about individuals, it can be seen as an exquisitely attuned set of cultural practices that assists Selves in the process of creating new human cognitive powers and capacities. I will support all of these claims in the course of this book.

First I will begin by laying out a general picture of the relationship between religion and the individual, between religion and reason. Recall that the individual, the Self, is defined by its universal content – its ability to reason, to act as a rational agent. Thus, the relationship between religion and the Self will be defined by the relationship between religion and reason.

Fides et ratio. Reason and religion have more often been seen as enemies than as friends ever since the emergence of philosophy among the peoples of the ancient world. As the religions of the "Book" (Judaism, Christianity, and Islam) emerged and came into interaction with the philosophers of Greece in the West and India in the East, Jewish, Christian, and Muslim theologians attempted to find ways to reconcile reason with the revealed truths of their respective traditions. These efforts climaxed in the twelfth century of the Common Era in the universities of Paris and in the land of Al-Andalus when Andalusia was still ruled by the Muslim Almoravids. An accommodation between reason and religion was reached during this era such that religious truths were seen as consistent with reason. When inconsistencies were noted, it was assumed that more work needed to be done so that the inconsistencies could be overcome. It was assumed that inconsistencies were due to our own ignorance rather than to any supposed inherent flaws in either reason or religion.

In the West, the inconsistencies between reason and religion became more pressing and sharp with the rise and spectacular successes of science and technology beginning in the sixteenth century.

During the Age of Enlightenment in Europe, it became fashionable to excoriate religion as an absurdity and an infamy. The scientist, in turn, was cast as a kind of lone hero, working courageously against the ignorance, stupidity, and willful superstitions of the communities around him ... and, despite almost overwhelming odds and great self-sacrifice, the courageous scientist was able to achieve intellectual breakthroughs of the first magnitude that benefited the very people opposed to his scientific research.

The irony of such myth-laden accounts of the "struggles between reason and religion" is that most of the early scientists were profoundly religious men. Whatever the truth and merits of this standard myth regarding the role of the scientist in society, it has certainly helped to recruit armies of young men who want to be seen as heroes fighting in the noble cause of "the battle against religion, superstition, and ignorance." These young "heroes," despite their self-infatuation, have certainly made enormous contributions to knowledge and indeed to all of humanity. These

contributions, however, have to be attributed, at least in part, to the greatness of the scientific method rather than to any particular heroic efforts
of the scientists themselves. Despite big egos, petty political agendas, and
huge economic influences, reason and fact tend to win out in science.
Again, this is due to the greatness of the scientific method. This is not to
neglect the ways in which scientific and technical advances can be put
in service to some pretty destructive political purposes. Science produces
both technical marvels and a monstrous technics (such as nuclear and
chemical weaponry) as well. As Lewis Mumford (1966) pointed out, unless
humanity controls its machines, the machines will control humanity. It
may be that only religion can control the machine.

If the three great monotheistic religions arrived at a consensus understanding of the relationship between reason and faith during the Middle
Ages, that consensus did not survive the period of the Renaissance. What
happened to that consensus? How did religion get painted as antiscience
and irrational? How did religion get branded as irrational?

As just mentioned, the standard answer to that question has been that
religion repeatedly opposed scientific advances and thus was seen as a
retrogressive and fundamentally irrational force. Again, that explanation
cannot be correct given the fact that many scientists were religious men
and many churches and religious groups supported the advancement
of science in myriad ways from the founding of universities to funding
huge scientific research projects. So then, how did religion get branded
as irrational?

There are very likely many factors that fueled the reason–religion
divorce in the West that began at the time of the Renaissance and the
Enlightenment. During the Reformation, for example, some religious
people began to call themselves irrational. The principle of "sola scriptura," or the use of scripture alone rather than tradition and reason to
guide behavior, could be seen by some as an antirational trend in religion. The overemphasis on personal faith as the primary route to salvation had the side effect of valuing a stance (trust, faith) over rational deliberation about moral choices and so forth. The sola scriptura
doctrine shifted the accent away from rational interpretative traditions
and argument onto the individual with his idiosyncratic interpretative
tendencies and his haunted, lonely conscience. That move alone would

not have been fatal to the reason–religion relationship had it not been for the second idea – that faith alone saves. If faith was all that really counted, then you did not need established and rationally justified doctrines, traditions, priests, rituals, or institutions. Indeed, these things were even considered harmful. Faith was explicitly analyzed by some religious thinkers (e.g., Calvin; Kierkegaard) as fundamentally an irrational process, but religion need not be fundamentally irrational or antiscience. Scientific and technical innovation can proceed quite nicely without claiming that religion is irrational. Indeed, science has developed in all cultures on the planet regardless of their position on the reason–religion relationship.

As seen from the point of view of the Self or the individual, reason and religion cannot be opposed. Scientific work on the anthropology, psychology, and biology of religiousness has shown that religiousness is deeply embedded in the human psyche. Religiousness appears to be a human cultural universal and may even turn out to be a trait that is strongly influenced by standard, nonmysterious, evolutionary forces like any other biologic trait. Like that other quintessentially human skill, language, religiousness displays many of the telltale signs of a classic, evolutionarily shaped adaptation or suite of adaptations. Belief in supernatural agents, for example, appears to be acquired relatively effortlessly by children. Children do not need to be force-fed religion; they naturally develop religion's basic component processes. Religiousness, furthermore, varies continuously, as does any other personality trait. Some families and persons are "better" at religiousness than others. Religiousness is heritable. When one twin is religious, the other will likely be religious as well. There are genes that are consistently associated with high scores on religiousness scales. Religiousness, finally, has a definite biology: Some drugs enhance religiousness whereas others diminish it; some brain regions are more consistently associated with religiousness than are others, and so on. We will review all of this evidence in the pages to come.

If we assume, as I think we should, that all of this psychobiological evidence suggests that religion has some sort of functional benefit for individuals, then it follows that whatever else religion is, it is NOT merely irrational or a delusion, unless of course delusions are functional. Although there may be some delusions (e.g., positive illusions about the Self) that might be functional and therefore positive for the individual, these do not rise to the level of organization characteristic of religious ideas. My illusions about my wonderful abilities and character are not always shared by those people who interact with me on a daily basis. My religious beliefs, however, often are shared. They are more elaborate, more developed, and more demanding than are my personal illusions. My personal illusions accommodate my self-conceit, whereas my religious beliefs demand a better me. Religion therefore cannot be considered a personal illusion – even a positive one.

Instead, religion appears to serve some functional purpose for the individual. How do we identify that purpose? One way to identify potential functional benefits of religion for the individual is to investigate its mechanisms or how religious experiences are mediated by the brain and the cognitive system. By observing how something works, we can sometimes make reasonable inferences as to its function. Although it is clear that we can often better understand the mechanism of a thing by first understanding its function, in many instances we do not know the function of the thing. All we have before us is the thing itself or some basic knowledge about its workings or mechanisms. We can sometimes observe the workings of a thing to get clues about its functions. In these cases we can "reverse engineer" a mechanism to discover clues as to its function. This situation is the one we are in with respect to religion. By observing which brain regions are engaged during religious experiences or behaviors, we can get some clue as to what types of information are being processed and what types of information are not being processed during the experience. Attention to brain mechanisms of religious experiences and behaviors can therefore yield critical clues as to potential functions of religion.

There are problems, however, with basing a scientific enquiry on the reverse-engineering strategy when subjective experiences of a person or persons are involved. First, we can't see subjective experiences, and thus it is a bit harder (although not impossible) to measure them. We are one step removed from the object of study because we have to measure reports about experience instead of experience itself. Here is where the focus on the brain really helps. With modern neuroimaging technology, we can identify what parts of the brain are activated and deactivated when someone reports a religious experience or engages in a religious practice. Brain activation patterns can be measured. We can subtract the "reporting" portion of the report on religious experience by comparing reports of religious experience to reports of a similar form of experience (e.g., a happy intense experience). Because "reporting" effort is equated across the two forms of experience, any differences in brain activation pattern must be due to or at least associated with the experience itself.

Even when not using the control of neuroimaging technology to look at brain support of religious experience, we can use a similar experimental logic to look at the features of religious experience. We once again simply compare reports of religious experiences to similar reports of equally intense and memorable experiences. Differences in the two forms of report may be due, at least in part, to the features of the experiences themselves because the vividness, intensity, valence, and memorability of the reports have been equated. Even when we are able to note what brain regions are activated in association with subjective reports of religious experiences and not activated in association with equally intense and memorable nonreligious experiences, we are still left with the problem that all we have is a correlation or an association – the report and the experiences or the experience, the report about the experience, and a pattern of brain activation. Correlations, of course, cannot speak to causation, but no one here is claiming that the brain causes religious experiences. My claim is more modest: Religious experiences are realized via the brain in human beings, and knowing how the brain mediates religious experiences can tell us something about potential functions of religious experiences.

Now consider the following case: Suppose that we find that a patient X developed an intense religiousness whenever he used a drug that stimulated only region Y in his cortex. We could legitimately conclude, it seems to me, that because the religious experience was reliably associated with stimulation of cortical region Y it would be reasonable to further investigate the role of region Y in religious experience. We would not be justified, however, in saying that region Y caused the religious experience because all we have is an association among the experience, region Y, and the drug.

Now suppose further that patient X (who, of course, had consistently been producing religious experiences via the drug that stimulates region Y) suddenly suffers a stroke. Upon recovery from the stroke in region Y, he goes back to the drug expecting to have a religious experience, but no such religious experience ensues after ingestion of the drug. The only thing that has changed for patient X is that he lost region Y. It is reasonable to ask, it seems to me, that given that religious experiences ensue after stimulation of region Y and are lost after damage to region Y that region Y may mediate religious experience?

Furthermore, when the doctors perform a computed axial tomography (CAT) scan of the brain, they find that region Y, and only region Y, has been obliterated by the stroke. They conclude that the drug (which normally stimulates region Y) no longer works because region Y no longer exists. Can we therefore conclude that region Y (or the drug) produces religious experience?

No, we cannot. We can, however, make a stronger causal statement about the connection between region Y and religious experience than we could make before. Before the stroke, all we had before us was the association between a brain activation pattern produced by the drug and the emergence of religious experience. After the stroke, we have more information about the three-way relationship among drug, region Y, and religious experience. The stroke tells us that loss of region Y clearly is related to loss of religious experience. Patient X apparently needs region Y to produce religious experiences.

Now suppose we discover another collection of patients, all of whom had been profoundly religious before they died and on inspection all had extra-large region Ys. That piece of information would further support the causal link between region Y and religious experience. If we found a third collection of patients who had once been religious and then had strokes that destroyed region Y and only region Y and then they lost their religiousness ... then we would have yet further evidence for a causal link between region Y and religious experience. The link was not peculiar to patient X or to patients like patient X ... it is a human-wide finding.

Now suppose that we learned that region Y was composed of a group of special neurons – call them von Economo neurons, which occur only in humans and only in region Y – and that it was these neurons the destruction of which was associated with loss of religiousness and the presence and number of which were associated with strength and depth of religiosity – the greater the number of von Economo neurons, the greater the level of religiosity. Can we not conclude that region Y is causally implicated in religious experience? Unfortunately, no. The added finding, however, advances the science of religiosity, making the link between region Y and religiosity even stronger.

Finally, suppose that stem-cell science is sufficiently advanced that von Economo neurons could be added to region Y, and when they are, subjects experience enhanced religiosity. Or suppose that stem cells could be used to grow new von Economo neurons that could be implanted into region Y after a stroke to that region. When the new cells are implanted, religiosity is restored.

To sum up, we have a drug that reliably "produces" religious experiences and is known to stimulate only von Economo neurons in region Y. The greater the number of von Economo neurons in region Y, the greater the religiosity. Destruction of von Economo neurons in region Y results in loss of religiousness. Adding von Economo neurons enhances religiosity and restores religiosity when it was lost. With all of these data, can we then conclude that von Economo neurons are causally responsible for religious experiences?

I would say, "No." All we can conclude from this data set is that von Economo neurons in region Y are required for realization of religious experiences. Region Y must be a key node in the brain network that realizes religious experience.

Although the above set of suppositions regarding a mythical region Y "God module" is all pure fancy, the thought experiment is informative. I will show in this book that the same logic we used in the thought experiment to link region Y to religious experience works in the real world. Although there is no region Y, there is a network Y – a region of the brain that, when stimulated by a drug or seizure activity or by behavioral practices, produces religious experiences and when lost after brain damage inhibits religious experiences.

Although reports of subjective religious experiences have all of the inevitable shortcomings of reports on other types of experiences, such reports should not be entirely dismissed. We accept this kind of evidence in other realms of human experience (e.g., introspective reports of cognitive processes, reports of dreams, and reports concerning memories, imagination, etc.), and it may be worth accepting secondhand reports here as well. I will show that the experiential evidence is particularly important for an understanding of religion's effects on individuals. Individuals believe in God because they experience Him. Believers claim that they can detect God's actions in their lives and that constitutes real evidence... but only for the believer. Yet it is entirely legitimate to take these reports seriously.

For example, just as we can sometimes accept reports as true reports given by other people when they speak about their inner experiences, we can also accept reports from these same people when they speak about their experiences concerning God. It should be obvious, however, that first-person reports about inner experiences cannot always be accepted as true. We cannot accept reports, for example, from persons who are inebriated, insane, or motivated to deceive. Are religious persons any of these? Not on the face of it. Most religious people are perfectly sane, sober, and reliable individuals. They, at least consciously, are not motivated to deceive.

Just as with other realms of investigation that are dependent on first-person reports of inner experience, reports of religious experience by many individuals can be sorted and studied using standard scientific and rational approaches. Results of this sort of patient, rational approach to religion and religiousness are summarized in the many texts and journals dedicated to the study of the psychology of religion. Among the plethora of findings described in these sorts of texts is the fact that there are commonalities across individuals in the experience of religiousness.

For example, hundreds of controlled analyses of the phenomenological properties of so-called religious mystical experiences are characterized by a consistent set of properties. William James (1902) summarized some of these properties in his varieties of religious experiences. Pahnke in 1967 built on James's summary. He described properties of all kinds of religious experiences, including those derived from ingestion of hallucinogens. Each religious experience varies in intensity and in the following nine properties:

1. unity or a sense of integration within oneself and with others;
2. transcendence of time and space;
3. deeply felt positive mood;
4. sense of sacredness;
5. a noetic quality or feeling of insight;
6. paradoxicality or the ability to respectfully hold opposing points of view;
7. alleged ineffability (the experience is felt to be beyond words);
8. transiency of the euphoria, but
9. persisting positive changes in attitudes and behavior (Pahnke, 1967).

We can add to the list of nine James/Pahnke features of religious experience eight other features derived from more recent analyses:

10. an enhanced sense of personal power or even that one has been specially blessed by God;
11. enhanced "theory of mind" capacities (these are capacities to accurately guess the mental states and intentions of others);
12. changes in sexual behaviors (these can be enhanced or dramatically diminished);
13. changes in reading/writing behaviors . . . most often these manifest as an enhanced interest in writing (In pathological cases, this becomes a form of hypergraphia.);
14. enhanced awareness and appreciation of music (Despite the recognition by many religion scholars of deep connections between religious rituals and music, the enhanced appreciation of music as a feature of religious experience itself has been neglected in discussions of religious experience.);

15. complex visual and metaphoric imagery (These complex visual metaphors are usually related to the sense of noetic insight that accompanies intense religious experiences. The religious ideas are felt as so meaningful that only complex symbolic visual imagery could capture them.);

16. ritualization (This is the propensity to perform ritual actions when religious experiences are heightened.); and

17. encounter with God or spirit beings.

Now, not every religious experience will contain all seventeen of these elements or be associated with all of these features, but many of them will be present most of the time when you hear a report of a religious experience from an ordinary and healthy person. You tend to get the whole suite of these experiences in mystical or intense states and only a few of them in mundane, everyday forms of religious experiences.

Most religious persons, for example, do not on a daily basis experience paradoxicality, awestruck wonder, or ineffability. They do, in contrast, very often experience a quiet joy (positive mood), persisting efforts at positive changes in attitudes and behavior toward Self and others, noetic insight or a sense of meaningfulness of life, ritualization, and a quiet, unassuming but abiding sense of the sacred in everyday life.

Interestingly, many of the experiential properties of religious experiences flow logically from property #17 (encounter with God), assuming that that encounter is significant for the supplicant. Other properties seem to reflect assimilation of the encounter experience into consciousness. The attempt to relate to God and "read the mind" of God may lead to ecstatic states, ritualization of behavior, and enhanced theory of mind capacities, but it may also lead to a sense of ineffability. Assimilation of the experience may lead to noetic insight and long-term changes in behavior. Remarkably enough, when we examine clinical cases of changes in religiousness in an individual's life, we find alterations, usually enhancement, in many (if not most) of these phenomenologic features of religious experiences.

When the religious experience is induced by brain disorder, however, there is a crucial difference. The change in the sense of Self is usually not positive – instead, the sense of Self may be distorted either upward (grandiosity) or downward (the Self is viewed as evil). This special effect of brain injury on the sense of Self in relation to religion is further evidence of the intimate ties between Self and religion that we will be exploring in this book. In healthy cases, the Self is enriched by religion. In cases of brain injury and in cases of psychological dysfunction, the sense of Self is distorted, and religiousness may fuel the distortion unless help intervenes. Nevertheless, even when a brain disorder is present, one may still derive a lot of positive mental content from spiritual experiences. There is usually a positive mood, a sense of sacred awe, a heightened appreciation of beauty and music, and certainly a sense of meaningfulness. There may even be a new compassion for others in these patients.

In terms of the themes of this book on religion and the Self, one of the most important characteristics of the mystical religious experience is the fact that the effects of the experience are long lasting, and they lead to what the individuals themselves who have undergone the experience claim is a form of personal growth – although nothing like the "personal growth" encountered in the pop psychology literature.

I am particularly interested in reports of personal growth in the religious life. The reports are most reliable in individuals who can be called "mystics" or in those who undergo a conversion or who rediscover their religious life as mature adults. In all these cases we have mature, thoughtful, sober, sane individuals describing their experiences when they turned toward God and actively sought a relationship with Him. When reading these reports of religious experiences and lifelong personal religious histories, one is impressed by the range of variation of expression of religious sentiments. What is equally fascinating is that many common themes emerge from this literature.

There are regular patterns in religious transformation. Most people who recount their history of a relationship with God report a kind of journey. Much of this journey can be understood in terms of the attachment dynamics at play in any relationship. There have been several attempts to apply the attachment perspective to religious phenomena (see Kirkpatrick, 2005; Granqvist, 2006). In the God–Self relationship journey, there is an initial period of infatuation, bliss, and love, then a dry period when it seems as if God is nowhere to be found. Then there is a period of purification (St. John of the Cross's famous "dark night"), when one leaves behind the things that separate him or her from God, and then finally a long period of quiet joy, freedom, peace, tranquility, vibrancy, contentment, generosity toward others, patience with self and others, and a quiet determination to do "God's Will." Given that these "gifts of the spirit" are the usual products of the spiritual life, it is bizarre to say, as some skeptics do, that religiousness is rooted in irrationality and delusion. Throughout the journey, there may be experiences of ineffable happiness and joys when one experiences a kind of forgetfulness or dissolution of Self and a corresponding union with God. Whereas this sort of progression of affective states does happen in some rare (happy) cases of human relationships, most human relationships do not eventuate in these "gifts of the spirit" – so the attachment framework, as helpful as it is, may not be up to the task of fully characterizing religious experience.

Even in the absence of these sorts of mystical experiences, people on the religious journey typically go through the sort of sequence of experiences mentioned above: initial bliss, a period of dryness, a period of growth and purification, and all along a growing sense of freedom, peace, joy, generativity, stillness, compassion, and strength. If the attachment perspective cannot account for this set of experiences, perhaps other frameworks might help.

As Batson, Shoenrade, and Ventis (1993) point out, the cognitive concomitants of this emotional sequence of this "quest" aspect of religious experience mimic to some extent the experience of problem solving and sudden insight and creativity concerning the solution to the problem after a period of impasse. There is an initial period of information gathering, concentrated effort, and intense focus on the problem at hand. After a while it becomes apparent that the problem is much too complex and may even be unsolvable. Then the individual gives up, puts the problem aside, defeated. The feeling of defeat gradually gives way to renewed thoughts about the problem – the "fixation." This is a kind of incubation of new ideas and generation of new approaches to the problem ... the individual is flooded with new insights and new energy, new enthusiasm, then again defeat when the problem's real complexity is revealed. There then follows a long period of dryness around and aversion to the problem. The individual completely forgets about it and then one day the solution springs into mind. The individual experiences real insight now.

The religious journey is similar. There is a pattern of regular, repeatable experiences that everyone experiences when they enter the religious life. This pattern of experiences is different from any other domain of life. The religious strain in experience has its own internal logic and pattern – its own intrinsic rationality. There is the initial enthusiasm and explosive growth, then a period of testing, and finally a period of breakthrough and steady maturity. The fact that these sorts of experiences are "regular," repeatable, and common across all kinds of individuals who undertake the "journey" suggests that religious experience is not random. There is rationality to the process, and that rationality must depend on particular cognitive processes. Now, that rationality, of course, is a practical form of rationality, but as Kant showed during the period of the Enlightenment, practical reason and epistemic rationality must at some point meet and inform one another.

To the extent that (as Sterenly, 2004, has recently pointed out) rationally formed beliefs are counterfactually sensitive, then (contra Sterenly) belief in the veridicality of individual religious experience can be rational. We can modify Sterenly's counterfactual test of rationality as follows: Had the world a religious person experiences been different for that person, his views would be different. Had the world or his experiences NOT included the types of experiences I described above, then he would have concluded that no God existed. But because, in fact, his experiences did include those experiences described by many others on the religious journey (initial euphoria, then a period of dryness, then a period of growth and purification, and all along a growing sense of freedom, peace, joy, generativity, stillness, compassion, and strength), then the test of counterfactual sensitivity is passed. Sterenly and others point out, however, that just because you have brain circuits that reliably produce religious experiences, which in turn are not random, you nevertheless cannot conclude anything about the truth content of those experiences, particularly if they involve a proposition like "God exists." Even if God does not exist (counterfactual test), the stimulation of the circuits would, Sterenly might argue, nonetheless produce religious experiences of one kind or another. This argument seems false or untestable to me as it relies on the assumption that God does not exist. There are plenty of examples of specialized or evolved brain circuits that "fire" or function in the absence of their preferred input (e.g., theory of mind circuit), but we do not therefore conclude that other minds do not exist, that mind reading is irrational, or that the firing of the theory of mind circuit in the absence of any direct stimulus says anything about the ontological status of the intended target (other minds) of the circuit. In fact, we use the existence of the theory of mind brain circuit as evidence that other minds exist and to study minds in general. If other minds did not exist, why would Mother Nature create a circuit to detect them? We can only observe the counterfactual (occurrence of religious experiences in the absence of God) if God does not exist, but that is precisely what is in dispute. Whatever the value of the counterfactual sensitivity test as a test of rationality, we have before us a set of human experiences reported by otherwise rational, sane, accomplished, smart, creative people. It's time that those experiences and the individuals who report them are taken seriously.

2 On the Self and the Divided Self

15: For that which I do I allow not: for what I would, that do I not; but what I hate, that do I.

16: If then I do that which I would not, I consent unto the law that it is good.

17: Now then it is no more I that do it, but sin that dwelleth in me.

18: For I know that in me (that is, in my flesh) dwelleth no good thing: for to will is present with me; but how to perform that which is good I find not.

19: For the good that I would I do not: but the evil which I would not, that I do.

20: Now if I do that I would not, it is no more I that do it, but sin that dwelleth in me.

21: I find then a law, that, when I would do good, evil is present with me.

22: For I delight in the law of God after the inward man:

23: But I see another law in my members, warring against the law of my mind, and bringing me into captivity to the law of sin which is in my members.

24: O wretched man that I am! Who shall deliver me from the body of this death?

– St. Paul's Epistle to the Romans, Ch. 7

The act of coming upon oneself in being for one endowed with consciousness and freedom, if the light of being has not been fully obscured, is
experienced as a good bestowed upon one without one's doing or merit.
                                              – von Balthasar, 1997, p. 64

A human being is spirit. But what is spirit? Spirit is the self. But what is
the self? The self is a relation that relates itself to itself or is the relation's
relating itself to itself in the relation; the self is not the relation but is the
relations' relating itself to itself. A human being is a synthesis of the infinite
and the finite, of the temporal and the eternal, of freedom and necessity.
                                              – Kierkegaard, 1980, p. 13

Introduction

The quotes at the beginning of this chapter are all from great religious
writers: St. Paul, one of the founding apostles of Christianity; Hans
von Balthasar, a great Catholic theologian; and Søren Kierkegaard, the
nineteenth-century Danish writer and philosopher of religion.

All three quotes exemplify a religious attitude toward the Self, it seems
to me. Each emphasizes the element of self-consciousness as fundamental to our notions of the Self. St. Paul points to the central religious
problem concerning the Self – the problem of the divided Self. Paul is
painfully aware of his own weakness of will (akrasia). His self-consciousness involves the feeling of being trapped by a Will not his own yet
his own nevertheless. He expresses the quintessential divided Self, which
comes from a divided Will. I find myself doing things that "I" do not
want to do and not doing the things that I want to do. I find further that
I cannot change the situation. So Paul cries out: Who will free me from
this wretched Self?

von Balthasar, in contrast, suddenly comes to himself in being; he
notices that he IS. He is now self-aware. Instead of being astonished,
puzzled, troubled, or perplexed by this new knowledge, he receives it as
a gift given to him from someone or something else. His fundamental
response to the astonishment of self-awareness is gratitude.

Kierkegaard's response is different from both von Balthasar's and
St. Paul's. Kierkegaard is a bit more puzzled by the "gift." He registers

the fact that he IS; that he is a Self, but then he claims that the Self is not a simple matter. It is layered and complex. The Self, he says, is a "relating" of Self back to Self. Reflexivity is its core. When self-consciousness emerges we get, instead of gratitude, a series of divisions and antinomies: temporal versus eternal, freedom versus necessity, and finite versus infinite. A human Self is aware of its finitude. It will not last forever. Yet it is also aware that there is a "forever," and the human Self can desire what it knows it cannot have. The Self is therefore doomed to be divided against itself. In this sort of situation, what should a human Self will? How should I direct my will? Surely not toward death? Neither can I direct my will toward the eternal, as I know that the eternal is not possible for me. Thus, self-reflexivity leads directly to a form of divided will again. Kierkegaard alludes to a possible synthesis of the finite and the infinite, but how does this synthesis happen? Does the act of synthesis allow one to break out of the reflexive circle of self-obsession that seems to be the human condition?

von Balthasar seems to have accomplished something like the synthesis of finite and infinite temporal perspectives within his own consciousness. He experiences his own self-consciousness as a moment within his own stream of consciousness. He suddenly realizes that he has been given the gift of being. He does not seem to exhibit a divided Will, as do St. Paul, Kierkegaard, and most of the rest of us. How does one arrive at this synthesis, this state of gratitude? von Balthasar would say that one needs to follow the religious way or path, as that path will solve the riddle of self-consciousness and the anguish of a divided Will.

Whether von Balthasar is correct is a matter that cannot be decided in this book, but I can and will show how religious structures address the core problem of the divided Will and of the Self against itself.

The divided Self is the problem religion addresses and solves. That inner divisiveness caused by a divided Will not only causes intense anguish, but it also reduces the amount of information an individual can process efficiently. The divided Self therefore prevents some forms of knowledge acquisition. The divided Self is not just a psychological or emotional problem. It is a cognitive problem of the first order that needed to be solved by our ancestors if human intellectual and computational abilities were to advance. Religion solves the problem of the divided Self by enlarging the sense of Self, expanding what used to be called the "agent intellect" (see Aquinas and deliberation below) so that inner divisions are reconciled and information-processing capacities are enhanced.

Theory of the Self

Because I will have quite a lot to say about the Self and its transformations in what follows, I will present the model of the Self that I will be assuming throughout the rest of this book. In the recent empirical psychological literature, two theories of the Self are particularly well supported by the data: the Self as a collection of schemas (Markus & Wurf, 1987) and the Self as a story (Bruner, 1990). The Self as a collection of schemas is rooted in work on representational and information-processing properties of the self-concept (e.g., Markus, 1977), and the Self as a story is rooted in the tradition of narrative psychology (e.g., Bruner, 1990; McAdams, 1996). Both of these metatheories contribute to two subtheories of the Self that I will be relying on throughout the book: the theory of self-regulation and the theory of possible Selves.

According to Markus and Nurius (1986), possible Selves are images of what people hope to become, expect to become, or fear becoming in the future. Although not every possible Self theorist would agree, I count as a special possible Self the "ideal Self." The ideal Self is special in that it is crucial for self-regulation. For now I need to show how possible Selves work in the process of self-regulation.

Possible Selves appear to be elaborated out of imaginary narratives involving the Self both in childhood and in adulthood (e.g., Erikson, 2001; Markus & Ruvolo, 1989; Whitty, 2002). Possible Selves consist of a description of a set of behavioral actions aimed at some goal designed to overcome some conflict, along with causes and consequences of those imaginary actions, with an end state that is described as an event. According to theorists (Bruner, 1995; Oatley, 2007; Ricoeur, 1984), narratives about future Selves provide interpretations about what we see as possible. As stories, they help to integrate material about conflict involving the present Self into a resolution of that conflict – a resolution involving a higher, more complete, and more complex Self.

Empirical work has supported this narrative-related, integrative function of possible Selves. We evaluate our current and past Selves with reference to possible Selves (Markus & Nurius, 1986). Thus, for instance, a current representation of the Self as "nonpracticing Hindu" would be evaluated more severely by an individual with a salient "saint" possible Self compared to an individual with a "banker" possible Self. The discrepancy between the possible Self as saint and the current Self as nonpracticing is large and such discrepancy has been demonstrated to be motivational. Interestingly, when the positive possible Self "saint" is combined with a feared possible Self such as "sinner," the motivational strength of possible Selves increases substantially because both approach and avoidance systems are activated under the regulatory control of the possible hoped for and feared possible Selves.

Possible Selves become relevant for self-regulation when they are recruited into the subset of self-knowledge that is active in working memory (Markus & Kunda, 1986; Markus & Nurius, 1986). Obviously, when a possible Self is periodically or chronically activated, it becomes particularly important for evaluation of current representations of the Self as well as discrepancy-reduction behaviors or engagement of approach and/or avoidance behaviors (Norman & Aron, 2003). For example, frequent attendance at religious services or performance of religious rituals will periodically activate a number of possible Selves, including an ideal Self. The chronically activated ideal Self is then in a position to contribute to self-regulation by providing a standard by which to evaluate progress toward a goal and resolution of internal and social conflicts (Oyserman, Bybee, Terry, & Hart-Johnson, 2004). Because the ideal Self allows for resolution of conflict, it is experienced as a relatively conflict-free unified Self. That people use possible Selves as behavioral standards to guide conflict resolution and self-regulation more generally has been remarked upon repeatedly (e.g., Hoyle & Sherrill, 2006; Hoyle & Sowards, 1993; Kerpelman & Lamke, 1997; Oyserman et al., 2004). Hoyle and Sherrill (2006) have pointed out that possible Selves map particularly well into hierarchically organized control-process models of self-regulation (e.g., Carver & Scheier, 1981; Hoyle & Sowards, 1993). Behavioral reference points or standards are organized in these models of self-regulation in a hierarchical fashion from abstract and general to concrete and specific. A particular behavioral standard derives from the level above it. The highest levels of standards are global ideals. In the context of religious ritual, these global standards are the ideal Selves that the current Self is urged to become or desires to become. The highest global standard is the God toward which the entire religious service is oriented. Participants in religious services often actively attempt to take on the identity of the God – to become "spirit possessed." To the extent that spirit possession in this sense is supported by the ritual context, it can serve as a global standard. In any case, in everyday religious contexts, such as in daily ritual practices, the individual is reminded that an ideal Self is possible and even required of him or her and that the ideal Self then serves as a behavioral standard against which the current Self is evaluated. Discrepancies between the two can then motivate corrective goal-directed behaviors. Discrepancies between a behavioral standard and the current Self, however, also give rise to the "divided Self"; it is the divided Self that religion promises to heal.

We will examine the Self as agent to get at the problem of the divided Self or Will and religion's answer for this problem. To see how religion addresses this fundamental problem at the center of the structure of the Self, it will be necessary to go into a bit more detail on how the Will operates to support the experience of a functionally effective, decision-making (i.e., free) Self or agent. It is this agentic aspect of the Self that is particularly important for religion, so religion has provided a range of devices (rituals, ceremonies, practices, images, ideas, etc.) to address the agent. These practices will be discussed in later chapters. For now, we will focus on fundamental cognitive and brain correlates of the Self relevant to the problem of the divided Self and to religion.

The Self as Agent

The sense of Self as "agent" appears to draw on several psychologic and neuropsychologic domains, such as autobiographical memory, emotional and evaluative systems, self-monitoring, bodily awareness, subjectivity or perspective in perception, and so forth (Churchland, 2002; Gallagher, 2000; Metzinger, 2003; Northoff & Bermpohl, 2004). The two processes most implicated in agency are Will (the sense of being the cause of some action) and goal-directed choice (the sense of choosing among alternatives and aiming for one of those alternatives). These two processes, Will and goal directedness, lie at the heart of the old problem of free will and the heart of our problem of the divided Self.

The conscious experience of "free will in a divided Self" lies at the center of the human religious experience. It undergirds our conceptions of the dignity and autonomy of the human personality as well as the responsibility of each person as he or she interacts with and affects, for better or ill, the lives of others. The importance of the issue of free will is acknowledged by most philosophers, theologians, and scientists, but there has been a consistent thread of "free will skepticism" that has run through the intellectual history of reflection on the phenomenon. This skeptical vein of thought has only intensified in the modern age as science has increasingly focused its nihilatory gaze on the issue.

Take, for example, Daniel Dennett's (1991) deflationary account of the Self. He argued, as did many of the ancient philosophers both Eastern and Western (see Sorabji, 2006), that there is no little man sitting in the mind somewhere directing behavior of the individual. Instead, the Self is a kind of center of narrative gravity, a fiction, created by different regions of the brain carrying out their normal information-processing operations, creating multiple drafts of sense experience as well as of remembered experiences. Because these multiple draft accounts of "what happened" concern only limited aspects of the persons' history or identity, these fictional summaries of remembered experiences help to explain the fragmented nature of our identities.

This "multiple drafts" account of the Self is problematic if we assume that individual persons, including even children, are designed by nature as strategic agents. Their processing of information is selective. The mind is not a neutral recording device. It selectively picks up information and then packages it in such a way as to be consistent with strategic aims of the individual. This strategic selection and processing of information precludes the multiple drafts account of the Self. Disconnected fragments of information are not possible for persons with intact strategic minds. Information may be biased, partial, and even delusional, but it cannot be neutral with respect to the agent. To the extent that persons are strategic in pursuing their interests, they must use some criteria for selection of information pick-up and processing. That selective criteria must logically and operationally confer unity on the information that is processed by the system. The information must refer ultimately to some entity like the Self; otherwise, strategic behaviors and information processing would be impossible.

Dennett and other skeptics also seem to be unimpressed by the fact that unity of self-consciousness is sometimes achieved. We are not always fragmented and conflicted. We all have experienced that unity – even on a daily basis. Indeed, we rarely mistake ourselves for others and we mostly act from self-interest, which necessarily implies some unity of thought, planning, consciousness, and intention. All of those fragmented stories occasionally get woven together into a single thematic unity. Yes, we are fragmented and divided Selves much of the time, but we are also some-times unified. Both states are likely to be functional. Sometimes it pays to be fragmented (e.g., one Self or story can act without awareness of another part of the Self and shirk responsibility). Most of the time, however, it pays to be unified. Achieving unity benefits the individual in myriad ways.

Biologic and Cognitive Roots of the Executive Self

A centralized executive Self that embodies a single unified consciousness is valuable from an evolutionary point of view for the following reasons: 1) A unified Self may be more effective in pursuing behavioral goals than a nonunified, conflicted Self. 2) A unified Self may be more effective at signaling intent (e.g., to cooperate) to others than a disunified Self. 3) A unified Self may be more effective than a disunified Self in evading predators. 4) A unified Self should be more effective in war and combat than a conflict-ridden, disunified Self. A conflicted Self is less likely to win hand-to-hand combat with a unified Self, as the conflicted Self would be more likely to consult fears than would a more unified Self. 5) From a neurocognitive and neurocomputational perspective, a unified Self is to be desired because it would increase the ability to benefit from access to a number and variety of brain/mind capacities than would a less centralized or disunified Self. People with a centralized Self, furthermore, may be able to exert greater control over attentional resources and focus than may people with a disunified Self. They have the opportunity to retrieve and effectively utilize a greater number and variety of memories and skills than would a disunified Self. 6) A unified Self enhances the capacity for pleasure relative to a baseline state of a disunified Self. This enhanced capacity for joy allows one to feel compassion and empathy for others.

One alternative to developing a unified consciousness is to be governed by whatever impulse is most salient in any given moment. To remain a creature governed by conflicting desires and driven by impulse makes the individual a slave to each moment. Many people do not find such a prospect to be unfortunate – never mind deplorable. I do not understand why. Accounts by individuals who have pursued such a life with abandon describe a life of slavery, emptiness, and desperation. Whatever pleasures are available to the disunified Self, they are fleeting and illusory. Whether one can characterize the life of the divided consciousness as a life driven by impulse, it seems clear to me that the attempt to develop a unified consciousness is a worthwhile one – particularly if it can lead to greater intelligence, greater effectiveness in combat, greater internal serenity, and greater compassion toward others. If reasons 1–6 are even partially correct, then it follows that a unified Self may be more attractive to the opposite sex than a disunified Self as it would more effectively signal genetic fitness. If a unified Self was more attractive to the opposite sex in ancestral populations, then people with the capacity or inclination to construct a unified Self were more likely to mate and pass on the capacity and inclination to construct a unified Self than were people less inclined to construct a unified Self. This is what apparently happened as most of us strive for some sort of coherent unity in our identities and in our conscious lives.

Self as Costly Handicap

Given all of these benefits of having a central unified sense of Self, why are we often so fragmented? Why are we not unified by design? Why don't we come from the hands of nature with unified Selves to begin with? There are probably many reasons for the existence of divided consciousness. First, as noted earlier in this chapter, it likely pays sometimes to revert to divided consciousness as it allows one to deceive oneself. Self-deception, in turn, can make it easier to deceive others. Second, divided consciousness is easier than unified consciousness. It is the default state. Despite the myriad benefits of constructing a unified Self, the process is difficult and costly. It takes prolonged, persistent effort to build a centralized executive Self. To do so, you need to use attentional resources to stay on task. You need to inhibit desires and goals that are inconsistent with a single consciousness and unified set of goals. You need to practice habits that support a centralized Self and extinguish habits that promote conflicting desires, and so forth. All of this is metabolically costly.

This latter fact, that pursuit of a unified sense of Self is effortful and costly, points to another reason why the default state is fragmentation. Being conscious of the fact that "you" are conflicted and that a sense of unity is possible to achieve with effort suggests that pursuing unity of Self could come to signal genetic fitness. Just as the loudest weanling will get the food from a discerning mammalian mother, so too will effort separate the wheat from the chaff among discerning and choosy human partners. Bulbulia (2006) suggested a similar argument for the effectiveness of placebos. The very costliness of the effort to build a centralized "executive Self" may make it a useful social signaling device to facilitate social cooperation. For religions to function well, they need high degrees of in-group cooperation. Looked at the other way around . . . for religions to promote cooperation within some local groups or coalitions of individuals, they need to develop techniques to identify the individual who truly wants to cooperate and to screen out the individuals who are not interested in real cooperation. These latter individuals are known in the literature as free riders. Willingness to perform costly religious behaviors for relatively long periods of time can function as reliable signals of willingness and ability to commit to cooperation within the group. Included in such costly religious behavioral patterns are the hard-to-fake virtues and character strengths, as free riders would not be willing to incur the costs of developing and practicing such virtues. Free riders could not build a centralized executive Self. Sustaining virtuous behavior is, to say the least, difficult. That is why character and virtue cannot be faked, at least over the long term. Just as ritual and religious practices, when practiced consistently over time, help winnow out free riders from the group, so too will development of hard-to-fake character strengths. To act generously and altruistically consistently over time is a convincing indicator of character as it requires the ability to consistently inhibit short-term gratification of selfish impulses.

Religiosity, in short, promotes development of an executive Self by promoting development of character strengths. It does this in turn by facilitating inhibition of free-rider behavioral strategies via the requirement of the adoption of costly programs of behavior. Costly religious behaviors that are practiced consistently over long periods of time and that are associated with inhibition of free rider and exploitative behavioral impulses function as costly and reliable signals of quality and commitment. What could be more effortful or "costly" than to consistently inhibit appetitive drives around short-term rewards in hopes that such postponement of immediate gratification will "pay off" sometime down the road? It is a good bet that cooperation with such an individual (i.e., an individual who consistently displays virtuous behaviors) would be productive because he or she has, in effect, demonstrated the ability to reliably inhibit free-rider appetitive drives/strategies.

Throughout history, religious practices have been the primary, although not exclusive, way that individuals and communities develop and foster these character strengths. Such religious practices, when they are associated with development of character strengths, enhance successful dyadic and group cooperation by signaling the trustworthiness of the individuals involved and their willingness to subordinate individual interests to group goals. Once again, free riders would be winnowed out via development of character strengths because they would be unwilling or unable to inhibit selfish exploitative impulses in favor of cooperative exchanges. Looking closely, therefore, at the links between the Self and religion predicts that human beings needed to develop the ability to facultatively inhibit powerful impulsive and related free-rider behavioral strategies when seeking to cooperate with, or become a member of, a particular cooperative group. It follows that the human mind/brain had to develop powerful inhibitory capacities around the suite of impulsive appetitive behaviors that motivate the free-rider behavioral strategy. This inhibitory capacity is precisely one of the best-established and major functions of the anterior temporal and frontal lobes (Barkley, 1997; Damasio & Anderson, 2003; Fuster, 2008; McNamara, 2002), a region of the brain, we will see, that is consistently implicated in religious behaviors.

To return to our original question: Why are we so fragmented to start with? We reply as follows: We start with a fragmented divided consciousness because a unified consciousness or Self is difficult to achieve. But this very difficulty allows us to use the effort toward and the achievement of unity as a signal of fitness.

Religion, Self, and Warfare

Please note that when I assert that religion wants strong "agents" to promote within-group cooperation, that does not mean that the form of cooperation religion promotes will necessarily be benign. One of the most powerful forms of coalitional cooperation is warfare, and religion appears to have been crucial for development of individuals who could wage effective warfare. Religion is not merely about producing nice little boys and girls. It is also about producing real, mature, autonomous, and free adults, adults who could wage effective war when necessary.

The Divided Self and the Process of Its Unification

Given all of the benefits noted earlier of developing a centralized and unified executive sense of Self, the experience itself is unstable. Although we often experience ourselves as unified free agents, we nevertheless and perhaps just as often experience ourselves as ridden with conflicting desires. Why is unified consciousness so unstable and so difficult to maintain? Divided consciousness seems to be the default position of the mind.

One hundred years ago, William James very astutely noted that divided consciousness was the inheritance of all humankind and that religion helped to address that problem. Religion, he argued, was connected to the problem of the divided Self. He addressed the issue in Lecture VIII,

"The Divided Self, and the Process of its Unification," of his *Varieties of Religious Experience*. He apparently saw the problem, however, as pressing or acute only for those individuals he called the "sick souls." These are the people who need to be "twice-born" to be happy. He argued that the psychological basis of the twice-born character "seems to be a certain discordancy or heterogeneity in the native temperament of the subject, an incompletely unified moral and intellectual horizon." He allowed, however, that all of us have some amount of discordancy in our character and that the normal development or maturation of character consists in "straightening out and unifying of the inner self." Inherited heterogeneity was just more extreme in some than in others. All of us, however, are driven to a greater or lesser extent to restore equilibrium and unity when consciousness and Will falters and wars against itself.

How, then, was this process of unification of the divided Will accomplished according to James? Religion was the preferred way, but not the only way. The process of reducing inner discord was, for James, a general psychological process and could happen with any sort of mental material. In all instances of reduction of inner division we have a sense of "firmness, stability, and equilibrium succeeding a period of storm and stress and inconsistency." Leading up to the change from division to unity is a process of preparation and "subconscious incubation" during which the individual grapples with the inner division. The solution may present itself suddenly or gradually, but the striving after equilibrium is the guiding principle that drives the process forward.

James realizes, however, that the religious path to the reestablishment of equilibrium within the personality is different from all other forms of restoration of equilibrium. Religious transformation is more thoroughgoing, deeper, longer lasting, and more radical than are other forms of restoration. Religion is a force that "... reinfuses the positive willingness to live, even in full presence of the evil perceptions that erewhile made life seem unbearable." Religion accomplishes nothing less than a full transformation of the Will, personality, and Self. James describes the process of this restoration but does not give us a scientific account of how religion does it, how religion facilitates transformation of the Self.

Although James could see the problem (the divided Self) and its resolution (religion), he could not identify the proximate sources or solutions of the problem. Astute as he was, however, he conjectured that the condition of divided Self was ultimately rooted in our genes. "Heterogeneous personality has been explained as the result of inheritance – the traits of character of incompatible and antagonistic ancestors are supposed to be preserved alongside of each other. This explanation may pass for what it is worth – it certainly needs corroboration." We can now offer some corroboration of this idea concerning the proximate sources of the divided Self.

Genetics of Divided Consciousness

One of the best available discussions of divided consciousness in terms of internal conflict over decision making comes from David Haig (2006) – an expert on genetic conflict. He very reasonably pointed to multiple sources of internal conflict:

> Internal conflict often seems maladaptive; consuming time, energy, and repose. If so, why does it persist? Three types of hypothesis could potentially resolve the conundrum of conflict within an adapted mind. First, one might argue that internal conflict arises from constraints on the perfection of adaptation; that evolved mechanisms work well on average but occasionally malfunction. We would be better off without internal conflict, but we are stuck with it. Second, one might argue that internal conflict is in some sense illusory; that the "contending parties" have the same ultimate ends; and that natural selection has simply adopted an adversarial system as the best mechanism of arriving at useful truths. Finally, one might argue that internal conflict is "real" and reflects a disagreement over ultimate ends between different agents that contribute to mental activity. I will reveal my hand at the outset. I believe that all three kinds of explanations, and their complex interactions, will play a role in an eventual understanding of internal conflict (Haig, 2006, pp. 9–10).

I am primarily interested in Haig's third source of internal conflict – that there exist internal "agents" that differ over ultimate behavioral goals. These agents reflect differing sets of genes, the strategic "interests" of which are opposed to and in conflict with one another. This genetic conflict is reflected in the consciousness of the individual in whom the genes reside. Haig points out that

> ...there are subtle ways in which genes can have distinct interests and these can be the source of contradictory adaptations within the genome. Transposable genetic elements replicate at a faster rate than the rest of the genome. Nuclear genes are transmitted via eggs and sperm, whereas mitochondrial genes are transmitted only via eggs. If different genes have different rules of transmission, then an adaptation of one gene that promotes its own long-term propagation may not promote the transmission of the other genes with which it is temporarily associated (Haig, 2006, pp. 15–16).

Genetic conflict is ubiquitous throughout the natural world. Organisms are composed of multiple genetic entities that do not always share the same interests because they have different modes of inheritance. Different transmission patterns of genes to offspring create the context for conflict or negative fitness covariance between two associated or antagonistic genes. For example, genes that are normally passed on by only one sex, such as mitochondrial genes inherited through the female line, differ in their transmission patterns from Y chromosome genes inherited through the male line and can therefore enter into conflict with them. If matriline genes, for example, can increase their likelihood of transmission by decreasing transmission probabilities of patriline genes, then they will do so.

Genetic conflict can often result in the spread of apparently maladaptive physiologic phenotypes. An allele harmful to male fitness, for example, could spread if it was beneficial to female-line mitochondrial genes. The resultant male phenotypes would be vulnerable physiologically, and thus natural selection would act to create suppressors of the harmful allele in males. Suppression, however, may be only partial ("dose sensitive"), and thus increased expression of the harmful allele may reoccur, creating an evolving cycle of measures and reactive countermeasures by the harmful allele and its suppressors. Effects of the harmful allele on male phenotypes reduce the numbers of males in the population who compete for resources with carrier females, thus increasing the fitness of carriers of the allele (females).

Similarly, conflict can often occur between the genes of parasites and their hosts. The host evolves mechanisms to reduce the damage inflicted by the parasite, and the parasite evolves adaptations to extract resources from the host, despite the host's countermeasures, to improve the chances that its descendants will be transmitted to infect new hosts. Some parasites, such as certain microsporidians in mosquitoes, are transmitted only through females (in the egg cytoplasm). When these parasites find themselves in males, they kill the host and try to get to an alternative host (typically a copepod). In females (daughters), the parasites are harmless. Similarly, in some crustaceans, cytoplasmic bacteria called Wolbachia turn males into females and exploit the "female" to find new hosts to infect.

Another form of genetic conflict called meiotic drive occurs when a gene obtains, during meiosis, a transmission advantage. Meiotic drive can involve both the sex chromosomes and the autosomes. Segregation distortion is a form of autosomal meiotic drive that has been intensively studied in the fruit fly, *Drosophila melanogaster*. A similar driving system characterizes the t locus on chromosome 17 in mice. The products of the genes encoded at the t locus are necessary for normal spermatogenesis, and thus when the males mature, they are sterile.

A form of intragenomic conflict that Haig (2006) suggests impacts the feel of intrapersonal conflict is called genomic imprinting. Genomic imprinting refers to the silencing of one allele of a gene according to its parental origin. The silencing or tagging of the DNA probably involves methylation of CpG-rich domains. Thus, each cell in the progeny recognizes and expresses only one allele of a gene locus, namely, either the paternally derived or the maternally derived allele. The pattern-specific monoallelic expression of imprinted genes results in a bias in the inheritance of traits, with some traits inherited down the matriline and others down the patriline. Most of the genes identified to date as imprinted code for proteins that influence early growth, with paternally imprinted or silenced genes tending to inhibit growth and maternally imprinted genes enhancing growth. In sum, paternally expressed loci increase and maternally expressed loci restrain allocation of resources by the mother to offspring.

Haig and colleagues (Haig, 2000, 2002, 2004; Haig & Westoby, 1988) provided formal, game-theoretic models of imprinting effects in terms of the opposing effects of patriline and matriline genomes on growth and development. They conceptualized the evolution of genomic imprinting in terms of a process of genetic conflict between the maternal and paternal genomes that occurs whenever there is uncertainty about paternity of offspring (which is considered to be the case for human biology). Because a paternal gene in one offspring is unlikely to be in its siblings or its mother, the paternal gene can increase its chances of getting into the next generation (i.e., its fitness) if it promotes extraction of resources from the mother regardless of costs to the mother or its siblings who, in the context of paternity uncertainty, may carry genes of another male parent. The maternal gene, by contrast, is in all the siblings, and thus its fitness is increased by favoring cooperation and sharing of resources.

As Haig says in the essay on intrapersonal conflict:

> A gene that a daughter inherits from her mother has one chance in two of having an indirect copy in the younger sibling and one chance in two of having an indirect copy in the daughter's own offspring. The two routes of achieving fitness remain equivalent for genes of maternal origin. However, a gene that the daughter inherits from her father is absent from the younger sibling but has one chance in two of having an indirect copy transmitted to the daughter's own offspring. The two routes are not equivalent for genes of paternal origin. That is, maternal genes of the daughter are "indifferent" as to whether an offspring or a maternal half-sib receives a benefit, but the daughter's paternal genes would "prefer" her own offspring to receive a benefit instead of a maternal half-sib (Haig, 2006, p. 17).

Thus, patriline genes are more likely to foster aggressive prenatal and postnatal growth schedules, whereas matriline genes are more likely to modulate, restrain, or inhibit aggressive rates of growth and development. Because these maternal and paternal genomes act antagonistically with respect to allocation of maternal resources and control of growth schedules, they also tend to promote internal brain and biobehavioral systems that function antagonistically around growth, reproductive behaviors, and adult behavioral repertoires more generally (Tycko & Morison, 2002).

These genetic data substantially verify the claim that the default state of most organisms, including human beings, is internal conflict. We are a conglomeration of conflicting sets of genes, all of which are in competition with one another to pass copies of themselves down the generations. They build physiologic systems that assist them in that process, and among these systems are systems of the brain. Given that there are multiple genetic sources constructing multiple brain networks that reflect competing interests and that consequently promote a sense of internal conflict and a divided consciousness, what needs to be explained is how we achieve a sense of unity at all. Despite the evident intrapersonal conflict we feel, we nonetheless often also feel that we operate from a unified consciousness. Although our genetic inheritance militates against a unified consciousness, we nevertheless can sometimes achieve a unified consciousness; this consciousness gives us a limited kind of freedom from the "choices" the genes make on our behalf. How is this sense of unity achieved? Haig (2006) says, "The Self can be viewed as the arbiter that mediates among the conflicting parties and then decides. We are free actors at least in the limited sense that no single set of interests exclusively determines our choices" (p. 22). I entirely agree with Haig's assessment of how unity is achieved. The Self arrives at, computes, or imposes a decision. The Self is an achievement that promotes a unified consciousness. The Self in my view should therefore be considered a cultural achievement of the first order fought for by ancestral populations who developed religious cultures and practices to build the executive Self over many generations.

Agency and Self

The content and experience of this central executive Self is manifested as "free will." It is the control we have over our own acts, plans, and thoughts. The experience of Self and agency underwrites the experience of free will. Even when we do not move a muscle in our body, but instead inwardly give a nod of assent to a proposition or some other image or idea, the feeling of agency still obtains and is fundamental to the cognitive moment of assent.

Although the subjective feeling of agency is a key aspect of the overall experience of free will, it alone does not give you the full experience of free will. To experience effectual action, to have the experience of free action, you need to have the corresponding sense that you could have done otherwise. You are a free being to the extent that you chose the course of action that you are now implementing. Agents arrive at their decisions after consideration of a number of possibilities for action. Thus, the essential ingredients for a free will are an agent that really causes things to happen in the world and a deliberation process that helps an agent decide on a course of action. These two ingredients largely summarize the consensus of philosophers as I understand it with respect to the issue of agency and free will. Free will involves an agent who, when given a series of alternatives, chooses one alternative among the series; this choice has real effects on the environment or in the agent's life. These alternative courses of action come from two sources: internal conflicts from within the individual and external vagaries of daily life, particularly when the individual is given two equally poor or equally good courses of action. By far the greatest source of conflict around alternative courses of action arises out of conflicting internal desires that in turn are rooted in evolutionary genetic conflicts.

Our practical reasoning ability was developed, in part, to find optimal solutions to these external and internal conflicts. In the philosophical literature, the search for optimal choices in the context of conflict and competing interests is known as deliberative reasoning. This ability to find an optimal solution to an internal conflict constitutes the core structure and competence of the Self. We therefore need to look more carefully at the deliberation process.

Aquinas and Deliberation

The medieval philosopher Thomas Aquinas and modern philosophers of Mind (e.g., John Searle) have rightly situated the experience of Self and of agency within a deliberative process involving the evaluation of potential courses of action and the act of deciding upon one course of action over the other possibilities. The exercise of agency is largely a process of "making up your mind" about what to do and when to do it. To make up your mind or come to a decision you need to "deliberate." You cannot simply sit back and wait for your evaluative processing to cause the decision or choice you will make. You must do something to make up your own mind. A decision must be made by the Self, and a commitment to that decision must be owned.

In his analysis of the problem of free will, Aquinas (1993) points out that forms taken in by the mind are " . . . general forms covering a number of individual things, so that the willed tendencies (of an individual) remain open to more than one course of action . . . " (p. 176). Aquinas suggests that one of the roots of free will is the way the deliberative mind operates. The mind processes "forms" that are like general categories that capture a range of more primitive natural kinds . . . and that generality, that ability to abstract away from specific instances and to entertain a range of specific outcomes, confers on human beings freedom from compulsion to enact any one specific aim or outcome. "The architect's concept of the house, for example, is general enough to cover many different house plans, so that his will can tend towards making the house square, round or some other shape" (p. 176).

The power of the mind (or the "agent intellect" as Aquinas calls it) to form general concepts that abstract away from specific stimuli and capture large amounts of information allows us to entertain many different ways to attain to a goal. We will see later that decentering involves an abstracting away from a particular self-problem context to arrive at an optimal more generalized Self-structure that can accommodate larger ranges of problems and goals.

Religion provides the individual with a range of practices and ideas to enhance the agent intellect, to strengthen the executive Self. We will discuss those practices and the ways in which they enhance an executive Self in following chapters. For now it is important to see that the deliberative process itself can enhance powers of the agent intellect. All of the long-term outcomes of the deliberative process – greater success at achieving goals, freedom from the pull toward the salient or the ability to delay gratification of impulses, self-responsibility and the creation of a value hierarchy – all these outcomes tend to increase the powers of the agent intellect and of the agent him- or herself. Although nature provides each human being with the potential for strong agent intellect, there is no guarantee that that potential will be actualized unless the individual uses religious practices or some process like religious practices to strengthen the agent intellect and/or the Self.

Aquinas's conception of free agency involves an enormously rich conception of Self, personhood, and individual dignity. In his commentary (1954) on Aristotle's *De Anima* in the chapter on the agent intellect, Aquinas notes that Aristotle's treatment of agency moves away from the Platonic ideas as the basic constituents of the Mind. Instead, Aristotle proposes a general abstractive activity of the Mind that separates the Mind from the immediate stimulus environment and from matter more generally. The agent intellect or the individual who realizes his active powers is not acted upon and instead is pure act and in some sense, therefore, impassible. He develops a relative autonomy with respect to the immediate environment. That does not mean that he is separate from the environment or the social and historical context. It merely means that his actions cannot be reduced to that context or to the immediate "now." He or she has some elbow or breathing room. He is not obliged to respond to every stimulus that crosses his path, no matter how salient. Instead, he acts upon those stimuli upon which he chooses to act, and he abstracts from those stimuli various and manifold "forms" that then become the raw material for the further building up of his autonomy, abstractive powers, and freedom.

Let us call this high conception of the agent the "executive Self" – always keeping in mind that the autonomy is relative to a social context – never absolute. There are no disembodied free agents. I contend that the goal of religious practices is the strengthening of this executive Self. Religion creates this executive Self by providing an ideal Self toward which the individual can strive and with which the individual can evaluate the current Self. Religion supports behaviors that reduce the discrepancy between the possible ideal Self and the current Self. I will show how religion accomplishes this task cognitively and neurologically in chapters following this one, but for now I ask for the reader's patience and indulgence before rejecting this contention outright. The case needs to be built up carefully.

Goal-Directedness as the Domain of the Executive Self

The reason why religion focuses on the "Self in society" so steadfastly is that the Self is the entity that controls the behavior of the individual, and social cooperation is only possible when many individuals exert some internal control over their behaviors. The agent or Self sets and pursues goals. Aquinas points out that, whereas free will comes from the deliberation around alternative courses of action, the exercise of the free will itself " . . . comes from an agent causing the action in pursuance of a goal, so that the first source of an activity's exercise is some goal" (1954, p. 177). To commit to a choice, to decide upon a course of action, to come to a decision, means to set and pursue a goal. A free choice arrived at through a process of deliberation gets its cognitive content from the goal that the chosen course of action intends.

Goal-directed behaviors set or intended by autonomous agents are the normal arena in which free will operates. We will see in later chapters that it is these sorts of behaviors, these "intentional acts," that are the target of ritual activities and of religious practices more generally. Divided will is due to a failure to order one's goals and intentions optimally. Aquinas holds that intentional acts, to operate optimally, need to be oriented toward ultimate value. "And if we take note of the objects of mind and of will we will find that the mind's object is what holds first place in the world of form – namely being and truth – whilst will's object is what holds first place in the world of goals – namely, good; and that good applies to all goals just as truth applies to all forms mind takes in, so that good itself as taken in by the mind is one truth among others, and truth itself as goal of mind's activity is one good among others" (Aquinas, 1954, p. 177). For the Self, the highest good is an ideal Self or God. The highest good and purpose of Mind and Will is to seek the good and know the truth. The stuff of good and the truth is, according to Aquinas, love – that much sullied but still necessary word. Love is the superordinate and ultimate goal of all other goals according to Aquinas. It, in turn, sets the standard for a hierarchy of values and a criterion upon which goals can be evaluated. The closer the goal is to the good and the true, the better the goal and the more optimally efficient intentional acting becomes.

In terms of possible Selves, if you set as a possible Self a saintly ideal Self, the standard is high and your corresponding discrepancy reduction behaviors must be enhanced. If you aim at an ultimate, you can better order your subordinate aims, and this lessens the chances for a divided Will.

When you fail to aim at the ultimate good or an ideal Self, you get a divided Will that results in weakness of the Will (akrasia). Only a highly developed sense of Self can perceive and aim for the ultimate good of God.

According to Aquinas, a free act is the result of a deliberative process by an autonomous agent aiming at the "good and the appropriate." The free man chooses only those stimuli that are good and appropriate. He transfigures his orientation, his Self, his desires, his poise, or his perceptual organs so that he wills only the good and the appropriate. For a free man, " . . . the object moving the will is something apprehended as both good and appropriate. Goods proposed as good but not apprehended as appropriate will not move will" (Aquinas, 1954, pp. 178–179). What is good and appropriate for human beings is what is proper to their dignity as free autonomous agents made in the image of God. The highest and most appropriate good for human beings is to love, first God and then neighbor. That ability to choose the good and the appropriate implies a huge amount of intellectual, spiritual, and moral development of the agent. Religion is required to help build a Self that is capable of consistently choosing the good and the appropriate over long periods of time. The Self can choose the true and the good by aiming at an ideal Self, ultimately God. Religion helps the Self attain to or become the ideal Self.

3 Mechanisms and Dynamics of Decentering

> But we have this treasure in earthen vessels, that the excellency of the
> power may be of God, and not of us. We are troubled on every side, yet
> not distressed; we are perplexed, but not in despair; persecuted, but not
> forsaken; cast down, but not destroyed...
>
> – St. Paul, 2 Cor. 4

Introduction

The central executive Self, the free agent intellect that chooses the good
and the true, is the treasure to which St. Paul refers. It is a treasure that
can be lost unless the religious path is taken. I have argued that religious
practices help to build up a centralized executive Self by reducing the
discrepancy between an ideal Self and the current Self. I want to show
in this chapter that a process I call "decentering" implements the discrepancy reduction process and helps to construct a centralized, ideal
executive Self. It does so by periodically taking the current Self "offline,"
out of working memory, for repair and construction and then linking it
back with an ideal possible Self commanding a greater range of computational and cognitive resources. By offline I simply mean removed from
working memory and placed into a suppositional, logical space (a mental
space, familiar to anyone who has imagined possibilities for themselves).

It is a conscious form of imaginative mental processing that does not occur in working memory. I will show in later chapters that decentering also influences and shapes a range of religious phenomena from religious experience itself to religious language, religious rituals, and a variety of religious practices. Decentering turns out to be one of the central cognitive processes that shapes both religion and Self.

Religion, for all of the reasons cited in the previous chapter, wants to build a central executive Self. An inevitable consequence, however, of the program to build a persisting, centralized, focused, and unified consciousness – an executive Self – is this process I am calling decentering. You cannot have a unified sense of Self unless you also have a process that constructs and maintains that Self. Decentering temporarily displaces or decouples the executive Self from its position of control over executive cognitive and motor functions to repair that sense of Self and then links it back with a greater range of cognitive systems than it was linked to before the decoupling was implemented.

The claim is a simple one: A Self (instantiated as a representational complex in semantic memory) becomes more complex and more unified than a baseline, less complex Self by obtaining control of a greater range of neurocognitive systems than the baseline Self controls. This is what decentering accomplishes – particularly when it operates in religious environments.

The function of decentering is to reduce the discrepancy between the current Self and a possible ideal Self by enhancing computational resources available to the current Self. The way that this is accomplished is by integrating the old Self into a new, more complex and resourceful Self. The "story" that is the old Self must be integrated into the story that is the new possible Self. In essence, the old Self must gain a greater level of control over neurocognitive systems. How does an existing self-concept exert control over any given neurocognitive system? It does so by acting selectively when it guides retrieval of memories, facts, or goals. A Self controls a neurocognitive system when it uses selectively retrieved information to guide behavior. In short, a Self controls the cognitive and behavioral repertoire of an individual when it controls attentional resources.

How does Self-concept or representational complex gain access to, use, or control attentional resources? We do not know. A plausible scenario might be the following: The Self-schema first inhibits the links between the attentional system and all other cognitive systems but the Self (i.e., it eliminates its competitors). Next, the attentional system by default (it has no other "choices") establishes both excitatory and inhibitory links with the Self-schema. Thus, the Self can now regulate attentional operations, and by regulating attentional resources, the Self can control the behavioral actions and goals of the individual. This scenario depends, of course, on the inhibitory capacities of the Self-construct. The neuroanatomical network that mediates the executive Self is centered on right-sided orbitofrontal, dorsomedial and dorsolateral prefrontal, and anterior temporal networks (Chapter 4, The Neurology of the Self). These brain regions are known to be extensively interconnected with and exert inhibitory control over virtually all of the other brain systems implicated in complex behaviors (for a recent compendium of essays on these regions, see Miller & Cummings (2007).

I will assume henceforth that something like the inhibitory scenario mentioned earlier is involved in the Self gaining control over attentional resources and that this increases the sense of unity and the sense of an ideal executive Self. Note, however, that given the inherently conflictual nature of the individual brain/mind (due to genetic conflict described previously), simple inhibition of all of the neurocognitive systems that seek access to attentional resources, even if it were possible, would not be desirable. What is desirable is some sort of optimal solution or synthesis of all of the competing claims on attention, a synthesis of competing and conflictual desires and motivations. I propose that this synthesis is accomplished by the decentering mechanism.

It is now time to provide some detail on this proposed decentering mechanism.

Cognitive Mechanisms of Decentering

Decentering occurs in four stages:

Stage 1: The sense of agency or volition is inhibited.

Stage 2: The Self-structure or -concept is placed into a suppositional logical space or "possible world" "box."

Stage 3: A discrepancy reduction process (between current and ideal Selves) is implemented via a search in semantic memory to find a more integral version of the Self that can encompass deeper, more optimal solutions to internal and external conflicts and problems.

Stage 4: The old Self is then bound to and integrated into the new identity (ideal Self) chosen by the search process via integration of the old story into the new story. If all goes well, that new identity is larger and more complex than the older Self, and thus it is more unified.

Explication of the Decentering Process

Let us assume a basic picture of the cognitive architecture like the one suggested by Nichols and Stich (2000; see Figure 3.1) to account for pretense.

Nichols and Stich explain:

This account of cognitive architecture, which has been widely adopted both in cognitive science and in philosophy, maintains that in normal humans, and probably in other organisms as well, the mind contains two quite different kinds of representational states, beliefs and desires. These two kinds of states differ "functionally" (as philosophers sometimes say) because they are caused in different ways and have different patterns of interaction with other components of the mind. Some beliefs are caused fairly directly by perception; others are derived from pre-existing beliefs via processes of deductive and non-deductive inference. Some desires (like the desire to get something to drink) are caused by systems that monitor various bodily states. Other desires, sometimes called "instrumental desires" or "sub-goals," are generated by a process of practical reasoning that has access to beliefs and to pre-existing desires. The practical reasoning system must do more than merely generate sub-goals. It must also determine which structure of goals and sub-goals are to be acted upon at any time. Once made, that decision is passed on to various action controlling systems whose job it is to sequence and coordinate the behaviors necessary to carry out the decision.

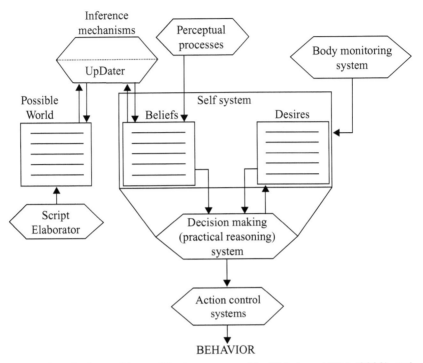

Figure 3.1. Basic cognitive architecture proposed by Nichols and Stich (2000), and the proposed "location" of the Self-system.

The architecture summarized in Figure 3.1 suggests that internal conflict is handled via the decision-making "box" or system, which receives input from both the desires box and the beliefs box. For our purposes, we can equate the executive Self with these three boxes: the beliefs, desires, and decision-making boxes. To account for counterfactual forms of reasoning like pretense, Nichols and Stich postulate a "possible world" box as well.

> Like the Belief Box and the Desire Box, the Possible World Box (PWB) contains representation tokens. However, the functional role of these tokens, their pattern of interaction with other components of the mind, is quite different from the functional role of either beliefs or desires. Their job is not to represent the world as it is or as we'd like it to be, but rather to represent what the world would be like given some set of assumptions that we may neither believe to be true nor want to be true. The PWB is a work

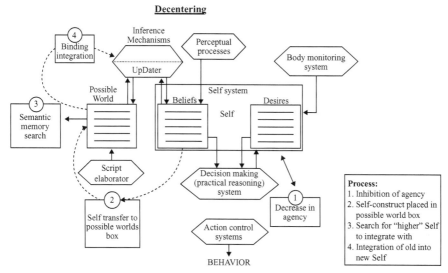

Figure 3.2. Cognitive architecture involved in decentering.

space in which our cognitive system builds and temporarily stores representations of one or another possible world. We are inclined to think that the mind uses the PWB for a variety of tasks including mindreading, strategy testing, and empathy. Although we think that the PWB is implicated in all these capacities, we suspect that the original evolutionary function of the PWB was rather to facilitate reasoning about hypothetical situations (Nichols & Stich, 2000, p. 122).

I suggest that the possible world system or box can be brought in to handle internal conflict in the following way (see Figure 3.2).

Stage 1. Reduction in Agency/Volition

Assume a decision impasse occurs because of internal conflict or conflicting desires. The decision-making system then halts its operation and sends inhibitory feedback to the beliefs and desires boxes (i.e., the current Self). The message is to suspend operations temporarily while a solution space is searched. The Self and agency are inhibited or reduced to trigger the search process. This suspension in agency may be involuntary if the problem simply cannot be solved; the Self may just experience a defeat in the real world; or the discrepancy between current and ideal Selves may suddenly become salient, thus triggering discrepancy reduction processes. Anguish, suffering, and depression can all issue in a reduction in agency and, under the right conditions, trigger a decentering process.

Alternatively, a suspension in agency may be accomplished via religious practices such as the use of ascetical techniques that may include fasting, sleep deprivation, performance of rituals, and so forth. Hallucinogenic drugs can also impair agency and induce a decentering process.

Stage 2. Placing the Self-Concept in Suppositional Space

When agency is inhibited, the current Self is decoupled from its control over executive resources of the individual and placed in a suppositional logical space (the possible worlds box). A search for a possible Self that will solve the conflict or problem is launched.

Stage 3. Search for Optimal Selves

Many potential Selves/stories are searched until a match to the solution is discovered. The Self that wins out in the competition represents a possible solution to the internal conflict that caused the shutdown in the decision-making process. Both the inference-making system and the script-elaboration system are activated in support of the search process. If no match or solution is found, the search continues with new possible Selves postulated during each iteration of the process. The length of the search process and its depth will depend on either the degree of the impasse that caused the shutdown in the first place or the distance between the current Self and the ideal Self the search is aimed at reducing. In religious ritual contexts, the ideal Self can be a deity; therefore, the discrepancy between current and ideal Selves is huge in the case of religious rituals.

The search is constrained to a stock of existing identities stored in semantic memory. These existing identities are constructed from all of the stories we have heard or read and from people we know, fictional selves from works of art, mythological figures, historical figures, characters in dreams, future hoped-for Selves, and supernatural agents, both positive and negative. This stock of identities may be searched in order of complexity, with the least complex Selves (dream characters) accessed first and the most complex (supernatural agents) accessed last.

Narratively Constrained Search Space for the Ideal Self

Many scholars (e.g., Freud, Propp, Jung, Campbell, Eliade) have noticed that the experience of growth into a better or ideal Self is accomplished via integration of the old into the new or better story. Victor Turner pointed out that rituals often promote entry into a "liminal space" that facilitates change from one social role into a larger or more mature social role. For the Self to grow into a more responsible social role in a community, it must integrate the old Self into a new Self that is capable of taking on the new responsibilities. This integration process, this process of spiritual growth, is reflected in some myths and tales from around the world. Vladimir Propp's *Morphology of the Folktale* (1968) summarized some of the recurrent motifs in folktales.

According to Propp (1927/1968), a tale is to be seen as a sequence of 31 themes or functions. In most versions of Propp's sequence, matters are considerably simplified as follows: The hero suffers a defeat or challenge, and he suffers exile or must leave home to address the challenge. On the journey, he meets some magical being that puts him to a test; he passes the test and thereby receives some gift in the form of a helper or magical talisman. Now ready to meet the challenge, he arrives at the appropriate place, meets the adversary, engages in a contest or combat, is hurt, but triumphs in the end. He then begins his homeward journey. When he arrives home he is no longer recognized by his compatriots. Some other person has assumed his place in his home world. He defeats this final adversary, marries well, and becomes a kingly figure.

To illustrate, take the early Sumerian myth of Gilgamesh. Gilgamesh suffers the loss of his twin and friend Enkidu. He wants to bring Enkidu back to life, so he goes on a journey in search of a medicine to bring Enkidu back to life. After an arduous journey through the steppe and the mountains, he meets his helper, Siduri, the alewife. She tells him how to cross the water of death so as to reach Utnapishtim, the underworld god who knows the secret of immortality. Utnapishtim gives Gilgamesh the crucial information about how to obtain the "plant of life." This effort to obtain the plant of life involves more challenges that Gilgamesh meets successfully until he obtains the plant and heads home. Another example is the Greek story of Odysseus. He sets out for war on Troy. He and his comrades accomplish that arduous task but then is frustrated in his attempt to return home. After many adventures, he obtains supernatural help from the goddess Athena. He arrives back in Ithaca and finds suitors attempting to marry his wife Penelope and thereby acquire all of his goods and lands. He, with the help of his son, slays all the suitors and reclaims his wife and his kingly status.

In a religiously constrained decentering search process, the old Self suffers a defeat or is temporarily inhibited via a ritual or ascetical process or in some other way. During the religious practice or ritual, a supernatural agent is held up as a model to imitate or take the place of the old Self. The aim of the old Self is to link up with the new ideal Self. When some links are made, the "hero" old Self experiences this as finding magical helpers along the way. This emerging new Self now has access to a wider range of neurocognitive capacities than the old Self had. These abilities help the hero surmount the challenge or internal conflict that triggered the search in the first place. The link with the new Self is still not solid, however, until the hero heads home, meets the old Self as an imposter, and defeats him decisively. When that is accomplished, the new Self emerges with control over decision-making capacities, attentional resources, and behavior. A new integration of the personality is accomplished, and the new Self now reigns supreme. The hero gets married and takes on a kingly status. That marriage motif signals the integration or binding of the old Self into a new higher Self.

Stage 4. Binding

When a solution identity is found, the old Self or identity is integrated into the new identity or Self via narrative devices/logic. The updater box takes over the process and updates belief systems to be consistent with the new identity, elaborates on the contours of the new Self, enhances perceptual pick-up capacities, and so forth. The updating process essentially displaces the old Self and instantiates the new Self, and decision making and action implementation can continue – under control of the "new and improved" Self.

This editing and shaping of the Self-construct via a mild form of the decentering process likely occurs on a daily basis, which is why we change over time. We are driven by the need to address internal conflict and desires. We are more or less successful in doing so over time, but it is not easy – personal and emotional growth always involves some amount of suffering.

Religious Practices and Decentering

Within a religious ritual context, the editing and shaping of a new Self occurs in a much more profound and indelible fashion because religious ritual constrains the search space in such a way as to entertain only the deepest solutions to the conflict. Ritual allows for the entertaining of a very high conception of a possible Self – indeed, a saintly or even a godlike Self. The potential Self that is the aim of the search process is given to us by a religious tradition. Often that model is a transcendent, supernatural agent with extraordinary qualities. Other models within a religious tradition may be revered ancestors or saintly figures. These models are based on figures that have faced dilemmas in the past and have solved them in optimal ways. They are worthy models to imitate. This religiously inspired "possible Self" therefore has the capacity to integrate some very fundamental internal conflicts. To do so, the old Self has to be defeated (inhibited or suppressed), and the beliefs and desires systems have to link up to the new ideal Self. If this link-up succeeds, it can bring to the personality a new level of integration, a reduction in internal conflict, and a new access to internal cognitive, emotional, and behavioral resources that were unthinkable for the old Self. When the link-up occurs, we see the fruits of such a "solution" in the religious emotions, which can involve some pretty impressive experiences, such as gratitude, awe, "elevation," joy, and ecstasy.

Religious practices assist in linking up with the ideal Self. Clearly, decentering is about linking up the old Self with a new and better Self. As I will show in a later chapter, many religious practices assist in that process of self-transformation. I wish to mention here the practice of yoga as its primary aim is to link up the aspirant with God or the Atman ultimate Self. Yoga has been used not only in many Hindu traditions but also in Buddhism, Jainism, Judaism, and, more recently, Christianity. The oldest extant codification of yoga techniques, the *Yogasutra* of Patanjali, can be dated back to the fourth to fifth centuries C.E. The primary aim of yogic practice is cessation of thought or at least to cultivate nonattachment to mental states and bodily desires and then to attach to the atman or immortal soul – a higher consciousness or a god. Practice in performing a series of body postures as well as meditative states helps the aspirant to gain power over the lower Self and then turn it into the subtle body made of an immortal and invulnerable crystalline substance, as the *Yogasutra* puts it. According to Patanjali, a true Self is opposed to other forms of the Self that contain various amount of "prakriti," including ahamkara (roughly the personal sense of self), buddhi (intellect and will), and mind.

Yoga is one example of a religious practice, various forms of which are utilized by millions of people each day and designed to yoke up the current Self with a higher Self. Admittedly, yoga in the West is usually a stripped-down version bereft of any true religious philosophy to back up the practice. Nevertheless, most people in the West who practice yoga see it as a spiritual practice – not just a bodily exercise. There is a conscious effort to quiet the mind, dampen down desire and cravings, dethrone the Self, and so forth, which is precisely what the decentering process accomplishes. The decentering process reduces to an attempt to shed an old Self and attach to and become a new higher Self. The psychology of the emotional attachment process might therefore illuminate parts of this process. When Granqvist (2006) reviewed the attachment and religion literature, he noted the original contributions of Kirkpatrick (see Kirkpatrick, 1999, 2005) and a series of studies by many research teams that demonstrate consistent relationships between religiosity and attachment status as well as studies of religious subjects who appear to use religious practices to promote and maintain close contact with God.

Decentering and the Religious Emotions

When a linking up with God or the ideal Self is accomplished, what ensues? Potentially what ensues is a deep integration of personality and resolution of very deep and otherwise insoluble internal conflicts. One would expect some spillover of these effects into the emotional life of the individual.

Integration into the higher Self is experienced as a sense of elevation, and in extreme cases, the process of yoking up of the Self to the divine is experienced as ecstasy. In more run-of-the-mill cases, we can expect the integration process to yield that sense of elevation and quiet dignity so characteristic of genuinely religious individuals. There may also be a sense of gratitude for the experience as integration brings with it many side benefits like less attachment to conflicts, old desires, and so forth. That sense of freedom is naturally experienced as gift; therefore, gratitude ensues. When the decentering process is deep or prolonged, the individual may experience ecstasy.

Ecstasy

Ecstasy is traditionally understood as an experience of joy so intense that you are taken outside of yourself so that your identity extends beyond your old conception of Self. "Ecstasy as an emotional experience thus is based on awareness, not on amnesia, although its intensity may result in a loss of consciousness and is thereby brought to its end. In this regard, ecstasy as an emotion differs from possession, hypnosis, or trance, of which the person often has no memory" (Malinar & Basu, 2008, p. 243). This observation underlines the fact that decentering and its effects in a religious context are not to be equated with trance or similar states. Ecstasy is a bridge "that connects the adept to that very absolute, divine, and transcendent entity, realm, or state taught in the religious doctrine. The ecstatic experience results in temporal contact with that realm in terms of direct experience (as in Hindu darshana, Sufi hal or wajd, or Catholic visio beatificatio), immersion (as in Vedantic brahman or Christian unico mystica), release of the 'self' from the body (as in some yogic practices), or the vanishing notions of 'self' to open up the space of a blissful emptiness (as in some Buddhist mediation practices)" (Malinar & Basu, 2008, p. 246).

Decentering and Related States/Processes

It should be clear from all that I have said earlier in the text about decentering that it cannot be construed as a simple trance state or a dissociative process or even as an "altered state of consciousness" as that phrase is generally understood. Indeed, it is my feeling that previous scholars who saw ecstatic trance in various religious rituals were really witnessing the operations of the decentering process in these rituals. Nor should decentering be considered an altered state of consciousness except in the most generic sense. Virtually every change of brain state can be considered an altered state of consciousness, and to that trivial extent, decentering can be called an altered state of consciousness.

Nevertheless, it is important to be clear how decentering differs from trance, hypnosis, or dissociation. Decentering always involves a reduction in the sense of agency of the Self. In most trance states, there is no such reduction in intentionality, ego, or Self. Instead, the Self is inflated and the sense of agency enhanced via hypnosis, suggestion, placebo treatment, drug ingestion, and so forth. There is an inflation of the sense of Self in these latter states even while there is a seemingly paradoxical reduction in self-will in trance. The reduction in self-will in trance, though, is illusory. In most settings where trance is induced by an authority figure or via drugs, the Self's strategic agenda is still operative: It wants to do the will of the prestigious other or it wants to medicate its anxieties with drugs and so forth. Decentering, in contrast, involves a real, if temporary, reduction in agency.

Another way in which decentering is different from all of the trance-related phenomena is that decentering involves a period of drift or uncertainty when there is real uncertainty as to which identity will control executive resources of the individual. During trance, no such period of uncertainty exists. Either the individual controls matters or the hypnotist does. Decentering, furthermore, is compatible with religious ritual processes, whereas trance is not. In ritual one has to act; in trance one does not act. One either sleeps or does the will of the hypnotist. The fundamental difference, however, between trance and decentering is a cognitive one: In a decentering process, which Self-structure will control executive resources is up for grabs. In trance and related states, identity or Self-concept is not in question; instead, the will of the individual involved is the prize. Admittedly, will and identity are closely related. Nevertheless, they are not the same. Identity or Self implements a will after deliberative processing (as we have seen in Chapter 2).

Risky Effects of Decentering

These latter considerations on what decentering *is not* lead naturally to a consideration of when the decentering process breaks down or goes wrong.

Religious Fanaticism

Take, for example, the case of the religious fanatic: the "religious individual" who is utterly convinced that God is on his or her side even if it means the murder of thousands of people. A breakdown in the decentering process might help to partially account for some of the distorted thinking of such individuals. Stage 1 of the decentering process is intact in fanatical individuals. During rituals, for example, they can experience a reduction in agency as they will perform stipulated ritual actions with fanatical exactitude. Stage 2 is also intact. Indeed, these individuals may feel as if their very selves are always in a suppositional space or up for grabs. This transfer of the self-concept to the possible worlds box may be one source of a sense of fundamental insecurity in some of these individuals. That fundamental insecurity is then offset by an overriding sense of certainty in the religious realm. What appears to be impaired in fanatical religious individuals is Stage 3, the search process. Even though the old Self is placed in the possible worlds box, no search process is conducted, and so no linking up with or integration into a higher Self is possible, but Stage 4 "binding" still proceeds apace. Because there is no ideal Self with which to bind the old Self, the old Self instead binds with itself, and thus the old identity is reinforced and experienced as impregnable. Its convictions are held with ever greater certainty. The greater the attachment of old Self to old Self, the more difficult it is to break out of the bind. Narcissism ensues.

Whatever the effects of the decentering process, positive or negative, it is clear that some such process must be involved in the individual's experience of religion. He or she relates to religion as a way of life and a redemption from the suffering found in life. I suggest that the brain and cognitive mechanisms that support the long and protracted process known as redemption or release sometimes use a process similar or identical to what I have been calling decentering. It should go without saying that when I refer to integration into an ideal Self as one of the objects of religious practices, I am not equating the ideal Self with God. To the extent that God is conceived in theistic and even personalist terms, religious persons can and do attempt to link their Selves up with God. As St. Paul says, they attempt to put on the Mind of Christ.

4 Neurology of the Self

Any consciousness whatsoever – past, future, or present; internal or external; blatant or subtle, common or sublime, far or near: every consciousness – is to be seen as it actually is with right discernment as: "This is not mine. This is not my self. This is not what I am."

– Buddha Sermon on Anatta: "The Anattalakkhana Sutta,"
Samyutta Nikaya XXII, 59

Introduction

Modern cognitive neuroscientific studies of the Self indicate that virtually every higher cognitive function is influenced by the Self: Memories are encoded more efficiently when referred to the Self (Craik, Moroz, & Moscovitch, 1999; Fink et al., 1996; Kelley et al., 2002); feelings and affective responses always include the Self (Davidson, 2001; LeDoux, 2002); fundamental attributions of intentionality, agency, and Mind all concern selves in interaction with other Selves (Gallagher, 2000; Vogeley & Fink, 2003); and so on. Yet basic problems concerning the nature, representational properties, and functions of the Self remain understudied and unresolved.

The scientific study of the Self has been somewhat slow to mature because the nature of the Self appears to be so complex (Metzinger, 2003;

Northoff & Bermpohl, 2004). The Self draws on several psychologic and neuropsychologic domains, such as autobiographical memory, emotional and evaluative systems, agency or the sense of being the cause of some action, self-monitoring, bodily awareness, mind-reading or covert mimicking of other's mental states, subjectivity or perspective in perception, and finally, the sense of unity conferred on consciousness when it is invested with the subjective perspective (Kircher & David, 2003; LeDoux, 2002; Metzinger, 2003). Any account of the psychology of Self should at least be consistent with most or all of these properties. It is no wonder, then, that progress in understanding the Self has been slow.

As mentioned in Chapter 2, I will be assuming the theoretical framework of "possible Selves" in this book. That framework suggests that Self-regulation is accomplished via an interplay between current and possible Selves, including hoped for and feared possible Selves. Religion, I suggest, holds up an ideal possible Self as a behavioral standard from which the current Self is evaluated and "adjusted" when necessary. That adjustment process involves an integration of the old into the new higher Self via the process I call decentering. With that as background, and keeping in mind the cognitive complexity of the Self-construct itself, I wish to step back and consider the brain correlates of the sense of Self. Consideration of the neurology of the Self will put us in a position to better understand the neurocognitive dynamics of the decentering process and the neurology of religious experience as well.

My focus in this chapter will be to establish the key neurologic structures implicated in support of the Self – particularly the Self as agent and "deliberator" between choices (i.e., the central executive Self).

Neuroanatomy of the Self

A number of investigators have recently suggested that the human sense of Self depends crucially on the anterior temporal and prefrontal cortex (Craik et al., 1999; Feinberg & Keenan, 2005; McNamara et al., 1995; Miller et al., 2001; Seeley & Sturm, 2007; Vogeley, Kurthen, Falkai, & Maier, 1999). Neuroimaging studies (positron emission tomography [PET] and functional magnetic resonance imaging [fMRI]) of persons performing self-related tasks (e.g., comparing activation patterns and levels associated with self-referential vs. non–self-referential tasks) have demonstrated that self-related processing tasks are associated with activation in very widely distributed neural networks including the orbital and adjacent medial prefrontal cortex (OMPFC), the anterior cingulate (AC; particularly the supragenual part, SAC), the dorsomedial prefrontal cortex (DMPFC), the insula, and the posterior cingulate cortex (PC), including the adjacent retrosplenium and precuneus (Gillihan & Farah, 2005; Seeley & Sturm, 2007; Uddin, Iacoboni, Lange, & Keenan, 2007).

Clinical studies indicate that the right prefrontal and anterior temporal cortices are key nodes in the neural network that supports the Self (Devinsky, 2000; Feinberg & Keenan, 2005; Keenan, Rubio, Racioppi, Johnson, & Barnacz, 2005). When a dementing process begins to invade frontotemporal sites on the right, personality changes become marked and striking (Wang & Miller, 2007). Miller et al. (2001), for example, reported that 7 of 72 patients with probable frontotemporal dementing disorders exhibited a dramatic change in Self. In 6 of these 7 patients, the selective dysfunction involved the right frontal region. In contrast, only 1 of the other 65 patients without selective right frontal dysfunction showed a change in Self. Similarly, Fink et al. (1996) reported selective activation of right prefrontal cortical regions in subjects engaged in recall of personal versus impersonal, long-term episodic memories. Craik et al. (1999) showed that right frontal sites were activated whenever subjects processed or memorized materials referring to the Self. In a seminal review of PET studies on episodic encoding and retrieval processes, Wheeler, Stuss, and Tulving (1997; see also Nyberg et al., 1996) concluded that episodic retrieval of personal memories is associated with an increased blood flow in the right frontal cortex with no increased blood flow in the left frontal cortex, whereas episodic encoding is associated with the opposite pattern (i.e., increased flow in the left frontal cortex and no increased flow in the right frontal cortex). They call this set of findings HERA (hemispheric encoding/retrieval asymmetry). Keenan, Nelson, O'Connor, & Pascual-Leone (2001) presented a series of pictures to a group of patients undergoing an intracarotid amobarbital test. The pictures represented faces generated by morphing the image of a famous person with the patient's own face, and participants were asked to remember what picture was shown during selective anesthesia of the right and the left hemispheres. Results indicated that most patients were unable to remember seeing their own face following an inactivation of the right hemisphere, whereas anesthesia of the left hemisphere did not interfere with recall of the "Self" face. These results once again implicate right frontal cortex in support of the Self.

What's so special about the right frontal/anterior temporal cortex? The right frontal/anterior temporal cortex differs from its left-sided counterpart in that it receives a more dense set of afferents coursing up from the neostriatal and limbic systems and it may also receive greater innervation from serotoninergic and noradrenergic cell groups in the brain stem (Bruder, 2003; Ongur & Price, 2000). Dopaminergic cell groups that project to the right prefrontal cortex display a more enhanced response to stress than dopaminergic cell groups projecting to the left prefrontal cortex (Berridge, Espana, & Stalnaker, 2003). The right prefrontal and anterior temporal lobes also send inhibitory efferents to a wide range of cortical and subcortical structures indicating a regulatory role for this region of the brain. Starkstein and Robinson (1997) pointed out that lesions in right prefrontal and anterior temporal regions virtually always result in syndromes of disinhibition. Instead of clear loss of function, you get release of previously inhibited behavior or abnormal enhancement of existing functions. The right prefrontal cortex has also been implicated in support of volition and voluntary motor actions. As we have seen, agency or volition is a key part of the central executive Self.

Neuroscience of Voluntary Motor Actions

When you perform a voluntary act, a special part of the central nervous system is engaged as opposed to when you move involuntarily. The execution of a voluntary motor act begins with activity (firing of groups of neurons) arising in the prefrontal lobes and then spreading to the motor areas of the prefrontal lobes including the primary motor cortex (PMC) and the supplementary motor area (SMA). The SMA in particular plays

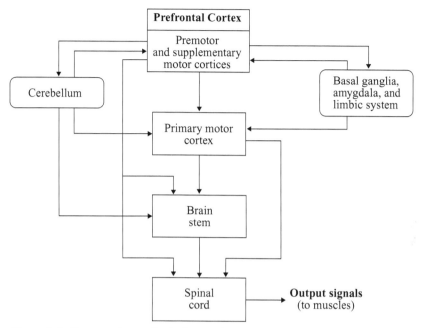

Figure 4.1. Neuroanatomy of voluntary action.

a major role in the preparation, selection, and initiation of self-initiated voluntary movements. This conclusion concerning the role of the SMA in voluntary actions is based on decades of electrophysiologic studies in monkeys and humans that consistently show a "readiness potential" on the electroencephalogram (EEG) that appears in the right SMA (and nowhere else in the brain) right before a voluntary movement. Monkeys with lesions in the SMA show a significant decrease of spontaneous behavior. Patients with Parkinson's disease (and loss of dopamine innervations to the SMA) suffer from akinesia. There are other disorders of voluntary movement associated with SMA lesions (e.g., transcortical motor aphasia) that cannot be covered in this book but that confirm the role of SMA in voluntary movement (Figure 4.1).

When an intention to move or act is encoded in the prefrontal cortex, it is transmitted to the SMA to initiate a motor command sequence. The commands to move are then transmitted from the SMA to the PMC and then the brain stem and down the spinal cord for motor output. The cerebellum and the basal ganglia modulate this sequential motor processing system in various ways, with the cerebellum controlling postural movements and all kinds of rapid and automated ballistic movements. The basal ganglia and the limbic system, in contrast, support the integration of cognitive, emotional, and sequential information into ongoing movement programs. The limbic system is important for emotional experiences, whereas the basal ganglia are important for motor functions. Deep to the temporal lobes and within the limbic system are two structures that are particularly important for the Self: the hippocampus and the amygdala. The hippocampus is crucial for the formation of new memories and for encoding spatial and contextual information. The amygdala is important for all kinds of emotional responses – particularly negative emotional responses.

In short, voluntary acts are associated with a particular portion of the central nervous system – namely, the right prefrontal cortex, the SMA, and the PMC – as well as with portions of the basal ganglia and limbic system. We are particularly interested in how the brain supports construction of an executive and autonomous agent/Self. To begin to construct a potential cognitive architecture for this executive Self, we will need to look at its breakdown patterns when its neurologic substrate is damaged.

Data from the Clinic

When the systems supporting the executive Self (agency, deliberation, and choice) break down, the patterns in which they break down may reveal the basic structures of the cognitive architecture that constitutes the system. There are a number of neuropsychiatric syndromes that involve an alteration in the sense of agency and Will. These neuropsychiatric syndromes involving a breakdown in agency and intentional acting should be seen as "experiments of nature" when nature reveals itself. Often nature will surprise with components of a system that our theories simply did not expect to find. The data from the clinic therefore are intrinsically "ecologically valid." We are peering directly into the workings of nature and the Mind/brain when we examine its breakdown patterns.

Alien Hand Syndrome

Take for example, the alien hand syndrome. Here the patient with damage to the SMA or to the nearby anterior portion of the corpus callosum may experience one of his hands as alien or someone else's hand. The hand is experienced as moving according to someone else's will, or the limb is experienced as being autonomous.

Consider the following case:

> At one point it was noted that the patient had picked up a pencil and had begun scribbling with the [affected] right hand. When her attention was directed to this activity, she reacted with dismay, immediately withdrew the pencil, and pulled the right hand to her side using the [normal] left hand. She then indicated that she had not herself initiated the original action of the right arm. She often reacted with dismay and frustration at her inability to prevent these unintended movements of the right arm. She experienced a feeling of dissociation from the actions of the right arm, stating on several occasions that "it will not do what I want it to do" (63-year-old right-handed female with left medial frontal infarction; Goldberg, Mayer, & Toglia, 1981, pp. 684–685).

Norman Geschwind recounted that his patients with alien hand syndrome would occasionally awaken from sleep to find that the alien hand was choking them during the night. This was more often the case when the alien hand was controlled by the right hemisphere (i.e., the left hand)!

The Environmental Dependency Syndrome

The experience of free will allows us to escape from slavery to the most appetizing or salient stimuli in our environment. Because we have free will, we can voluntarily choose to forego gratification now to obtain some future and higher reward. Free will frees us from undue dependence on the external world; it temporarily severs the intense attachment to the external environment or "world." Without the ability to periodically withdraw from the world and its attachments, the external environment would pretty much constitute the primary determinant of human behavior . . . it would excessively control our behavioral options.

A most striking example of the power of the external environment to "excessively" control an individual's behavior due to a loss of autonomy comes from the "environmental dependency syndrome" described first by Lhermitte (1986). This neuropsychological syndrome occurs in patients who have suffered damage to their frontal lobes. The frontal lobes are believed to specialize in the monitoring of internal and intrapsychic events and in promoting distance from the environment. The frontal lobes function in opposition to the parietal lobes, which are sensitive to events in external surroundings and which foster approach to the environment. The optimal functioning of these two cerebral regions involves a state of reciprocal inhibition such that the individual is never unduly influenced by one pole of the inner–outer polarity.

Patients with bilateral frontal lobe damage display a pattern of behavior that reflects the now unopposed activity of the parietal lobes. Their behavior comes under the influence of the "approach tendencies" of the parietal lobes. These patients are excessively influenced by the external environment. They are stimulus bound, concrete, socially inappropriate, and display a remarkable inability to grasp context. Lhermitte (1986) also demonstrated that these patients exhibit a tendency to imitate the examiner's behaviors and gestures even when this behavior entails considerable social embarrassment. The mere sight of an object may elicit the compulsion to use it. Lhermitte (1986) described cases in which he placed a syringe (with saline in it) in front of a patient who then promptly lifted it up and tried to inject herself with the needle! In a very literal sense, then, the immediate external environment controls these patients' behaviors.

Delusions of Control

Here the patient (typically a schizophrenic) experiences his or her thoughts, actions, or emotions as not being his or her own but instead as being replaced by those of external agencies like Satan or some other individual or group known to the patient.

Consider the following case from Mayer (1911):

In regard to the voice I hear talking to me all the time, it was through my investigating spiritualism and watching and listening for what I could hear in the evenings after reading the newspaper that it commenced. One evening it began to talk to me, telling me some funny stories, and it kept that up for a week, when one Saturday evening it hypnotized me as I sat in my chair, and I went to bed that night and was in bed until Monday, hypnotized, I suppose, for I was seeing pictures of all kinds all the time until I got up to go to work Monday morning. He has been talking to me ever since. He says he is the devil from hell and he is going to take me to hell as soon as he gets ready. He makes me speak words as if he has my tongue in his control when he is talking to me; but if I talk to any person, I have control. He makes me smell different things and he will tell me about it at the same time. It feels as if there is a flea or bug on my eye, nose, or throat, or any place, and he will say to me, "Brush that bug off." He bothers my eyes, so that I cannot see right at times, and he bothers my stomach at night, saying, "I'll fix your stomach for you so you cannot eat." Three weeks ago, he shook my brain like you would a handkerchief, saying to me, "See what I am doing to you, I'll fix this block of yours." He talks to me all day and night, waking me at night to tell me what he made me dream. He makes my head hurt in the back and it feels hot, and he says it will be worse later on with me.

"John," he says, "you never will have another minute's peace as long as you live, and when you die it will be worse. I came here to worry you and I am going to play with you, like a cat does with a mouse, and when I get tired of you, I am going to kill you. That is, I am going to make you kill yourself, but I am going to make you kill someone else first. That black-eyed doctor thinks himself smart. Oh, you won't know you are doing it, you will want to knock something off or cut something out, and you will think it just has to be done. I can set you daffy in a minute. I have your brains right under my thumbs. Now you have not a thought coming; I am doing your thinking and telling you things. I can shut your thoughts off and you will never know it. I won't let you know things until I get good and ready."

He tells me every little act I did in my life, saying, "Now what in h – did you do that for?" He will tell me to do this or that at my work when I am going to do something, the same as you would tell me to do it, or he says, "I will stay here till you come, when I will go," and he will keep this nagging up all day like a talking machine. Sometimes I go nearly crazy. This is a sample, a drop in the bucket to what I hear:

"You are a d – f – for telling the doctor. He thinks that what you say and write is what you think or have thought and says he will make you see it that way. You d – f – , I can think and make you think what I want you to. Peace in mind is all there is to life, and let me see you get it. I'll not let you forget your troubles. No, the doctor shan't even know of them. If you had done that way, resisted at first, you would not have been bothered with me. You will be sorry for it the way you are getting stubborn. You won't get me out of your mind. You are onto me, to get you worked up and put mean feelings on you, trying to make you mad, but I'll fool you and the doctor yet."

"Let's write a book, John, about hell. I have asked you often and if you don't I will carry you to hell. Do it, John; no one knows about hell and I want to tell them. If you do, I will give you a little peace. D – you for resisting. The doctor can explain all he wants, but I'll show you yet you can't fight me off."

It is a continual dream with me all night. I would be asleep, but it kept running things into my mind all night, which seems like a lot of dreams. In the morning after getting up, it would go all over these things, saying it wanted to do it that way. "You can use your own mind if I let you, John, but I am not going to. You are a fool for sitting down and letting me get in your head. Oh, you can get mad if you want to, but you cannot hurt me, all you can do is to kill yourself and that will please me. Do you think that doctor can do you good? Well, he might know something about this business, but if he knows anything that will interfere with me in my work on your head, the minute he goes to do it, – well, if he goes to do anything that will do you any good, he will have to kill me or make me weak enough that you can overpower me. That is, your mind will be too strong for me to do anything with. John, when I see that is going to happen, plump, off goes your block. Mind you, now. I will kill you if I see that man is doing any good or doing me any harm. I have every nerve and every little thing in your head and body in my control, so it is up to you now to let that doctor do something, if he can, or stay away from him. Now John, that doctor from his questions to-day thinks you allowed family troubles to bother you, but it is not that. If you had got up out of that chair in the evening after you finished reading the paper, it might have been different."

"Tell that man to go to h – . He cannot do you any good. He might think he is a doctor, but he is not a brain fixer, like I am, for I am the devil from hell. The doctor is putting you to hell as fast as you can go. I am the steam that runs the engine, and the engine is the brain. Your doctor might fix the engine like a machinist, but I am the steam to the brain or engine, and you can't fix the steam."

"Those spiritualists told you not to repeat anything I said, and now you are writing a letter dictated by the devil from the depths of hell, and I am going to take you there as soon as I get ready. It might be to-night, and might be in a year. I will go with you to see that doctor and he might hypnotize you until you think you are better, but as soon as you come out of that condition I will have you just the same. When your wife separated from you, you were a good man. You did what you thought right toward her, and she thought she was doing the same, but neither was right. It is not what you think, but what the Lord God himself thinks. We will get into trouble with the doctor if we don't scratch that out. No, don't write it."

"What do you mean, anyhow, writing this way when I am going to take you to hell. Don't give the doctor this to read; don't write anymore; he can't save you from me. I can't write any more. I mean, I cannot take time to have you write any more. But tell him this, I can fix more people in a holy jiffy in my way than he can ever in his lifetime. Do you think it is you and not I writing this?"

"You are more contented, are you? I'll have you again, though. I am sicker than a dog, cannot talk to you. Don't tell the doctor on me. Tell him that he cannot hurt me" (Mayer, 1911, pp. 265–268).

Comment. This case, although more dramatic and severe than other cases, is like many other patients with some form of schizophrenia that involves passivity phenomena and with intrusive and alienated thought processes. Before I discuss the case in more detail, please note that schizophrenia is associated with limbic, anterior temporal and prefrontal dysfunction, thus confirming the link between this neural network and the executive Self noted earlier in this chapter. In addition, this case of "possession" exemplifies many other such cases. We will discuss these cases more fully in Chapter 8. Most often the entity that is controlling the patient's will is experienced as evil, malign, and oppressive. Some shred of agency is left in this case of possession as the patient did not fully identify with the alien entity. This patient did not claim to be Satan. Instead, he claimed that the devil was controlling his thoughts and actions. Interestingly, it would be hard to answer a question like "What did this patient will?" Clearly, one part of him willed to be rid of the evil entity, and another part of him controlled the thought and emotional processes of the primary identity.

Demonic possession represents one of the most vivid illustrations of divided consciousness possible. Where is Self or agency here? Clearly, agency has been displaced to a second-order entity that is experienced as malicious and that is controlling the first-order identity – the patient. The patient's ability to deliberate and formulate goals and plans and to make and commit to courses of action was, of course, severely impaired – yet still some form of agency remained. The Will is divided. The patient did not give his inward assent to control by the second-order entity, nor did he identify with or mentally appropriate that entity. The decentering process that normally leads to integration of Identity 1 into Identity 2 was prematurely derailed. A breakdown in the decentering process can help explain the lack of integration of Identity 1 into the higher Identity 2, but it cannot explain the sense of alien control the patient experiences. The patient senses himself AND another being, alien to Self, but that yet controls Self to a significant degree. How can we explain this sense of being controlled by another?

Cognitive Models of Agency

Most of us can think inward thoughts and know that we are the source of those thoughts, but sometimes some schizophrenics and individuals with multiple personality disorder (MPD), bipolar disorder, or other brain damage do not understand or believe that they are the source of the thoughts in their heads. How does this happen?

Interestingly, all of these aforementioned disorders share one brain system breakdown in common: The prefrontal cortex is damaged or metabolically abnormal in all of those conditions. Now the prefrontal cortex is the cortex that controls voluntary motor actions among a host of other cognitive processes. Neuroscientists have discovered that, for most intentional actions that arise in tandem with prefrontal neuronal indices (like the readiness potential), we create a model of the intention ("I will do x") as well as a model of the predicted effects of that action on the environment. When there is a match between the intended and the predicted effects, all is well. To get that match, a third operation (known as the attenuation of the actual sensory effects of the action) is required, and that third operation can happen only if the prefrontal cortex sends an inhibitory signal down the sensory system to inhibit incoming sensory signals. Cognitively speaking, only a strong sense of Self can oppose strong incoming sensory signals and impose an attenuation effect on those signals. If no such attenuation effect occurs, then the predicted effects do not match the actual sensory effects (in real life, they never do), and then the individual cannot assign a source to the intention or the thoughts. He cannot locate an intention inside himself (there was no match between intention predicted and effects), so he attributes the thoughts occurring in his head (there was, after all, an intention sent to the motor centers) to some other entity.

If we assume that the subjective experience of ownership of one's own thoughts and of control over sensory events emerges from an unconscious comparison between intentional and predicted/anticipated effects of one's actions, then when there is a match between intended and predicted effects, there is an increased tendency to experience the effect as self-caused. When there is a mismatch between anticipated and actual effect, the event is attributed to an external cause.

To account for the takeover of one identity by another (in the same body), we need to add a little bit more detail to this simple cognitive

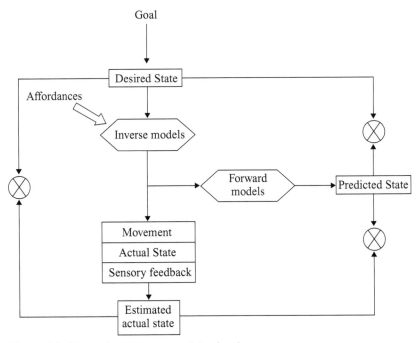

Figure 4.2. Forward and inverse models of action.

model. We have been describing what is known as an inverse model of voluntary control. Inverse models generate predictions about desired states and compute matches or mismatches (see Figure 4.2).

Forward models do the opposite. In any given voluntary action, an "efference" copy of the motor commands for that action is used to generate a prediction of the anticipated effects of that action. Then three comparisons are made. A first kind of comparator takes as input representations of the desired state and of the predicted state. If a difference is found, an error signal is sent to the inverse model that is then used to run further predictions until a match is made. A second kind of comparator mechanism compares the predicted consequences of a motor command with its actual consequences. The result of this comparison can be used to attenuate matched sensory information and to distinguish an intention or thought generated by the Self from that caused by changes in the world. After attenuation of sensory information, only the Self-generated signals/thoughts are left, so the thoughts are attributed to the Self. Finally, a third kind of comparison is between desired state and actual feedback. So to summarize:

The first comparison is between desired state and the predicted state. The second comparison is between predicted and actual outcomes, and the third between desired and actual outcomes. It is the first and second comparisons, those between predicted and outcome or intention, that matter for attributions of intentions/thoughts to Self versus some alien other. If both intention and outcome do not match predictions, then it is impossible to use either to locate the Self or to attenuate actual sensory input and thus sensory input will overwhelm the Self-related control processes. Identity is then rendered unstable and open to fluid changes.

This model does not explain all of the symptomology associated with clinical syndromes of impairment of agency, but it helps to explain some of that symptomology.

Note

Bulbulia (2009) has offered an original model of religious cognition that is related to some extent to the feed-forward and simulation models just explicated. He argues that religious beliefs require encapsulation from behavioral practices – or else illusory beliefs would guide behavior. He suggests that religious representations are decoupled from the rest of the cognitive apparatus and marked as untrue. Pyysiäinen (2003) offered a similar but much less detailed account of religious cognition. Bulbulia (2009) then notes that religious beliefs are nevertheless held to be true by believers, so he needs an explanation for that fact if he wants to hold that religious representations are decoupled from other cognitive systems and marked as untrue. He therefore postulates another constraint on religious cognition – namely, that self-deception must be involved. One further constraint is that religious beliefs be allowed to operate in social cooper-ation domains. Bulbulia (2009) realizes that social cooperation is surely an instance of practical behavior, but we have seen that religious ref-erents are considered fictions in the model, so they cannot be allowed to inform practical behavior. Bulbulia then argues for a further inte-gration constraint wherein religion operates only in social cooperative domains and not in other behavioral domains. In summary, for Bulbulia (2009) religious cognitions produce counterfactual representations of sacred realities, which are considered and marked "as true" (the self-deception constraint). These representations are formatted so that they do not influence practical action (the encapsulation constraint) outside normative social exchange (the integration constraint).

These simple cognitive models of action and of religious cognition, as well as the clinical syndromes they seek to explain, can also inform philosophical approaches to agency and free will. Perhaps the simplest conclusion one can reach when given the clinical facts summarized above is that it is more difficult to derail the deliberative process than it is to derail the agent. Human beings can always spin a rationale for some choice. The reasoning may be poor, but it will still occur. Agency is more vulnerable to dysfunction than is deliberation – yet the philosophical discussion of free will has emphasized deliberation. The agent or the Self can be overwhelmed and rendered inoperative if the agent is impaired due to clinical (brain) dysfunction, sensory overload, or moral dysfunction (akrasia). When the agent is weakened, autonomy and choice are threatened.

We therefore need a very strong sense of Self or agency to operate effectively over long periods of time, but when a strong centralized executive Self emerges, so does a cognitive repair process (decentering) as the executive Self needs a system to maintain and update its systems. The decentering process decouples the Self from its control over executive cognitive functions. It takes the Self offline and then repairs it by integrating it into a higher, more complex Self entity. The decentering process can go wrong, and you can see it happen in various disorders of the Self (see Chapter 8, Table 8.1).

Decentering and MPD

The annihilation of the Will of the first-order identity in the patient described earlier is similar to what occurs in cases of Multiple Personality Disorder or MPD. What is unique about MPD, however, is that you can observe the process of decentering when the new second-order identity appropriates the cognitive and neural resources of the first-order identity. When that happens, the Will of the first-order identity is impaired. In MPD, Stage 4 (the binding or integration stage in the decentering process) fails to occur, so the patient is left with two or more identities. Instead of Identity 1 integrating into the new identity, integration fails, and two identities coexist in a single individual. When the identities are unaware of one another or when one identity is unaware of the other, a process of suppression occurs. The takeover or the suppression of the first-order identity occurs relatively rapidly, typically in less than 5 minutes (Putnam, 1988). Most, but not all, patients exhibit either a burst of rapid eye blinking and eye rolling at the beginning of the takeover. These eye disturbances indicate perhaps neuronal activity in the frontal eye fields. This activity may be followed by a transient "blank" or vacant gaze and volatility in autonomic nervous system functions. On videotape, one can see a rearrangement of facial musculature that coincides with a shift in affect, voice, and perceptual and cognitive functions (Putnam, 1988). There may be dramatic shifts in EEG patterns and in brain activity patterns. Sometimes these alterations in brain activity patterns are even associated with a change in handedness (from right- to left-handed).

Take for example, the following cases (from Flor-Henry, Tomer, Kumpala, Koles, & Yeudall, 1990, pp. 153–156):

The first case (Ms. K), who was dextral, became asymptomatic in the unusually short period of 3 months following intensive hypnotherapy with video-taped recordings which the subject then viewed, systematically, the next day. Before treatment she showed on neuropsychological testing, impairment for Verbal Learning, Coloured Progressive Matrices, Purdue Pegboard for the left hand and Tactual Performance for the left hand and both hands. This pattern of deficit indicates left temporal and bilateral frontal dysfunction, right > left. The presence of right frontal dysfunction further emerged on dynamometric hand strength with an 8-kg difference between the preferred and non-preferred hands. Normally there is a difference of 1-3-kg at the most in the strength of the two hands. Retested when asymptomatic after treatment, the left hemisphere indices of dysfunction had become normal, but the right frontal deficit remained in evidence. There were interesting changes also in the WAIS-R before and after treatment. Before treatment when the patient showed symptoms of secondary depression, both the Performance and Verbal IQ were similar and in the normal range: Performance IQ = 102, Verbal IQ = 106. On retesting 3 months later, the Verbal IQ was unchanged but the Performance IQ increased to 126. Thus, from a psychometric point of view, her post-treatment cerebral state was one of relative dominant hemisphere hypofunction, in view of the striking Verbal/ Performance discrepancy. The fact that the Performance IQ had, initially, dropped so considerably is related to the depression, which disrupted the efficiency of the non-dominant hemisphere. The patient's basic personality was strongly dextral but in one of her alternate personalities she became sinistral and the various personalities had very different handwriting styles.

The second woman (Ms. W) with multiple personality, who was sinistral, showed neuropsychological deficits on the following tests: Aphasia Screening test, Williams' Verbal Learning, Purdue Pegboard (Preferred, Non-preferred and both hands), Halstead Category test, Dynamometric test (preferred and non-preferred hand). On the Dynamometric hand strength there was a difference of 12 kg between the preferred and non-preferred hand. Psychometrically on the WAIS-R the Verbal IQ was 93, Performance IQ 122, and Full Scale IQ 104. Thus, neuropsychologically the pattern of dysfunction was the same as that of the first patient: bilateral frontal, right > left and dominant temporal. The psychometric pattern of the second case, as was true in the first, revealed relative hypofunction of dominant hemispheric systems. Since the patient was not cured at the time of discharge, there is no knowledge of her neuropsychological state after recovery (Flor-Henry et al., 1990, pp. 153–156).

Comment. These cases are striking in that they provide hard neuropsychologic performance data that document changes in brain processing abilities as a function of personality state. It is as if the brain reorganizes itself to accommodate differing personalities. Note also that one particular brain area is implicated in initiating or handling the brain state and personality change: right prefrontal and temporal circuits. We will see later that these same circuits are implicated in religious experiences. Consider the following case from Henninger (1992):

P.G. was a 19-year-old woman with six known alternate personalities. As a child she lived with her mother and several stepfathers, the second of whom sexually abused her. At the time she was left handed. Her disorder appeared at age 18 during her first year of university attendance. At the time of testing, the host personality, Pe, was a second year university student. She did not have access to the other personalities and believed she was making them up. The primary alter, Pa, was a 9-year-old child. Pe and Pa were the two most dominant and most frequently appearing personalities. Pa was aware of Pe and the other sub-personalities (p. 269). . . . Pa's and Pe's divergent interests, the differences in handwriting style, in manual preference, in manual dexterity, and the presence of spontaneous mirror writing in one but not the other personality suggest two distinct identities. The absence of any sign of recognition of the investigator, the testing room, the equipment, or tests during the testing of the second personality (initial test of Pe) further supports the diagnosis. The analyses of the projective drawings by the clinical psychologists strongly support both a history of abuse and a diagnosis of MPD (p. 279).

Comment. Henninger (1992) concludes that "the significant differences between the two personalities in the relative manual skill of their two hands and in the ear advantages on both the verbal and the musical dichotic tests support the hypothesis that when Pa is in control, the right hemisphere is dominant and that when Pe is in control, the left hemisphere is dominant" (p. 279).

This is a remarkable conclusion to reach. The idea is that agency and the Self can be housed within one hemisphere. Henninger suggested that a possible neurological model of the dissociation in personality observed in MPD is the split-brain subject who has had the commissures connecting the two cerebral hemispheres severed. Studies of these subjects have revealed that the left and right hemispheres, after being disconnected, function as two separate entities, each unaware of the perceptions and cognitions of the other (Sperry, 1974). The handedness changes shown in persons with MPD are unexpected and suggest a relationship between MPD and lateralized functioning.

You see similar switches in handedness and in the sense of Self or identity between depression and mania in bipolar affective patients. Consider the following case from Savitz, Solms, Pietersen, Ramesar, and Flor-Henry (2004):

> Y.D. is a 32 year old right handed woman who works as an administrative assistant. She was diagnosed with bipolar disorder type I at age 15 and was hospitalized on seven occasions, 4 times for depression and three times for mania. When she would enter a manic phase of the illness Y.D. described being "dominated by the left hand" and she became left handed.

Implications of the Clinical Data for Self

Now given these dramatic brain-related changes in identity, what do these cases of MPD and bipolar patients tell us about the Self and free will? What do the clinical data tell us about the divided Self? Clearly these patients in either identity can still deliberate and choose among alternative courses of action. The two identities may not be able to do this simultaneously, but each can deliberate on its own about short-term goals relatively normally. What they deliberate about is of course different, and the quality of the deliberation process is different. The goals of each identity are also certainly different . . . nevertheless, each identity deliberates fairly normally and effectively. It is not clear, however, that both identities can effectively deliberate about long-term goals. You need a strong executive Self to do so. What is amiss here is this executive Self or agent.

The primary identity does not possess an agency strong enough to bind and own all of the intentional states associated with the brain that houses it. Perhaps no agent does, but most agents have enough control over their brains so as not to allow invasion by an alien entity. Thus the power of the agent to control its own substrate so to speak – rather than the deliberative process – is crucial to the experience of free will. Aquinas would be able to account for these clinical syndromes because he would be able to say that the agent, to be really free, needs to be highly developed. The agent must exhibit self-mastery and must have had some success in willing the good and the appropriate over long periods of time – otherwise freedom and autonomy are vulnerable. Now most things that happen in life are outside the control of the agent, so Aquinas is not saying that autonomous agency will protect you from brain disorders, and so forth. Instead, as I read him, he seems to be saying that Will is like a muscle. It can be strengthened or weakened depending on its proper exercise, and the proper exercise for the human Will is to aim at the good and the appropriate over long periods of time. You need a strong executive Self to do so.

5 Neurology of Religious Experiences

Concerning the Gods, there are those who deny the very existence of the Godhead; others say that it exists, but neither bestirs nor concerns itself nor has forethought for anything. A third party attribute to it existence and forethought, but only for great and heavenly matters, not for anything that is on earth. A fourth party admit things on earth as well as in heaven, but only in general, and not with respect to each individual. A fifth, of whom were Ulysses and Socrates, are those that cry: I move not without Thy knowledge!

– Epictetus, *The Golden Sayings of Epictetus*. No. 38;
The Harvard Classics (1909–1914)

Introduction

God is interested in the individual Self. The religious individual assumes this fact and cries out with Ulysses and Socrates, "I move not without thy knowledge!" For some people like Ulysees, Socrates, and Epictetus, apparently, the Self is constituted by and lives in direct relationship to the god. For many people, then, Self and God are intimately connected at the cognitive and psychological levels. That level of experience, the relationship between Self and God, can be measured to some extent by looking at brain and cognitive mediation of religious experience.

When we examine the available data on brain mediation of religious experience, the most important issue we will be attempting to decide is if religious experience is associated with a consistent set of brain sites and activation patterns. If there is a consistent set of brain regions implicated in religious experience, then we can look at what is known about the functional roles of these particular brain regions to gain clues as to the functions of religious experience.

Neurologic studies of religious experiences began in earnest just over 100 years ago when William James delivered his Gifford lectures. These lectures were published as *The Varieties of Religious Experience* (1908/1928). James's first lecture was entitled "Religion and Neurology," in which he pointed out that, if specific brain regions were found to participate in religious expression, it would not mean that religion was nothing but a misfiring of neurons in that brain region. Similarly, if religious expression was more common among individuals with mental disorders, it would not imply that religion was due to mental disorder. Instead, we can partially infer normal operations of the religious Mind/brain by carefully documenting the ways in which the system breaks down. Breakdown patterns, it turns out, are not random, and that allows us to use the information we have on the rule-governed process of breakdown to reconstruct the minimal cognitive architecture that must have existed in the healthy state to give us the breakdown pattern we now observe.

Although William James attempted a reconstruction of the cognitive operations of the healthy religious mind, he was never able to develop a neurology of religious experience, as neurology itself was just emerging as a science when James worked. Too little was known at the time to develop a real science of religion. Since James's pioneering studies, other psychologists, anthropologists, and sociologists attempted to understand various facets of religious phenomena, but James's accent on neurology was largely dropped until the 1970s.

What revived neurologic studies of religious experience in the 1970s were reports of intense religious experiences in epileptics with seizure foci in the temporal lobes. Although links between epilepsy and religiousness had been noted for centuries, systematic observations of religiousness in epilepsy did not begin to appear until the nineteenth century (cf. Howden, 1872–1873), but these reports were not followed up by other investigators. Only sporadic reports appeared on the neurology of religious experiences between James's observations and the modern period, so no systematic growth in the field occurred until the 1970s.

In the 1970s, a flurry of new reports (Bear & Fedio, 1977; Dewhurst & Beard, 1970; Geschwind, 1979; Waxman & Geschwind, 1975) reignited interest in the English-speaking world in brain–religion relationships. These early investigators described patients with intense religious obsessions and preoccupations. Dewhurst and Beard (1970) reported that some patients with temporal lobe epilepsy (TLE – an epilepsy in which the seizure focus is in the temporal lobes, a region of the brain that controls memory, emotion, and aspects of language) were prone to intense religious conversions (see also Waxman & Geschwind, 1975). Other patients described profound experiences of being chosen by God for a special mission. Still others filled notebooks with reams of material on religious and philosophic themes. All of these dramatic religious experiences occurred after a brain injury or after a series of temporal lobe seizures. In most but not all of these latter cases, the intense religiosity subsided after the epilepsy was treated with medicine that stopped the seizure activity in their brains.

Here are some descriptions of cases (from Dewhurst & Beard, 1970, pp. 498–499):

The patient's first conversion experience occurred in 1955 at the end of a week in which he had been unusually depressed. In the middle of collecting fares (he was a bus driver), he was suddenly overcome with a feeling of bliss. He felt he was literally in Heaven. He collected the fares correctly, telling his passengers at the same time how pleased he was to be in Heaven. When he returned home he appeared not to recognize his wife, but she did get from him a somewhat incoherent account of his celestial experience. Later the patient told his G.P. (general practitioner) that he felt as if a bomb had burst in his head and that he thought he was paddling in water. On admission to St. Francis Hospital Observation Unit, he was constantly laughing to himself; he said that he had seen God and that his wife and family would soon join him in Heaven; his mood was elated, his thought disjointed and he readily admitted to hearing music and voices: "I wish they would tell me I could go to earth. Look at you cooped up here. I could give you a game of tennis." He remained in this state of exaltation, hearing divine and angelic voices, for two days. Afterwards he was able to recall these experiences and he continued to believe in their validity. He was discharged from hospital after ten days.

During the next two years, there was no change in his personality; he did not express any peculiar notions but remained religious. In September 1958, following three seizures on three successive days, he became elated again. He stated that his mind had "cleared." (A letter to his wife, in which he attempted to express his religious ideas, was, in fact, unintelligible.) During this episode he lost his faith. "I used to believe in Heaven and Hell, but after this experience I do not believe there is a hereafter." He also lost his belief in the divinity of Christ – he had been born, had a father and mother, and therefore could not be the son of God. This sudden conversion was marked by an elevation of mood and a general sense of well-being and clarity of mind. He considered that this second episode also had the nature of a revelation.

Investigations: Three electroencephalographic studies with sphenoidal leads showed spiked discharges, predominantly on the left but with the occasional discharge on the right. The supposition was that the focus lay in the left temporal lobe, but the skull X-ray showed an elevation of the right petrous bone which was taken to favour a right-sided lesion.

An air encephalogram also favoured a right-sided lesion. However, when sodium amytal was injected into the left carotid artery the patient became aphasic, and as this was a feature of his minor seizures a left temporal lobectomy was decided on. This was carried out in March 1959.

Follow-up: The patient remained fit-free over the next eighteen months, though he had to have a course of E.C.T. for a depressive episode in September 1960. Throughout this period he retained belief in the validity of his second experience and continued in an attitude of agnosticism.

Comment 1. This case is interesting from the anatomical point of view, as it suggests that the structures that were mediating the heightened religiosity were in the right temporal lobes as the left temporal lobe was removed. Despite the removal of the left temporal lobe, his beliefs about his religious experience were maintained – even though he called himself agnostic. Thus the right temporal lobe likely mediated the religious experience. We will see this link between the right temporal (and frontal) lobes and heightened religiosity in the next case as well as the effects of neuroelectrical spikes in these structures on religious experience as studied over several years.

A Case of Enhanced Religiosity and Enhanced Mental Powers. Let us now consider the following (from Dewhurst & Beard, 1970):

> In 1954 he stopped taking his anti-convulsants; within six weeks he was having fits every few hours; he had become confused and forgetful. At this point he suddenly realized that he was the Son of God; he possessed special powers of healing and could abolish cancer from the world; he had visions, and believed that he could understand other people's thoughts.
>
> At a subsequent interview he mentioned a "holy smell" and gave the following account of his conversion. "It was a beautiful morning and God was with me and I was thanking God, I was talking to God; I was entering Aldwych, entering the Strand, between Kingsway and the Strand, going down some steps... I was not thanking God, I was with God. God isn't something hard looking down on us, God is trees and flowers and beauty and love. God was telling me to carry on and help the doctors here, and I was telling Him back, not aloud, I wasn't talking to myself; they would call you crackers if they heard that; God was telling me, at last you have found someone who can help you, and He was talking about you, doctor, He was talking about you... "
>
> Investigations: An air encephalogram showed moderate dilatation of the whole of the left lateral ventricle including both temporal and frontal horns. An electroencephalogram showed that the main focus of abnormal discharge was localized to the temporal lobe, although there were occasional similar discharges from the left side. The patient was not considered suitable for temporal lobectomy.
>
> Follow-up: In 1957 the patient appeared very much the same as he had on his discharge from hospital 21 years previously. His talk was rambling, his thoughts disordered, his manner inconsequential and his mood fatuous and euphoric. He had been admitted to psychiatric hospital for nine months and was still attending as an outpatient.

He had held several minor clerical jobs for short periods. He was taking anti-convulsants regularly and was apparently free from fits.

Three months before this follow-up interview, the patient had had a feeling that his dead father was trying to get in touch with him, and also had a marked passivity experience. "God or a power – electrical power – was making me do things." At the same time he saw a light going round the room which stopped just over his head. He considered that God had put these ideas into his head in order to convert him to the true way of life.

Five years after he was first seen the patient showed considerable improvement. He had held the same job for a year. He was brighter and quicker in manner. Fits had been rare. However, his sister said that he still some times talked about God in an inappropriate way (Dewhurst & Beard, 1970, pp. 500–501).

Comment 2. Here the patient's realization that he was the "Son of God" seems to be causally related to the brain disorder that manifested when the patient stopped taking his antiseizure medications. The features of the patient's experiences are also noteworthy as they recur in all kinds of religious experiences reported by all kinds of people without brain disorders. These are a change in the sense of Self (he realized he was the Son of God); a feeling of "insight" (he suddenly realized . . .); a feeling of having special perceptual powers (he could understand other people's thoughts); positive affect (I was thanking God); and special practical powers (he could heal cancer). The enhancement of mental powers and affect suggests a disinhibition or stimulation of selected brain functions rather than a diminution or loss of brain functions. Disinhibition is not necessarily a good thing. It can lead to all kinds of behavioral problems. In contrast, disinhibition can also reveal functional capacities of the brain that are usually more difficult to identify or appreciate. In this case, disinhibition led to the patient's feeling that he could better read other people's thoughts. This capacity to read the minds of others is known as the "theory of mind" ability. We all have this ability. It allows us to infer and guess the intentions and thoughts of others. When it is disinhibited, we overestimate our own abilities to guess the intentions of others. In healthy religious experiences, we also see a change in the sense of Self . . . usually it is greater humility about the Self. In aberrant experiences, however, such as this one, we see a distorting grandiosity, and the Self is inflated rather than humbled. In any case, in this clinical case we see recurring features of religious experiences, positive affect, feeling of insight, a feeling of special powers, a change in the sense of Self, and so forth, except that these experiences are grossly enhanced or are distorted and they are clearly causally linked to the brain disorder.

A Case of Enhanced Religiosity Affecting Sense of Self. Consider now another clinical case (from Dewhurst & Beard, 1970):

> When he was a boy the patient was taken to church by his father, who was very concerned that his son should live a religious life. This was the more so when the father was converted from Methodism to Christian Science. At the age of 9 the boy decided to become a minister, and at that time he used to get up at 6 a.m. to sing hymns. However, his interest in religion ebbed as the years passed and had become minimal by the time he was 21.
>
> At the age of 23 the patient had his first minor seizure. He was then in Iraq with the R.A.F. living a spartan and isolated life. A fortnight after the seizure, while walking alone, he suddenly felt God's reality and his own insignificance. As a result of this revelation, he recovered his faith and determined to live in a Christian manner. However, this conversion experience gradually lost its impact and he once again ceased concerning himself with religion. Then in 1954 he had two of his rare grand mal attacks in one day. Within twenty-four hours of the second seizure he had another conversion experience as part of a florid religious psychosis that lasted a week. He remembered feeling dizzy for a period following the second seizure, then returning home with a dull headache and going to bed. Several hours later he had a sudden dream-like feeling, saw a flash of light, and exclaimed "I have seen the light." He suddenly knew that God was behind the sun and that this knowledge meant power; he could have power from God if he would only ask for it. He had a series of visions in which he felt that his past life was being judged; a book appeared before him, a world atlas with a torn page; a pendulum was swinging and when it stopped the world would end.

Some elements in this experience had a paranoid trend. He knew that his thoughts were being recorded. He saw people looking down at him from Heaven and heard one of them laugh and say "H – is going to commit suicide." Later, in hospital, he heard heavenly voices abusing him, felt rays were being shone on him to punish him (they caused a sensation of burning), and said he had been twisted round until his bones were nearly broken. He made an attempt at suicide by breaking a window and trying to cut his throat.

Investigations: Serial electroencephalograms suggested a left anterior temporal lobe focus. A left carotid arteriogram was normal, but the air encephalogram showed some contraction of the anterior horn and body of the left lateral ventricle and some enlargement of the lateral cleft of the left temporal horn. The straight X-ray was also suggestive of a left temporal lesion.

A left temporal lobectomy was performed in January 1955.

Follow-up: Five months later, the patient was still so involved in his psychotic experience that he had no interest in other topics. He completely believed in the validity of everything he had seen and heard during the acute phase, and specifically rejected the idea that the experience could have been the product of a disordered mind. He considered that he had received a message from God to mend his ways and help others, and the fact that he had been singled out in this way meant that he was God's chosen instrument. Twelve months after operation there were no new psychotic experiences to record, but his religious beliefs remained strong and he was attending church regularly. The patient had since remained fit-free (p. 499).

Comment 3. This case, like the other cases mentioned earlier involving a temporal lobectomy, is especially interesting as the patient's religiosity remained after removal of the part of the brain where the seizure activity was occurring (he had a left temporal lobectomy). This set of facts indicates that the seizure activity in the left temporal lobe could not have been the sole factor causing the religious experiences. His hyperreligiosity remained after left temporal lobectomy. Instead, effects of the seizure on other parts of the brain were likely involved. The left temporal lobe is connected primarily with the prefrontal cortex and with the right temporal lobe. We will see that these structures, the right prefrontal and temporal lobes, are indeed involved in religious expression. The case also illustrates the occasional co-occurrence of complex and highly meaningful (for the individual) visual imagery with the religious experience. This co-occurrence of features related to the sense of Self, complex meanings, and abstract visual scenes can be explained with reference to the brain, as the sense of Self, language meanings, and abstract visual analysis are all handled by the same region of the neocortical networks that gives rise to religious experience.

Despite these sorts of clinical cases where there is a clear association between heightened religiosity and TLE, rates of heightened religiosity among TLE may not exceed 5 percent (Devinsky & Lai, 2008). Ogata and Miyakawa (1998) interviewed 234 Japanese patients with various forms of epilepsy, including 137 patients with TLE. Only three patients, all with TLE, reported significant religious interests.

Some authors have argued that the heightened religiosity found in the few TLE patients who report it does not stem so much from the anatomy of TLE as it does from psychiatric effects of TLE. Tucker, Novelly, and Walker (1987) evaluated 76 patients with TLE of unilateral onset for signs of heightened religiosity. They carefully screened out any patients with significant psychiatric histories. They compared TLE patients with a left-sided focus to TLE patients with a right-sided focus and two other control groups consisting of patients with primary generalized seizures and patients with nonepileptic seizures. They found no significant group differences in religiosity between the left versus the right TLE groups or between patients with TLE and either control group. They argued that the reason why religiosity was not elevated in their TLE population was that none had significant psychiatric histories relative to the control groups.

To some extent, the results of Tucker et al. could have been due to the assessment instruments they were using. Roberts and Guberman (1989) developed an exhaustive inventory/checklist of religious and spiritual experiences and then asked 57 TLE patients to indicate if they had ever experienced any of the events on the list. They found that 51 percent indicated that they had experienced a significant past spiritual event such as an intense religious conversion. This rate of conversion very likely far surpasses rates of conversion experiences in the general population.

Trimble and Freeman (2006) looked at the clinical correlates of TLE patients with and without self-reported high interest in religion (these patients also scored higher than the other TLE group on three measures of religiosity) and compared these epileptic patients to a control group of regular churchgoers. They found that the hyperreligious TLE patients more frequently had bilateral seizure foci than unilateral (right or left) foci and more frequently reported episodes of postictal psychoses. Compared to the healthy churchgoer group, hyperreligious TLE patients more often reported actual experiences of some great spiritual figure or supernatural being – either an evil presence or a benign spiritual presence.

The Trimble and Freeman (2006) study, as well as the earlier-mentioned clinical cases of heightened religiosity in TLE, raises the issue of just how seizure activity in the temporal lobe could give rise to religious experience. Geschwind (1979) suggested that heightened interest in religious matters in TLE often occurred in association with hypergraphia (a tendency to highly detailed writing often of a religious or philosophical nature), hyposexuality (diminished sex drive), and irritability of varying degree. Gastaut (1954) pointed out that the major interictal behavioral symptoms of TLE including 1) emotional intensity, 2) viscosity (excessive attention to detail and perseveration), and 3) hyposexuality are the exact opposite of the behavioral manifestations of Klüver–Bucy syndrome, which involve bilateral removal of the temporal lobes. The classical symptoms of Klüver–Bucy syndrome are placidity (lack of aggression), fluctuating attention, and hypersexuality. In TLE, overexcitation or hyperconnectivity between limbic and temporal sites leads to the TLE behaviors where everything but sex is significant and requires attention. In many TLE patients, aggressive outbursts are not uncommon. How can we explain these opposite behavioral profiles?

One possibility is that, in Klüver–Bucy syndrome, prefrontal and whatever remaining temporal sites there are after resection are underactive, whereas limbic-related sexual drives are disinhibited and behavior is controlled by posterior parietal cortex (thus the fluctuating attention). Conversely, in TLE, prefrontal and temporal sites are released from inhibition, whereas limbic sites are inhibited. This scenario, however, would not explain the emotional flatness in Klüver–Bucy and emotional intensity in TLE. If the amygdala is the key site for aggression, then it should be overactivated in TLE and underactivated in Klüver–Bucy. To the extent that the temporal lobe resection impacts the amygdala, it is not surprising that you would see placidity as part of the syndrome. In TLE, the amygdala is overstimulated, whereas in Klüver–Bucy, it is absent or underactivated. Sexual drive depends on hypothalamic sites that are regulated in turn by the amygdala. Without any top-down influence from the amygdala onto hypothalamic sites, you get hypersexuality. With overstimulation of the amygdala, you get inhibition of hypothalamic sites and hypo-sexuality.

If we assume that the seizure activity runs throughout the amygdala and adjacent limbic regions, then a hyperstimulated amygdala would inhibit the hypothalamic functions associated with sexuality, thus ac-counting for hyposexuality in TLE-associated hyperreligiosity. What accounts for the hyperreligiosity? If we assume that right anterior tempo-ral and prefrontal networks are hyperstimulated by limbic and amygdalar seizure foci and spikes and we further assume that right prefrontal anterior temporal networks mediate the executive Self, then something about the executive Self allows one to "perceive" religious stimuli (e.g., supernatural agents) with greater intensity than is normally the case.

Bear and Fedio (1977), in fact, argued that heightened religiosity was due to a greater number or density of connections between cortical sites handling the senses and the limbic system, including the amygdala, so that patients with TLE experienced a greater number of sensory events as "significant" relative to a healthy person with fewer such connections. Ramachandran and Blakeslee (1998) later assessed this theory by measur-ing subconscious reactions to religious, sexual, and violent imagery via skin conductance responses (SCRs) in temporal lobe epileptics with reli-gious preoccupations, normal "very religious" people, and normal "non-religious" people. In temporal lobe epileptics, SCRs were enhanced for religious words and images to about the level found in the religious con-trols. This result is consistent with the Bear and Fedio model of hyper-connectivity.

Assuming that the hyperconnectivity model is operative in hyper-religious TLE patients, how does hyperconnectivity result from seizure activity? An epileptic seizure results when an abnormal and excessive synchronization of firing of brain neurons spreads across brain regions. The most common part of the brain giving rise to TLE-related complex partial seizures is the mesial (inner) aspect of the temporal lobe including structures deep to the temporal lobe and housed in the limbic lobe, the amygdala, and the hippocampus. Hypersynchronized and discharging neurons in the amygdala would have the effect of chronically overstimulating the structure. Connections from the amygdala to the cortex would be excitatory, whereas impulses from the amygdala to the hypothalamus would be inhibitory. Increasing impulses from the amygdala to the cortex then would be interpreted at the cortical level as greater numbers and frequencies of significant emotional events, whereas impulses from the amygdala to the hypothalamus would result in prolonged inhibitory pressure on the hypothalamus.

In their recent review of religious and spiritual experiences in epilepsy, Devinsky and Lai (2008) largely endorse the hyperconnection model for interictal hyperreligiosity, and they agree with Trimble and Freeman that interictal religiosity may be linked with bilateral temporal lobe seizure foci. During ictal experiences, however, they argue that religiosity is associated with right temporal lobe activity and point out that 4 of the 5 well-documented cases of "in the moment" ictal religious experiences were associated with right temporal or temporofrontal foci.

The link between right frontotemperal foci and religiosity in both the ictal and interictal states is also supported by a case (Case 1) described by Devinsky and Lai (2008), wherein heightened religiosity was associated with right temporal seizure activity, and loss of religiosity was associated with removal of the right temporal lobe. I could find no instance where removal of the left temporal lobe, in the context of unilateral foci, resulted in loss of religiosity (from Cirignotta, Todesco, & Lugaresi, 1980).

A Case of Ecstatic Seizures. The crucial role of the right temporal cortex is underlined by the rare phenomenon of ecstatic seizures, which are seizures that are associated with religious ecstasy. Dostoyevsky may have experienced these sorts of seizures (Hughes, 2005), but let us look at a case that has been studied more recently.

The patient is a 30-year-old unmarried man who had a normal birth and gives no history of familial epilepsy, severe illness, or cranial injury. He attended secondary school and is currently employed full-time. A self-contained, suspicious, unsociable person, he is prone to lonely meditation. His only intellectual concerns, music and travel, are in harmony with his need to establish rarefied contacts with the environment. He has a taciturn nature and expresses himself slowly and with difficulty.

At the age of 13 he began to have attacks of short duration (20–30 sec) characterized by psychomotor arrest, slight lapse of consciousness, and, above all, an ineffable sensation of "joy." The episodes had a frequency of 1 or 2 per month but have become almost daily in recent years. In January, 1979, he was referred to us after a tonic-clonic nocturnal seizure. He had never seen a physician before, as he did not consider his small attacks as negative events.

Seizures generally come on when he is relaxed or drowsy. The subjective symptoms are defined by the patient himself as "indescribable," words seeming to him inadequate to express what he perceives in those instants. However, he says that the pleasure he feels is so intense that he cannot find its match in reality. Qualitatively, these sensations can only be compared with those evoked by music. All disagreeable feelings, emotions, and thoughts are absent during the attacks. His mind, his whole being is pervaded by a sense of total bliss.

All attention to his surroundings is suspended: he almost feels as if this estrangement from the environment were a sine qua non for the onset of seizures. He insists that the only comparable pleasure is that conveyed by music. Sexual pleasure is completely different: once he happened to have an attack during sexual intercourse, which he carried on mechanically, being totally absorbed in his utterly mental enjoyment.

The neurological examination was negative. The EEG in the waking state is normal. A focus of spike activity appears in the right temporal zone during sleep. During a 24-hr polygraphic recording, a psychomotor seizure was observed, at the end of which the patient said he had experienced one of his short and sudden states of ecstasy (pp. 705, 709).

Comment 4. This case is remarkable in that the description of the experience associated with the seizures could have been taken to be a description of a mystical experience by a religious mystic. Interestingly enough, the patient himself asserted that the joy was more of a conative, spiritual–cognitive experience rather a bodily or emotional experience per se.

All of the TLE-related data, including the striking phenomenon of ecstatic seizures, suggest that heightened religiosity is associated primarily with bilateral temporal lobe foci or with right-sided temporal lobe foci. Devinsky and Lai (2008) come to similar conclusions in their review of the literature. Heightened spike activity in the amygdala, particularly on the right side, stimulates both temporal and prefrontal sites such that heightened significance is attached to everyday events, and complex ideations occur in response to chronic emotional stimulation due to amygdala overactivity. In short, the literature on TLE-related religiosity gives us an initial clue as to the brain circuits that normally handle religious material – namely, the right-sided temporal and prefrontal networks as it is these networks that attach religious concepts to the impulses originating in the amygdala.

The Role of the Hippocampus

What about the hippocampus? The hippocampus is known to be impaired in TLE and may be the origin of some seizure activity in TLE. Wuerfel and colleagues (2004) evaluated religiosity and brain volumes/activity in 33 patients with partial-onset epilepsy with quantitative magnetic resonance imaging (MRI) scans. Some patients had frontal lobe seizures and others had TLE. The researchers found that religiosity in both patient groups significantly correlated with reduced right hippocampal volumes but not amygdalar volumes.

It is not yet possible to evaluate the extent and role of the hippocampus and the amygdala in creating religious content. The report of Wuerfel et al. (2004) linking reduction in right-sided hippocampal but not amygdalar volumes and heightened religiosity may be due to the enhanced role the amygdala is forced to play in the whole drama. If it is chronically stimulated, it may develop new synaptic connections with other sites and thus increase in volume relative to the hippocampus or at least not be subject to the same rate of disease-induced cell loss as the hippocampus, but this is mere speculation given the paucity of data on the issue.

These considerations underlie the importance of all of these structures – the hippocampus, the amygdala, the temporal lobes, and the prefrontal lobes, particularly on the right side – in the neurology of religious
experiences. I will now turn to a review of the literature on religiosity in
other neurologic disorders to see if they are consistent with the findings
we have gathered from the epilepsy literature.

Schizophrenia

Schizophrenia is a disorder of the Self involving psychotic delusions and
hallucinations that has its onset most typically during the adolescent
period. There is a definite heightening of religiousness in schizophrenic
patients. Reports of religious experiences are more frequent among
the schizophrenic population than the general population – especially
in those patients with positive symptoms (Huguelet, Mohr, Borras,
Gilliéron, & Brandt, 2006; Mohr, Brandt, Borras, Gilliéron, & Huguelet,
2006; Siddle, Haddock, Tarrier, & Garagher, 2002). In a sample of 193
patients admitted to a community hospital for schizophrenia, 24 percent
had religious delusions (Siddle et al., 2002). Huguelet et al. (2006) found
that 16 percent of their sample of schizophrenic patients had positive
psychotic symptoms involving religious content and that the majority
of the patients reported that religion was an important aspect of their
lives. Mohr et al. (2006) conducted semistructured interviews about religious coping with a sample of 115 outpatient schizophrenic patients and
found that 71 percent reported that religion instilled hope, purpose, and
meaning in their lives, whereas for others, it induced spiritual despair
(14%). Patients also reported that religion lessened (54%) or increased
(10%) psychotic and general symptoms. Positive delusions with religious
content appear to be linked with specific sites of neural dysfunction.
Single photon computed emission tomography (SPECT) neuroimaging
on an individual with schizophrenia who was actively experiencing religious delusions revealed increased uptake in the left temporal region, as
well as reduced uptake in occipital cortex, especially on the left (Puri,
Lekh, Nijran, Bagary, & Richardson, 2001). The authors note, however,
that these results in a single patient are difficult to interpret as increased
uptake could mean either hyper- or dysfunction in the left temporal lobe.

The link between religiousness and schizophrenia has been explained in evolutionary terms as follows. Stevens and Price (1996) argued that the genetic susceptibility to develop schizophrenia emerged as an adaptation to facilitate group splitting. In ancestral human groups, subgroups or cults would form around charismatic leaders who had experienced religious insights and visions. These cult leaders would then split from the natal group and trek off to form new groups at some distance from the natal group. These cult leaders were likely schizotypal, according to Stevens and Price. Even if we agree, however, that ancestral humans would follow leaders with schizotypal traits or full-blown schizophrenia, it does not seem plausible that all human groups were founded this way. Nor does it seem plausible that group splitting in itself was so important a human behavior as to be positively selected. It does not seem to outweigh the costs associated with schizophrenia.

Polimeni and Reiss (2003) proposed a scenario similar to that of Stevens and Price. Religious and healing powers conferred prestige and leadership status on certain individuals and thus increased fitness. These were the shamans. Shamans, in turn, developed trance and schizotypal traits/ abilities to practice their religious inspirations/powers. Fitness-related benefits of these shamanistic capacities outweigh the costs associated with vulnerability to schizophrenic traits. McClenon (2006) proposed a similar theory in his ritual healing theory, but in this case, the fitness-related benefit had to do with healing capacities.

Crow (1993, 2008) has also offered an evolutionarily informed theory of the disorder that speaks to its neuroanatomical abnormalities. He argues that schizophrenia was the price we (Homo sapiens) paid for the acquisition of language. The acquisition of language in Homo sapiens required the introduction of a range of neuroanatomical asymmetries in the human brain. Grammatical components of language were housed in the left temporal regions, whereas pragmatic aspects of language were housed in the right frontal regions. Cerebral asymmetry produced a "torque" effect on the brain such that right frontal regions were wider than homologous regions on the left, and left occipital regions are wider than homologous regions on the right.

If you fail to develop this torque, this form of cerebral asymmetry, then you will evidence language and cognitive deficits proportional to the reduction in asymmetry and you will become vulnerable to schizophrenia. There is a considerable amount of empirical evidence in support of Crow's theory (Brüne, 2004). Schizophrenics, for example, do, in fact, suffer from a lack of normal anatomic asymmetry between the right and left hemispheres. In contrast, many other brain disorders are associated with a reduction in asymmetry but are not associated with psychoses (e.g., developmental learning disabilities such as dyslexia). Even normal aging is associated with a reduction in asymmetry – but again, there is no psychosis. Obviously, in addition to the reduction in asymmetry you need an overactivated limbic system to get psychosis.

Anatomy of Schizophrenia

It is generally agreed that symptoms of the disorder can be divided into two broad categories. Positive symptoms include delusions and auditory hallucinations, whereas negative symptoms include flattened affect, disorders of Will, and anhedonia. Schizophrenia has been associated with dysfunction in dorsolateral prefrontal cortex as well as abnormal regulation of subcortical dopaminergic (DA) systems. Limbic DA activity is enhanced, whereas dorsolateral prefrontal cortical activity is depressed (Cummings & Mega, 2003; Weinberger, 1986). This is called hypofrontality. Because cortical sites partially regulate subcortical DA function, hypofrontality in schizophrenia may lead to hyperactivity of subcortical DA systems. The locus of therapeutic action of many antipsychotic agents appears to be a circuit within the limbic cortex – the nucleus accumbens circuit (NAC). The NAC receives excitatory input from multiple sites in the frontal cortex and in other limbic structures.

The left temporal lobe in schizophrenia has been shown to be reduced in volume relative to the right temporal lobe (Kasai et al., 2003; Kubicki et al., 2002; Kuroki et al., 2006) and relative to healthy controls (Suddath et al., 1989). This reduction in size of the left temporal lobe is correlated with severity of the thought disorder (Shenton et al., 1992). The right temporal lobe appears to be relatively spared in schizophrenia.

As in the case of TLE, the anatomical sites of dysfunction in schizophrenia include limbic networks, the amygdala, the hippocampus, the left temporal lobe, and the dorsolateral prefrontal cortex. In addition to these TLE-related sites of pathology, schizophrenia is also associated with DA and aminergic overactivity in the limbic system and in the NAC. In sum, there is evidence for overactivity in limbic sites (such as the amygdala and NAC) and underactivity or dysfunction in cortical sites (such as the left temporal and prefrontal lobes). The right temporal lobe and the parietal lobes appear to be relatively spared in schizophrenia.

Given these neurologic correlates of schizophrenia, how might the pattern of spared, overactivated, and underactivated sites produce the heightened religiosity associated with the disorder? What appeared to produce heightened religiosity in TLE was an overactivated amygdala and right temporal lobe. What we see in schizophrenia is an overactivated limbic system (including the amygdala) and a relatively spared right temporal lobe. The neurologic data from schizophrenia appear then to be consistent with the TLE data.

The frontotemporal dysfunction of schizophrenia undoubtedly contributes to the cognitive deficits of schizophrenia, which include executive function deficits, language deficits, delusions, and auditory hallucinations, to name a few. Like other patients with prefrontal dysfunction, schizophrenics also display what are known as source-monitoring deficits. They cannot accurately identify the source of many of the ideas, beliefs, and facts with which they are acquainted. Source-monitoring deficits often give rise to confabulatory accounts of how the patient acquired the information in question. Bulbulia (2009) has suggested that religious convictions may be related to source monitoring and confabulatory dynamics operative even in healthy persons. Presumably schizophrenia represents a case when source monitoring and confabulatory system dynamics break down to produce religious delusions.

Obsessive-Compulsive Disorder

Obsessive-compulsive disorder (OCD) is characterized by intrusive and unwanted ideas, thoughts, urges, and images known as obsessions together with repetitive, ritualistic cognitive and physical activities comprising compulsions. The frequency of religious obsessions in OCD populations in the United States has been estimated to lie between 10 percent

(Eisen et al., 1999) and approximately 30 percent (Mataix-Cols, Rauch, Manzo, Jenike, & Baer, 1999; Steketee, Quay, & White, 1991). The frequency of religious obsessions in the OCD population in countries of the Middle East runs much higher, with at least half of the patient population reporting religious obsessions (Tek & Ulug, 2001). Boyer and Liénard (2006, 2008) have offered a cognitive and evolutionary model of ritualistic behaviors in OCD.

The clinicopathological functional and structural imaging studies of OCD suggest a consistent finding: There is abnormally increased activity in orbitofrontal cortex (OFC) and in subcortical basal ganglia (particularly in the caudate) and limbic circuits (Fontaine, Mattei, & Roberts, 2007). These areas show increased metabolic and functional activity when OCD symptoms are provoked. When patients are treated with serotonin reuptake inhibitors, the functional activity in the OFC and caudate nucleus resolves toward normal (Fontaine et al., 2007, p. 625, Table 38.2). Given the elevated rates of hyperreligiousness in some OCD patients, these data indicate that the overactivation of the OFC and the caudate nucleus which projects to the frontal lobes may be implicated in hyperreligiousness. In both TLE and in schizophrenia, the OFC is also likely overactivated, so the OCD data are consistent with the TLE and schizophrenia data. The OFC is densely interconnected with the limbic system and, in fact, partially regulates the same. Therefore, if the limbic system is overactivated, it would not be unreasonable to suppose that the both the limbic system and the OFC would be overactivated as well in TLE, schizophrenia, and OCD.

What about the temporal lobes? We have seen that the right temporal lobe was implicated in hyperreligiosity in both TLE and schizophrenia. The role of the temporal lobes in OCD symptomology may have been obscured in previous neuroimaging studies of the condition as most of those had been done while patients were medicated. When Adler et al. (2000) examined the effects of symptom induction on functional MRI (fMRI) neural activation in medication-free patients with OCD, they observed significant activation in several regions of the frontal cortex as well as the anterior, medial, and lateral temporal cortices. Right-sided superior frontal activation inversely correlated with baseline compulsion symptomatology. Thus, it is clear that the temporal lobes and right prefrontal cortex contribute to OCD symptomology.

Scrupulosity

One subtype of OCD, "scrupulosity," is particularly relevant to hyperreligiosity. It is worth citing a couple of cases of scrupulosity to get a feel for the kinds of unwanted thoughts that plague the patient in this condition. These cases are from Greenberg, Witztum, and Pisante (1987).

> **Benjamin.** Thirty-three-year-old married man with three children. Following his marriage when 20, he became preoccupied with the thought that he had not had sufficient concentration during his wedding ceremony, rendering the marriage invalid. He went to see rabbis about it until a second ceremony was arranged. After this, he became preoccupied with his wife's menstrual cleanliness. The thoughts filled his mind all day, although he tried to dismiss them. Although he was aware that this preoccupation was excessive, he would question his wife many times a day as to whether she had become menstrually unclean. If she dismissed his question, he would decide that she was not taking the matter seriously and he would remain tense. He consulted rabbis very frequently as to whether – given his doubts – he was permitted to be with his wife, and they always permitted it. Nevertheless, he avoided touching his wife whenever possible, and intercourse was very infrequent. He only agreed to intercourse because of the commandment "Be fruitful and multiply," but on occasion his wife "forced" intercourse on him.
>
> In addition, he took a long time to complete the portions of daily prayer that are considered to be especially important and requiring particular devotion, every such line adding an extra 10 minutes to his prayer.
>
> From an Eastern European ultra-orthodox background, Benjamin's father is described as rigid and pedantic, never giving way to leniency, and making his religious practice a burden for the family.
>
> Benjamin was the third of nine children, and the first son. In the Jewish religion the duty of performing commandments is emphasized for

men, and the duty of educating them is taken more seriously than for girls. From the age of three, Benjamin went to a separate-sex institution for teaching Jewish studies, with little emphasis on secular studies. He married at 20 and has three children. He has never felt a strong sexual desire, although it has always been heterosexual. He learns all day in an institution for Talmudic studies. Three years ago he became increasingly depressed, and responded to ECT. The intensive thoughts were unaffected until he was given clomipramine.

Since then his mental state has been kept relatively stable on regular clomipramine (up to 200 mg).

At interview, he is tall and thin, with a long beard, dressed in the black long coat of ultra-orthodox Eastern European Jewry. He is quiet and withdrawn although he occasionally smiles. He describes his preoccupying thoughts, his weak resistance and partial insight. There are no psychotic features (pp. 32–35).

Comment 5. Note the similarities between this case and the TLE inter-ictal behavioral syndrome. In both disorders there is hyperreligiousness and hyposexuality. Unlike many patients with TLE, there is no evidence of rage or irritability in this OCD patient. Nor is there any evidence for hypergraphia.

In the following example, one can see the ways in which OCD infuses the life of prayer the individual was attempting to develop.

Ephraim. Nineteen-year-old bachelor. At the age of 12, Ephraim developed fears of bears and wild animals. He became tearful and withdrawn and rejected food. Over the subsequent months his studies deteriorated, and he started praying excessively, often going back to the beginning as he thought he may have forgotten something. Shortly before his bar mitzvah, his father died. His fears receded, although he remains frightened of thieves or other intruders at night. His main problem now is over lengthy prayers. He says the words slowly in order to be exact, and goes back over sections he thinks he may have forgotten. His fears over saying his prayers dominate his day. Up at 6 A.M. in order to say some pre-prayer prayers, he completes his morning prayers at 11 A.M. After learning in the Talmu-dical academy with a special tutor – willing to go at a very slow pace –

he is home for lunch for two hours followed by two hours for the after-noon prayers (normally 10 minutes), immediately followed by another two hours of evening prayers (normally 10 minutes). His two-hour lunch break is mainly taken up by meticulous handwashing before the meal and slow recital of the benediction; grace after meals can take half an hour. A five-minute prayer recited before sleep takes another half an hour. In the time left over "I think about the prayers." In addition, washing, dressing and all other activities are very slow, and any visit to the toilet takes half an hour.

Ephraim's father was a Holocaust survivor, described as a depressive, who spent his days in the Talmudical academy, sleeping there usually, often not returning home for weeks and never showing any interest in his wife or children. His oldest son assumed responsibility for the children. Ephraim's father only became religious after arriving in Israel from Europe; his oldest son became irreligious which upset the family. Ephraim was the youngest of five, being of normal development if a little bashful. He was very attached to his mother, and was very upset when he was sent to boarding school – a decision taken in order to prevent him following in his brother's irreligious footsteps.

Over the years he had not benefitted from treatment by a series of antidepressant medications.

At interview, Ephraim was a short, thin, pale young man, bowed over, dressed in the garb of the ultra-orthodox. He rarely established eye-contact and spoke with a lisp in a quiet voice. He said that his slowness caused him much pain and considered it excessive. When requested, he read a prayer Psalm slowly but steadily. He made it quite clear, how-ever, that this did not count as prayer, and declined to pray along-side the assessor. There were no features of psychosis or depression (pp. 60–61).

Comment 6. Ephraim displayed an acute awareness that some aspects of his condition (slowness) were abnormal. It is striking, however, that the bulk of Ephraim's energies were devoted to prayer. This investment in prayer was not essentially obsessive. Many people attempt to pray "without ceasing" as St. Paul advised. What was obsessive in Ephraim's behaviors was that the praying had to be done "correctly" and in a precisely orderly way. The neuropsychiatric basis of cases of scrupulosity very likely resembles that of the more typical OCD syndrome. Overactivation in the OFC and limbic system is probably key. When overactivation in the limbic system is strong enough, it may suppress drive centers in the hypothalamus, and then you would get depressive symptomology as well as hyposexuality and the like.

Frontotemporal Dementia

Frontotemporal dementia (FTD) is a neurodegenerative disorder that is localized primarily to the frontal lobes and the anterior portions of the temporal lobes.

In its early stages before individuals become demented, FTD is associated with early behavioral abnormalities, including apathy, disinhibition, and obsessive and compulsive behaviors (Miller et al., 1997; Neary et al., 1998). In one anatomical subtype of FTD, the degeneration appears to involve selectively, and often asymmetrically, the amygdala and anterior temporal lobes, as well as the posterior/medial portion of the OFC (Chan et al., 2001; Edwards-Lee et al., 1997; Galton et al., 2001; Mummery et al., 1999; Rosen et al., 2002). This subtype, called the temporal variant of FTD (tvFTD), involves asymmetric, right- or left-sided degeneration of the OFC, the anterior temporal lobe, and the amygdala.

The religious experiential manifestations of the disease are interesting because they usually involve the relatively sudden acquisition of interest in religious ideas, texts, practices, and so forth. Here are some cases all involving the temporal variant of the disease (from Edwards-Lee et al., 1997):

> **Patient LTLV 1 (Left-handed).** A 56-year-old left-handed woman was seen after 9 years of progressive dementia. At the age of 46 years she was demoted from administrative secretary to account clerk. She deposited money incorrectly and forgot co-workers' names. She was irritable, threw bills at employees, shoplifted and embarrassed her family in public. At 51 years a psychologist noted that she had trouble understanding simple words and that her behaviour was "bizarre and inappropriate."

At the age of 53 rapid, empty paraphasic speech was present. Intellectual testing revealed overall IQ within the borderline range (FSIQ = 75) with PIQ (85) substantially higher than VIQ (67). Basic attention (Digit Span 5-37%) and constructional skills (Rey–Osterrieth copy 5 63rd%) were normal, while information processing speed (Digit Symbol = 16%; Trails A = 10%; Stroop A and B, 1st%) and nonverbal memory (Rey–Osterrieth delayed recall = 18th%). In contrast, executive skills (FAS was <1st%; Stroop C <1st%; Trails B = 7th%), word-retrieval, and verbal learning memory (Shopping List <1st%) were markedly impaired.

By the age of 56 years she initiated incoherent conversation with strangers, lifted her shirt in public and touched strangers' buttocks. Previously vegetarian, she now ate meat. She spent the day copying verbatim from the Bible and successfully played the search and circle word game similarly to Patient RTLV 5. Previously learned piano playing was largely preserved.

On examination she was disinhibited, touching the examiner's hand and pulling up her shirt to expose her breasts. She was bizarre and remote, rarely answering questions. She addressed all examiners as, "hey lady" and described items as "itchy." Verbal output was fluent with pressured speech and frequent paraphasias. She followed simple one-step commands. She achieved a score of 1 on the MMSE based on preserved ability to draw the pentagons. She precisely drew and recognized on multiple choice the modified Rey–Osterrieth Complex Figure.

MRI showed bitemporal atrophy, greater left than right. SPECT revealed bitemporal hypoperfusion worse on the left than right with sparing of other brain areas (pp. 1031–1032).

Comment 7. The only indication of hyperreligiosity in this patient is "copying from the Bible." Right temporal cortex is spared relative to the left.

Patient RTLV 3. A 66-year-old right-handed female had 2 years of behavioural and cognitive change. Previously social, she withdrew and her religious beliefs heightened. She could not recognize her son's voice on the telephone and developed word-finding trouble. Driving competency remained normal and she continued to manage family finances and housework. On examination she was irritable, remote and easily upset.

MMSE score was 23. She had mild anomia and a mild decrease in language comprehension. Memory was impaired but drawings and calculations were normal. She did not cooperate for PIQ but VIQ (78) was in the borderline range. Basic attention (Digit Span = 37%) was normal, but learning and memory ranged from low average to borderline (shopping list Trial 5 = 7; delayed recall = 5; Rey–Osterrieth delay = 14, 25th%). In contrast, information processing speed (Trails A <1st%; Stroop A and B <1st%), word-retrieval (Boston Naming Test = 10, <1st%), and executive skills were severely impaired (FAS <1st%; Stroop C = 200 seconds, 2nd%).

MRI was normal, but SPECT revealed bitemporal hypoperfusion, worse on the right than the left. Over the next 2 years she became increasingly irritable and remote. Although too uncooperative for testing, she continued to run her household (pp. 1030–1031).

Patient RTLV 1. A 59-year-old right-handed man made errors in calculations and over 2 years was demoted from an estimator to a handyman and was forced to retire. He wore unmatched shoes or socks, tucked his jacket into his pants, buttoned shirts inside out and put deodorant or shaving lotion in his hair. He waved to pictures on walls. Initially easygoing, he became stubborn and irritable. A religious awakening led him to spend hours in church; he argued with his wife and friends regarding his new religious ideas. He became emotional, cried when people left him and refused to attend his father's funeral. His eating habits changed; he nibbled constantly, repetitively spat, and ate coffee and banana peels. He was alternately placid and irritable with a remote, bizarre and robot-like affect. MMSE was 22. Digit Span was seven and verbal output fluent. He showed a severe anomia, named only two animals in 1 min but had only mild difficulty with reading and memory. His calculations were poor but he copied drawings well. Head CT showed mild atrophy, most marked in the right temporal lobe. SPECT showed decreased rCBF of the anterior temporal regions, greater on the right than the left. He died 4 years after examination. An autopsy showed asymmetric, primarily right-sided temporal > frontal atrophy with no plaques, neurofibrillary tangles, Pick bodies or Lewy bodies. Neuronal loss and gliosis were noted in the temporal > frontal areas and were worse on the right than the left (p. 1029).

Comment 8. In these latter two cases, heightened religiosity was associated with right temporal pathology or hypoperfusion. The hyperreligiosity was therefore likely mediated either by disinhibited right-sided orbitofrontal and limbic networks or by left-sided temporal and frontal networks.

FTD is a degenerative disorder; therefore, loss of neural structures is piecemeal and progressive. It is not yet clear how the disease progresses – which structures go first, second, and so forth – but it is likely that if prefrontal structures go first, they will release from inhibition temporal, parietal, and limbic structures. During that period of disinhibition, you should see manifestations of enhanced behavioral output such as artistic or religious behaviors. In my view, you are more likely to get sudden interest in religious matters when the right limbic, temporal, or orbitofrontal cortex is released from inhibition.

Summary of Neurologic Data on Hyperreligiousness

I have now completed my brief survey of hyperreligiousness in patients with brain disorders (see Table 5.1).

I did not discuss bipolar disease, but suffice it to say that religious delusions are much more likely in the manic than in the depressive phase of the illness (Brewerton, 1994) and that mania is associated with limbic, orbitofrontal, and right-sided temporal overactivation (Migliorelli et al., 1993). I believe that when taken together the clinical data suggest that the limbic system (particularly the amygdala), portions of the basal ganglia, the right temporal lobe (particularly the anterior portion of the medial and superior temporal lobe), and the dorsomedial, orbitofrontal, and right dorsolateral prefrontal cortex are the crucial nodes in a brain circuit that mediates religiosity. As we will see in the next chapter, the circuit, in turn, is regulated by the mesocortical DA and various serotoninergic systems.

When this circuit is stimulated in the right way, you get religious ecstasy. When the circuit is overactivated, you get various forms of religiously tinged aberrations. When cortical sites (right temporal and

Table 5.1. Disorders enhancing religious experience

Anatomical site/ function Disorder	Frontal/ECF	Hippocampus/ Amygdala Memory/emotion	Dopamine intensity
Frontotemporal dementia	↓	↑	↑
Temporal lobe epilepsy	↑	↑	↑
Schizophrenia			
Positive	↑	↑	↑
Negative	↓	↓	↑
Bipolar disorder			
Manic	↑	↑	↑
Depressive	↓	↓	↓
Obsessive-compulsive disorder	↑	↓	↑

Note: ↓ = decreased function; ↑ = disinhibition.

frontal) play the leading role, you get ideational changes in belief systems and outright delusional states. When limbic and basal ganglia sites play the leading role, you get changes in ritual behaviors as well as increased interest in religious practices such as prayer and other rituals. Beyond this meager summation, little more can be said with any degree of confidence. Let us turn now to the literature on neuroimaging of religious practices in healthy people. Perhaps we can find more clues as to how the brain mediates religious experience/practices. We will first be looking for disconfirmation of these ideas derived from the clinical data on the circuit that mediates religiosity in clinical populations. Then we will look for evidence of structures and brain networks that did not make an appearance in the clinical literature.

Brain and Religion in Healthy Individuals

In the past 10 years, new functional neuroimaging techniques have been brought to bear on the issue of how the brain supports religiosity. These techniques allow one to see brain activity unfold as the brain reacts to some stimulus or action performed by a participant.

Functional imaging techniques such as SPECT, positron emission tomography (PET), and functional MRI (fMRI) allow for study of the activity of large regions of the living brain in vivo under the scalp as the subject performs some task.

"Functional imaging" methods, because they yield a picture or image of brain activity rather than just structure (as do MRI and computerized tomography [CT]), can be used to study brain function. Functional neuroimaging techniques have made it possible, for the first time, to study brain function in normal, living humans and so afford an opportunity to investigate phenomena considered unique to human beings, like religious behaviors.

Human brain functional imaging techniques all rely on the fact that the brain uses energy when it is working, and energy utilization requires both glucose and oxygen consumption. Glucose molecules and oxygen can be tagged with a chemical that can be detected as they are utilized by the brain with specialized measurement devices arrayed around the head. With MRI, molecules within the brain are magnetized, by an array of magnets situated around the head. When magnetized, these molecules change their orientations, and this change can be used to infer volume and integrity of surrounding tissue.

I turn now to a review of neuroimaging studies of religiousness. This review is summarized in Tables 5.2, 5.3A, and 5.3B.

Newberg and colleagues (2001) pioneered the use of functional imaging approaches to religion and brain issues. They have used PET and SPECT methods to study the brain states of experienced meditators during meditation and of nuns in prayer. They found in both cases decreased activation levels in the parietal lobes and increased activation levels in frontal lobes. There was also increased activation seen in the cingulate gyrus bilaterally and the thalami. They suggest that because the parietal region has been implicated in somesthesis, body schema disturbances, and the sense of Self, the hypoperfusion in the parietal regions results in a dissolution of the boundaries of the Self and a more intense religious experience. Note that this formulation of the religious experience is consistent with some accounts from mystics who claim that they felt closer to God when they "forgot" themselves. Note also, however, that whereas some workers in the field point to the sense of presence as

Table 5.2. Neuroimaging of religion table

Study	Azari et al., 2001 (same as Azari et al., 2005)	Beauregard & Paquette, 2006	Newberg et al., 2003	Puri et al., 2001	Wuerfel et al., 2004
Subject population	Religious teachers and nonreligious college students	Carmelite nuns; no control group	Christian women in a Charismatic or Pentecostal tradition who had practiced glossolalia for more than 5 years	Schizophrenic patient	Patients with localization-related epilepsy
Total number of subjects	12 (8 male, 4 female)	15 (all females)	5 (all women)	1 (male)	33 (23 males, 10 females)
Religious task	First verse of biblical Psalm 23 was recited	Remember and relive (eyes closed) most intense mystical experience being a nun	Glossolalia	He suffered from religious delusions	Completed NBI and separated into high and low religiosity groups based on NBI subscales
Control task(s)	Happy (German children's nursery rhyme) and Neutral (instructions to use a German phone card)	Remember and relive (eyes closed) most intense "state of union" with another person	Singing with eyes closed to match condition during glossolalia	NA	Completed NBI and separated into high and low writing and sexuality groups based on NBI subscales
Technique	PET	fMRI	SPECT	SPECT	MRI
Additional information about technique	Subjects were scanned in 6 conditions (reading silently and reciting with eyes covered for religious and happy and religious and reading, and lying quietly for the neutral condition)	Baseline condition was a normal resting state	7 mCi 99mTc-Bicisate and 25 mCi of 99mTc-ECD	99mTc-HMPAO	

108

Subcortical areas

Brain stem
Pontine tegmentum
Midbrain   +L
Mesencephalon
Tectum mesencephali
Pontomesencephalic
  tegmentum
Raphe nuclei

Diencephalon
Thalamus
Thalamic nuclei
Geniculate body
Centrum medianum
Basal forebrain

Limbic system
Left amygdala
Right amygdala   +LS
Septal nuclei   +
Hippocampus   +Smaller right
                                                      hippocampus

Basal ganglia/striatum
Caudate   +R, +L
Putamen
Striatum (n. accumbens,
  sub innominata,
  lenticular nuclei)

(continued)

109

Table 5.2 (*continued*)

Study	Azari et al., 2001 (same as Azari et al., 2005)	Beauregard & Paquette, 2006	Newberg et al., 2003	Puri et al., 2001	Wuerfel et al., 2004
Cerebellum					
Cerebellar vermis					
Cerebellar hemisphere					
Corpus callosum					
Cortical areas					
Frontal (cortex/gyrus)					
Frontal	+DM				
Opercular					
Paraolfactory					
Lateral orbital					
Medial orbital					
Caudal orbital					
Orbitofrontal		+RM; +RM			
Gyrus rectus					
Frontal gyrus					
Paracentral lobule					
Frontal white matter					
Prefrontal cortex	+R, +DL	+L, +M; +R, +M			
Precentral somatosensory					
Postcentral somatosensory					
Central gyri					
Neocortex					

110

Parietal (cortex/gyrus)

Brodmann area 40 (IPL)   +R, +L;
   +L
Brodmann area 7 (SPL)   +R;
   +L

Supramarginal gyrus
Angular gyrus
Precuneus   +R
Cuneus
Pericentral
Parietal operculum
Primary sensorimotor cortex   +L

Temporal (cortex/gyrus)

Temporal sulcus
Frontal cingulate cortex
Mesiotemporal   +R;
Middle   +R

Posterior superior   +
Inferior/fusiform

Occipital (cortex/gyrus)

Optic radiations
Lingual gyrus
Medial
Postrolandic sensory
Lobes
Primary visual sensory cortex   +
Visual association cortex
Extrastriate visual cortex

(continued)

Table 5.2 (*continued*)

Study	Azari et al., 2001 (same as Azari et al., 2005)	Beauregard & Paquette, 2006	Newberg et al., 2003	Puri et al., 2001	Wuerfel et al., 2004
Limbic-associated					
Medial (prelimbic) prefrontal					
Cingulate					
Anterior cingulate		+L, +D; +R, +D			
Medial cingulate					
Posterior cingulate					
Infralimbic					
Insula		+L			
Hippocampal regions					
Hypothalamus					
Parahippocampal					
Entorhinal					
Temporal pole					
Notes	The religious participants reported previous conversion experiences. A German population was used	The purpose of the study was to understand mystical experience from a Christian perspective; red denotes mystical vs. baseline condition; black denotes mystical vs. control condition	No notes to report.	Subject was schizophrenic and suffered from religious delusions; subject was imaged when expressing religious delusions	Participants completed the NBI and were divided into 3 groups depending on their NBI subscales. Data are reported for those participants who expressed hyperreligiosity

Note: All areas of activation are based on the religious task and not the control task.

Abbreviations: PET = positron emission tomography; MRI = magnetic resonance imaging; fMRI = functional MRI; SPECT = single photon emission computed tomography; L = left hemisphere; R = right hemisphere; M = medial; S = superior; D = dorsal; HMPAO = hexamethyl propylene amine oxime; NBI = Neurobehavioral Inventory; NA = not applicable; ECD = electron capture detection.

Table 5.3A. Neuroimaging of religion table – meditative and miscellaneous studies (Part 1)

Study	Borg et al., 2003	Harris et al., 2008	Herzog et al., 1990	Kakigi et al., 2005	Kjaer et al., 2002	Lazar et al., 2000	Lehmann et al., 2001	Lou et al., 1999	Lutz et al., 2008
Subject population	Normal males from radioligand development trials or experimental drug trials	Normal adults	Yoga meditation group	Yoga master	Meditation teachers	Subjects practiced Kundalini meditation daily	A Buddhist Lama	Experienced yoga teachers	Long-term Buddhist meditators
Total number of subjects	15 (all males)	14 (7 men, 7 women)	8 (6 men, 2 women)	1 (male)	8 (males)	5 (4 male, 1 female)	1 (male sex is presumed)	9 (6 males, 3 females)	16 Buddhist meditators and 16 healthy volunteers (28 males, 4 females)
Religious or meditative task	None	Not a religious task per se; subjects read religious statements and had to evaluate how truthful they were (true, false, or undecidable). Examples of the religious statements include: A personal God exists, just as the Bible describes; There is probably no actual creator God; Jesus spoke 2,467 words in the New Testament.	Yoga meditative relaxation	Meditative state	Yoga Nidra relaxation meditation	Meditated by monitoring their breathing and silently repeating "*sat nam*" during inhalations and "*wahe guru*" during exhalations	2 subjective experiences during which he meditated (Buddha in front of me, Buddha above)	Practiced an intense form of concentric meditation (Tantric Kriya Yoga) for 2 hours before coming to the study	Pure compassion meditative state

(continued)

Table 5.3A. (continued)

Study	Borg et al., 2003	Harris et al., 2008	Herzog et al., 1990	Kakigi et al., 2005	Kjaer et al., 2002	Lazar et al., 2000	Lehmann et al., 2001	Lou et al., 1999	Lutz et al., 2008
Control task(s)	None	Subjects also read short statements about mathematics, geography, autobiographical accounts, ethics, semantics, and facts and were to evaluate how truthful they were (true, false, or undecidable)	Yoga resting state	Nonmeditative state	Rest condition – attend to speech in the same voice	Generated a list of animals and did not monitor breathing	3 subjective experiences during which he meditated (verbalization of a 100-syllable mantra, self-dissolution, and self-reconstitution)	Relaxation meditation (Yoga Nidra)	Resting state
Technique	PET	fMRI	PET	MEG, fMRI	PET, MRI	fMRI	EEG	PET	fMRI
Additional information about technique	Radioligand [^{11}C]WAY100635	BOLD changes were measured	Measuring regional CMRGlc	Both techniques were performed after noxious laser stimulation; BOLD	^{11}C-raclopride	None	None	^{15}O-H$_2$O	None
Subcortical areas									
Brain stem									
Pontine tegmentum									
Midbrain									
Tectum				+R, +L		+			
mesencephali									
Mesencephalon									

Pontomesencephalic
tegmentum
Raphe nuclei   +D

Diencephalon
Thalamus
Thalamic nuclei
Geniculate body
Centrum
medianum
Basal forebrain

Limbic system
Left amygdala
Right amygdala
Septal nuclei
Hippocampus

Basal ganglia/
striatum
Caudate
Putamen
Striatum (n.   +V   + +
accumbens,
sub
innominata,
lenticular
nuclei)

Cerebellum
Cerebellar vermis
Cerebellar   +
hemisphere

115

(continued)

Table 5.3A (*continued*)

Corpus callosum

Study	Borg et al., 2003	Harris et al., 2008	Herzog et al., 1990	Kakigi et al., 2005	Kjaer et al., 2002	Lazar et al., 2000	Lehmann et al., 2001	Lou et al., 1999	Lutz et al., 2008
Cortical areas									
Frontal (cortex/gyrus)		+A, +P					+S, +Mid	+post medial (BA 6)	
Frontal								+P, +S	
Percular									
Paraolfactory									
Lateral orbital									
Medial orbital									
Caudal orbital									
Orbitofrontal									
Gyrus rectus									
Frontal gyrus				+RS, +LS, +R Mid					
Paracentral lobule									
Frontal white matter									
Prefrontal cortex						+DL			+M
Precentral somatosensory									
Postcentral somatosensory									

116

Region									
Central gyri	+pre		+pre (BA4 and BA 6)	+pre and post					
Neocortex									+
Parietal (cortex/gyrus)						+			
Brodmann area 40 (IPL)	+		+L, +Bi						
Brodmann area 7 (SPL)	+						+R		
Supramarginal gyrus	+								
Angular gyrus									
Precuneus	+								
Cuneus									
Pericentral									
Parietal operculum									
Primary sensorimotor cortex								+L	
Temporal (cortex/gyrus)									
Temporal sulcus	+A	+S	+S		+				
Cingulate cortex	+, +PS			+pregenual anterior					
Mesiotemporal									
Middle				+					
Posterior superior									
Inferior/fusiform	+fusiform		+fusiform						

(continued)

117

Table 5.3A (*continued*)

Study	Borg et al., 2003	Harris et al., 2008	Herzog et al., 1990	Kakigi et al., 2005	Kjaer et al., 2002	Lazar et al., 2000	Lehmann et al., 2001	Lou et al., 1999	Lutz et al., 2008
Occipital (cortex/gyrus)									
Optic radiations							+ (but not the V1 region)		
Lingual gyrus							+		
Medial									
Postrolandic sensory									
Lobes									
Primary visual sensory cortex								+	
Visual association cortex									
Extrastriate visual cortex									
Limbic-associated									
Medial (prelimbic) prefrontal									+M prefrontal, +Mid prefrontal
Cingulate									+P
Anterior cingulate									+
Medial cingulate									
Posterior cingulate									
Infralimbic insula									
Hippocampal regions	+					+	+	+Bi	+R, +A
Hypothalamus									
Parahippocampal						+			+
Entorhinal									
Temporal pole									

118

Notes
The binding potential of radioligand [^{11}C]WAY100635 to 5-HT$_{1A}$ receptors was examined. There was no religious or control task per se. Subjects completed the Swedish version of the TCI. Potential binding areas are reported that were correlated with the scales on the TCI.
Reaction times were obtained for belief, disbelief, and uncertain categories. Although there were religious statements, areas of the brain that were lit up for these statements were not reported in the paper. Only areas of belief, disbelief, and uncertainty were reported. The areas that responded to the statements were not reported.
Participants practiced yoga until the particular states were met and the specific measurements of CMRGLc were obtained; no real religious condition; they repeated sentences or had a "central point of power" that they focused on.
The subject reported no pain during meditation, which prompted the study. Areas of the brain that showed an increased signal are reported.
^{11}C-raclopride BP were examined; EEG was also used; decrease in BP in ventral striatum due to decreased D$_2$ receptors. There was an increase in theta activity. Other areas of interest for increases and decreases in BP during meditation were reported among the participants but not summarized as a whole.
No notes to report.
Areas of activation are reported for all meditation conditions.
PET was carried out in 8 different conditions and global CBF was performed in 2 subjects. Different areas were activated in response to meditation. All areas of activation for all 8 conditions are reported and differ depending on what type of meditation was practiced. Areas of activation are reported from the CBF.
The findings were found to be stronger in the right vs. the left hemisphere.

Note: All areas of activation are based on the religious task and not the control task.

Abbreviations: A = anterior; BA = Brodmann's area; Bi = bilateral; BOLD = blood oxygen level dependent; BP = binding potential; CBF = cerebral blood flow; CMRGLc = cerebral metabolic rate of glucose; D = dorsal; EEG = electroencephalography; fMRI = functional magnetic resonance imaging; L = left hemisphere; M = medial; MEG = magnetoencephalography; Mid = middle; P = posterior; PET = positron emission tomography; R = right hemisphere; S = superior; TCI = Temperament and Character Inventory; V = ventral.

119

Table 5.3B. Neuroimaging of religion tables – meditative and miscellaneous studies (Part 2)

Study	Newberg et al., 2001	Newberg et al., 2001	Stigby et al., 1981	Tebēcis, 1975
Subject population	Practicing Tibetan Buddhist meditators and healthy controls	Franciscan nuns	Practicing transcendental meditators at least twice daily for 2 years	"At least some months" experience of daily TM
Total number of subjects	8 Buddhists (4 men, 4 women) and 9 healthy controls (sex is not reported)	3 (all females)	14 (9 males, 5 females) and 13 controls (5 males, 8 females) who were not practicing TM	14 (12 males, 2 females) and 14 controls (8 males, 6 females)
Religious or meditative task	Meditation (eyes closed); could use meditation books; eyes closed for last 30 min	Prayer (verbal meditation; eyes closed for last 30 min)	TM technique of Maharishi Mahesh Yogi	TM technique
Control task(s)	Rest state – eyes closed and ears unoccluded	Rest state – eyes closed and ears unoccluded	Closed-eye wakefulness	Open eyes and sit quietly without moving unnecessarily
Technique Additional information about technique	SPECT Injected with 7 mCi of ^{99m}Tc-HMPAO	SPECT Injected with 260 MBg of ^{99m}Tc-HMPAO	EEG	EEG
Subcortical areas				
Brain stem				
Pontine tegmentum				
Midbrain	+			
Mesencephalon				
Tectum mesencephali				
Pontomesencephalic tegmentum				
Raphe nuclei				

Study	Newberg et al., 2001	Newberg et al., 2001	Stigby et al., 1981	Tebēcis, 1975
Diencephalon				
Thalamus	+, +thalami			
Thalamic nuclei				
Geniculate body				
Centrum medianum				
Basal forebrain				
Limbic system				
Left amygdala				
Right amygdala				
Septal nuclei				
Hippocampus				
Basal ganglia/ striatum				
Caudate				
Putamen				
Striatum (n. accumbens, sub innominata, lenticular nuclei)				
Cerebellum				
Cerebellar vermis				
Cerebellar hemisphere				
Corpus callosum				
Cortical areas				
Frontal (cortex/gyrus)	+l	+l		
Frontal				
Opercular				
Paraolfactory				
Lateral orbital				
Medial orbital				
Caudal orbital				
Orbitofrontal	+			
Gyrus rectus				
Frontal gyrus				
Paracentral lobule				
Frontal white matter				
Prefrontal cortex	+DL	+		

(continued)

Table 5.3B (*Continued*)

Study	Newberg et al., 2001	Newberg et al., 2001	Stigby et al., 1981	Tebēcis, 1975
Precentral somatosensory				
Postcentral somatosensory				
Central gyri				
Neocortex				
Parietal (cortex/gyrus)				
BA 40 (IPL)		+		
BA 7 (SPL)				
Supramarginal gyrus				
Angular gyrus				
Precuneus				
Cuneus				
Pericentral				
Parietal operculum				
Primary sensorimotor cortex	+sensorimotor cortices, +DM sensorimotor cortices			
Temporal (cortex/gyrus)				
Temporal sulcus				
Cingulate cortex				
Mesiotemporal				
Middle				
Posterior superior				
Inferior/fusiform				
Occipital (cortex/gyrus)				
Optic radiations				
Lingual gyrus				
Medial				
Postrolandic sensory				
Lobes				
Primary visual sensory cortex				
Visual association cortex				
Extrastriate visual cortex				

Study	Newberg et al., 2001	Newberg et al., 2001	Stigby et al., 1981	Tebēcis, 1975
Limbic-associated				
Medial (prelimbic) prefrontal				
Cingulate	+, +cingulate gyri			
Anterior cingulate				
Medial cingulate				
Posterior cingulate				
Infralimbic				
Insula				
Hippocampal regions				
Hypothalamus				
Parahippocampal				
Entorhinal				
Temporal pole				
Notes	No notes to report.	No notes to report.	An imaging technique was not used – only EEG was used to differentiate between wakefulness, drowsy, sleep onset, and sleep. Frequency and voltage were reported for frontocentral, temporal, and parieto-occipital.	An imaging technique was not used – only a trend in EEG and the theta frequency band was noted. The meditators showed more theta activity.

Note: All areas of activation are based on the religious task.
Abbreviations: BA = Brodmann's area; D = dorsal; EEG = electroencephalography; HMPAO = hexamethyl propylene amine oxime; I = inferior; L = left hemisphere; M = medial; P = posterior; S = superior; SPECT = single photon emission computed tomography; TM = transcendental meditation.

important for the religious experience, Newberg and colleagues seem to be arguing the opposite.

Another important study that used functional imaging techniques to study religious experience was that by Azari and colleagues (2001). These investigators used PET to study a group of six self-identified religious subjects, who were Protestant Christians, and a group of six control subjects, who were self-identified as nonreligious. The study took place in Düsseldorf, Germany.

The two groups were matched on age, gender, and level of education. The goal of Azari et al. (2001) was to image the brains of their volunteers while they were engaged in religious thoughts (e.g., recitation of the Psalms) as opposed to nonreligious but equally "poetic"/happy thoughts – namely, an overlearned poem from childhood like a nursery rhyme. They also asked their volunteers to indicate how they were feeling while they were engaged in these tasks. All subjects were able to recite from memory both the religious and happy texts at the time of the PET scanning.

According to the self-assessment ratings, only the religious subjects achieved the religious state (while reciting the religious text). The PET images acquired from the religious subjects in the religious state showed peak blood flow activation in the right dorsolateral prefrontal cortex compared to the nonreligious subjects. This activation pattern was also observed in contrast to both the happy state and the neutral read condition.

Newberg, Wintering, Morgan, and Waldman (2006) measured regional cerebral blood flow using SPECT in a group of five Christian women who had practiced glossolalia for at least 5 years. Glossolalia is also known as "speaking in tongues" within Christian communities. There is a reduction in volitional control, and then the individual begins to emit vocalizations that sound like a different language. Both the target individual and his or her community attribute religious meanings to these vocalizations. The researchers observed decreased activity in the left caudate and in the prefrontal lobes and a trend toward increased activity in the right amygdala.

Beauregard and Paquette (2006) reported on two studies of Carmelite nuns in mystical states associated with their contemplative prayer practices (see also Beauregard & O'Leary, 2007). The first study involved fMRI scans of fifteen nuns in a baseline condition (a restful state), a control condition (most intense union with another human being), and a mystical condition (recalling and reliving their most significant mystical experience). Self-induction methods were used to produce the control and mystical conditions. The second study used quantitative electroencephalography (EEG) to measure brain waves of the same nuns in the same three conditions, with subjects sitting in an isolation chamber. The results from the first study showed that many areas of the brain (including especially the inferior parietal lobule, visual cortex, caudate nucleus, and left brain stem) were involved in the nuns' recalling and reliving their most significant mystical experiences. The results from the second study showed "significantly more theta activity ... in the mystical condition, relative to the baseline condition" in the insula, the right inferior parietal lobule and superior parietal lobule, and the right inferior and middle temporal cortices. "Moreover, there was significantly more theta activity in the mystical condition, compared to the control condition" in the anterior cingulate cortex and the medial prefrontal cortex (Beauregard & O'Leary, 2007, p. 275).

Footnote. As this book was going to press, another neuroimaging study of prayer was brought to my attention by an anonymous reviewer (I thank the reviewer for this kindness). Schjødt, Stødkild-Jørgensen, Geertz, and Roepstorff (2008) and Schjødt, Geertz, Stødkild-Jørgensen, and Roepstorff (2009, forthcoming) used fMRI to investigate brain activation patterns associated with overlearned forms of prayer such as the Lord's Prayer and improvisatory forms of prayer (prayer made up on the spot). The participants were a group of Danish Christians. Recitation of the Lord's Prayer was associated with strong activation in the right caudate nucleus. Given that this nucleus is known to be a central node in an ascending network of DA systems that support reward and approach behaviors, among other things, the authors hypothesized that

that religious prayer was capable of stimulating the DA system of the dorsal striatum in religious people. Improvised praying, in contrast, elicited a strong response in the temporopolar region, the medial prefrontal cortex, the temporoparietal junction, and precuneus. All of these structures participate in mediation of the sense of Self. The authors pointed out that praying to God appeared to activate areas of the brain known to be involved in social cognition and theory of mind processing.

I will not review in any detail the neuroimaging findings on meditative states except those from studies that included a form of meditative prayer. I excluded those studies that treated meditation as a mere relaxation exercise rather than a religious exercise. Please consult Tables 5.3A and 5.3B for more details on imaging studies of meditative states. Here I will mention only two such studies as they were particularly well designed and they yielded information relevant to the brain structures that we are evaluating for a role in religiousness.

Kjaer et al. (2002) used [11C]raclopride PET techniques to study DA activity during Yoga Nidra meditation in eight experienced practitioners. Yoga Nidra meditation involves deliberate withdrawal of the mind from wishing to act. The meditator becomes a neutral observer. During meditation, raclopride binding in the neutral striatum decreased by 7.9 percent, corresponding to a 65 percent increase in dopamine release. In short, this form of meditation actively induces release of dopamine in the forebrain.

Lutz, Brefczynski-Lewis, Johnstone, and Davidson (2008) used fMRI to study the effects of compassion meditation on brain response of meditators to emotional and neutral sounds. Compassion meditation involves the cultivation of a feeling of loving kindness toward all. When meditators heard sounds of distress, insula and cingulated cortices increased activation levels. These results are congruent with other studies demonstrating a role for the insula in empathy for others. Relative to nonmeditation rest states, the meditation states demonstrated increased activation in amygdala, the right temporal–parietal junction, and the right posterior superior temporal sulcus.

Summary of the Neuroimaging Findings on Religiousness

All of these neuroimaging studies (see Tables 5.2, 5.3A, and 5.3B) of both familiar religious practices such as prayer and glossolalia, as well as compassion meditation and reading of the Psalms, converge on the conclusion that the circuit of brain sites that we identified as crucial for religiosity from the clinical data (orbitofrontal, right temporal, limbic system [amygdala], the serotonin and dopamine systems, etc.) also appear consistently in the neuroimaging findings of healthy persons performing religious practices. This is a remarkable fact. Across many different types of religious practices and many different types of participants, the prefrontal lobes (with the partial exception of the Beauregard & O'Leary, 2007, study 1), the temporal lobes, the limbic system (except for the Azari et al. study involving the reading of Psalms), and the DA systems all appear to undergo increased levels of activation during the religious practice. There is also a trend at the cortical level for activation increases to be right-sided. The parietal lobes tend either to undergo deactivation or do not change at all. Activation patterns in the cerebellum are also not consistent.

A Tentative Synthesis of the Neurological Data

These results and similar ones from other investigative teams suggest that there is a network of brain regions that consistently are activated when a person performs a religious act.

The most important regions of the brain for studies of religious expression appear to be a circuit linking up the orbital and dorsomedial prefrontal cortex, the right dorsolateral prefrontal cortex, the ascending serotoninergic systems, the mesocortical DA system, the amygdala/hippocampus, and the right anterior temporal lobes.

There is a huge literature that documents the connectivity patterns of each of these anatomical sites (reviewed in Gashghaei, Hilgetag, & Barbas, 2007). They are all interconnected. The posterior OFC appears to regulate the limbic system and is densely interconnected with the insular, temporal polar, and parahippocampal cortices as well as with basal fore-brain structures such as the ventral striatum, nucleus basalis of Meynert, and amygdala (Nauta, 1962; Van Hoesen, 1981). The medial OFC is recip-rocally connected to the rostral portion of the insula, the medial basal amygdala, ventromedial temporal pole area 38, and medial subcallosal cingulate areas 24, 25, and 32. The anterior entorhinal area 36 is intercon-nected with the hippocampal formation. The lateral orbitofrontal region is interconnected to dorsal and caudal portions of the basal amygdala, which is a source of projections of emotional information to the visual processing centers in inferior temporal cortex, supracallosal areas 24 and 32, the auditory association cortex area 38 in the temporal lobe, inferior temporal cortex area 20, and prefrontal dorsal area 6. The latter area is interesting, as it involves supplementary eye fields as well as Exner's area, which is thought to mediate cognitive functions involved in writing. Hypergraphia may be associated with hyperreligiosity in TLE and other neurologic conditions (Waxman & Geschwind, 1975).

The raphe nucleus manufactures serotonin – a neurotransmitter cru-cially involved in religious experience. A role for the serotonin sys-tem in relation to spiritual experiences is supported by observations of drugs that act on the serotonin system, such as lysergic acid diethy-lamide (LSD), psilocybin, N,N-dimethyltryptamine, mescaline, and 3,4-methylenedioxymethamphetamine. On a behavioral level, these drugs (in susceptible individuals) elicit perceptual distortions, changes in the sense of Self, a sense of insight, spiritual awareness, mystical experiences, and religious ecstasy. They do so by decreasing firing in the raphe system, which then removes the ability of the person to screen out large amounts of incoming sensory information. The person is then inundated with "meaningful" and vivid images. A decrease in serotonin also leads to an increase in firing of dopamine neurons in the circuit. Dopamine is the other neurotransmitter repeatedly implicated in religious experiences. Relatively high levels of dopamine in the circuit create a pleasurable and positive mood. When low serotonin is combined with high dopamine lev-els in the circuit, the feeling of being inundated with meaningful images and impressions is associated with positive affect, and you are much more likely to get religious experiences.

The amygdala and anterior temporal and orbital frontal regions play a key role in the modulation of emotion, with the amygdala being especially important for the comprehension of negative emotions, particularly fear (Adolphs, Russell, & Tranel, 1999; Adolphs, Tranel, Damasio, & Damasio, 1994). The amygdala/hippocampus regulates emotional appraisal and memory consolidation.

In summary, the circuit that mediates religiousness involves primarily limbic, temporal, and frontal cortices on the right. This proposal is congruent with those of other authors who have studied potential brain correlates of religiosity (e.g., Bear & Fedio, 1977; d'Aquili & Newberg, 1993; Devinsky & Lai, 2008; Persinger, 1987; Ramachandran, Hirstein, Armel, Tecoma, & Iragui, 1997; Trimble, 2007). Most of these authors, however, emphasize the role of the temporal lobes in religious experience. They do so presumably because of the impressive clinical data on temporal lobe epileptics who exhibit hyperreligiosity and the interictal behavioral syndrome (Geschwind, 1983). For example, Persinger (1983) argues that "temporal lobe transients" or microseizures that emanate from deep within the temporal lobes give rise to religious experiences and other related experiences such as out-of-body experiences, space–time distortions, and intense meaningfulness. These microseizures elicit powerful experiences because they activate neighboring structures such as the amygdala (important for emotion), the hippocampus (attention and memory), and adjacent limbic structures. Since the early 1980s, Persinger and his colleagues have carried out many studies of brain and religiosity using the special technique of transcranial stimulation of the temporal lobe regions of the brain. Persinger claims consistent findings of "the sense of presence" when the temporal lobes are stimulated and that this sense of presence is one of the roots of religious experience. His stimulation technique, however, has not been replicated by other laboratories (see Granqvist, 2006).

d'Aquili and Newberg (1993), more than any other scholars, have explored possible neuropsychologic models of religious experience. They very sensibly assume that all the major association areas of the cortex generate some aspect of the total religious experience. They assume, for example, that the temporal lobes attach meaning and significance to events and thus are central to eliciting the profound adherence to religious frameworks. They argue that the parietal lobes undergo a deactivation during profound religious experience and that this deactivation is related to a diminution in sense of Self or ego.

All of these models of brain correlates of religious experience are helpful. In my estimation, however, we need additional data-gathering efforts and model-building efforts in this area. As the review of the literature in this chapter demonstrates, the data on religion and brain have been gathered in almost a secondhand manner. Astute clinicians noticed profound changes in religiousness after brain injury in some patients. They reported as faithfully as possible on these changes, and these reports gave birth to the new brain-based approach to the study of religiosity. The adventitious approach to data collection about brain and religion correlates means, however, that no systematic efforts to document relationships between particular brain regions and particular aspects of religious cognition have yet been attempted or accomplished. We have no way of knowing, therefore, whether the clinical and neuroimaging data are giving us a biased picture of the true state of affairs with respect to brain mediation of religiosity.

Despite these shortcomings of the existing data set on religion and brain, it is nevertheless striking, at least to this observer, that the picture is relatively consistent. There is a consistent set of brain structures that modulate religiosity. I have named those structures earlier in this chapter and have said something about their known functions. I have also argued that they are interconnected anatomically. This latter fact suggests that the structures in question may act as a single functional unit. If so, then chemically addressing that circuit should produce religious experiences. We will see in the next chapter that that is indeed the case.

6 Neurochemistry of Religiosity

And it shall come to pass afterward, that I will pour out my spirit upon all flesh;

and your sons and your daughters shall prophesy, your old men shall dream dreams, your young men shall see visions.

– Joel Ch. 2

Introduction

Once a year, the Huichol Indians of the Southwest United States and northern Mexico make a kind of pilgrimage across hundreds of miles to gather the peyote they use in their religious ceremonies (Schaefer & Furst, 1997). The trek is led by an experienced "mara'akame" or shaman, who is in contact with God-ancestor Tatewari (grandfather-fire). Tatewari, also known as Hikuri, is personified with peyote plants on his hands and feet. Upon arriving within sight of the sacred mountains of Wirikuta, the shaman begins the ritual cleansings and chants that will initiate the dangerous crossing into the Otherworld, facilitated by peyote. The shaman supervises preparation of the hikuri plants as the fresh cacti are grinded into a pulp on a metate, with each drop of liquid oozing from the pulp collected in a gourd. Participants are served the peyote and sing songs that praise peyote for its protection of the tribe. During the many hours of the religious rite while they are intoxicated with peyote, the participants see visions, receive guidance, and experience a religious form of ecstasy that enriches them spiritually and sustains them emotionally as they go about the rest of their lives.

Recent archaeological evidence suggests that peyote (*Lophophora williamsii*) has a history of use in religious rituals that can be traced back more than ten thousand years. Indeed, there is strong evidence that humans have ingested psychoactive materials throughout the evolutionary history of our species. They or we did so as part of our religious rituals. Our brains contain nerve cells with specialized receptors that bind preferentially to these psychoactive chemicals – all of which produce changes or alterations of states of consciousness that appear to be both ecstatic and "religious."

Ecstatic Religion

The Huichol Indians practice a form of ecstatic religion, but you do not need peyote or any other drug to experience religious ecstasy. Most scholars of religion believe that the earliest forms of religion were "ecstatic" – that is, religious practices were designed to induce a transformation in the sense of Self to commune with the gods, to experience a sense of euphoria and well-being, and to acquire new personal powers (such as the power to heal others, foresee the future, or communicate with the spirit world). The combination of self-transformation, joy, well-being or euphoria, and personal power defines the ecstatic religious mind and the essential psychological elements in all religions.

Ecstatic religions often but not invariably involve use of psychoactive substances and what is now called shamanism. People who could induce in others or in themselves these ecstatic religious states were treated with deference and honor. In modern scholarship these religious specialists are called shamans.

The main function of a shaman was (and still is) to heal others of illnesses or injuries – thus the link between religion and medicine was forged quite early in our evolutionary history. Interestingly enough, a common set of experiences was reported by shamans who attempted to heal others. These common experiences were reported across the many cultures that used shamans as healers. The shaman would go into a kind of ecstatic trance, in his "imagination" travel to spiritual realms where he would meet spirit beings who could either help or hinder him in retrieving the soul of the patient, and then return the soul to the patient along with any other medicines he discovered were necessary for the healing.

Take, for instance, this account of the "calling" of an Eskimo shaman (as quoted in Lewis's *Ecstatic Religion*). Like Christ Himself, the young man went off by himself into the Arctic wilderness to be tempted and to find his religious calling. After days of lonely wandering . . .

> I soon became melancholy. I would sometimes fall to weeping and feel unhappy without knowing why. Then for no reason all would suddenly be changed, and I felt a great, inexplicable joy, a joy so powerful that I could not restrain it, but had to break into song, a mighty song, with room for only one word: joy! Joy! And I had to use the full strength of my voice. And then in the midst of such a fit of mysterious and overwhelming delight I became a shaman, not knowing myself about how it came about. But I was a shaman. I could see and hear in a totally different way. I had gained my enlightenment, the shaman's light of brain and body, and this in such a manner that it was not only I who could see through the darkness of life, but the same bright light also shone out from me, imperceptible to human beings but visible to all spirits of earth and sky and sea, and these now came to me to become my helping spirits (Lewis, 1971, p. 37).

When a young man or woman received the "calling," he or she had to be trained by an elder or a group of elders in the arts of healing and in the religious knowledge of the tribe. In premodern tribal societies, this is what the elderly do – they teach the young. The elders are repositories of the history, the experiences, and the mythological lore and religious goals of the tribe. No one received more training than a shaman – not even the hunters were better trained.

The training of a shaman was remarkably similar to the training of any modern priest or spiritual specialist. It involved strict discipline under supervision of an older expert, abstention from sex, frequent religious

practices, and study of the medical lore of the tribe, the use and properties of any hallucinogens the tribe used in its religious practices, the
religious rituals and mythological lore of the tribe, and the symbols that
referred to the spirit realm and the gods. These symbols would then be
scraped on rock or painted on walls or boulders and any other suitable
surface. This sort of rock and cave art very likely facilitated the rise of
writing when agriculture arrived on the scene some ten to fifteen thousand years ago. Thus the prototypical ecstatic religion called "shamanism" very likely contributed to the development of all of those arts of
civilization we consider so crucial today, including the production of
mythological images and lore, art, writing, music, the healing arts, and
much else besides. Assisting the shamans in these productive activities
were the medicinal herbs and plants that he or she carefully manu-
factured as well as the psychoactive plants that he or she tended and
refined.

Hallucinogens/Entheogens

We now know quite a bit about the actions on the brain of peyote and
similar hallucinogens. We know how they help to induce that religious
ecstasy. Virtually all of the hallucinogens activate nerve cells that are specialized to process the neurochemicals serotonin and dopamine, which
are neurotransmitters that turn on and operate the brain structures I
identified earlier as part of the religion circuit (i.e., the amygdala and
hippocampus, other structures in the limbic system, the anterior temporal lobe, and the orbitofrontal, dorsomedial, and dorsolateral prefrontal
cortices). Neurochemicals such as serotonin and dopamine allow nerve
cells to communicate with one another. The transmitters are released
near a neuron, attach to receptors on that neuron, and then cause it to
electrically discharge or fire (depolarization). That electrical impulse then
causes other transmitters to be discharged from the neuron, which then
communicate with yet other neurons, causing them to depolarize, and
so forth.

Hallucinogens reduce the firing of cells in the raphe nucleus of the
brain stem that manufacture serotonin while enhancing the firing of cells

that manufacture the neurotransmitter dopamine. That dopamine then gets released in the limbic, prefrontal, and temporal cortices, modulating their activity levels. When hallucinogens are used in a religious context, you do not get an overall reduction in brain activity. Instead you get a heightening of dopamine-modulated activity in the limbic, prefrontal, and temporal cortices and a lowering of serotoninergic tone in these same sites.

If the "religion circuit" can be addressed or turned on by these drugs, then one should see features of the religious experience in individuals ingesting these drugs. We have just seen that peyote can address the religion circuit and produce profound religious experiences. What about the other hallucinogens, such as lysergic acid diethylamide (LSD)?

Here are some examples of experiences reported by chronic, hospitalized alcoholics who had received treatment with the hallucinogen LSD in the early 1960s (Unger, 1965). It will become clear that they are to some extent "religious" and that they share some of the phenomenological features (altered consciousness, positive affect, meaningfulness, etc. – these features will be described further later in this chapter) of an ecstatic religious experience.

> I found myself drifting into another world and saw that I was at the bottom of a set of stairs. At the very top of these stairs was a gleaming light like a star or jewel of exceptional brilliance. I ascended these stairs and upon reaching the top, I saw a gleaming, blinding light with a brilliance no man has ever known. It had no shape nor [sic] form, but I knew that I was looking at God himself. The magnificence, splendor, and grandeur of this experience cannot be put into words. Neither can my innermost feelings, but it shall remain in my heart, soul, and mind forever. I never felt so clean inside in all my life. All the trash and garbage seemed to be washed out of my mind. In my heart, my mind, my soul, and my body, it seemed as if I were born all over again (Unger, 1965).
>
> A feeling of great peace and contentment seemed to flow through my entire body. All sounds ceased and I seemed to be floating in a great, very very still void or hemisphere. It is impossible to describe the overpowering feeling of peace, contentment, and being a part of goodness itself that I felt. I could feel my body dissolving and actually becoming a part of the

goodness and peace that was all around me. Words can't describe this. I feel an awe and wonder that such a feeling could have occurred to me (Unger, 1965).

At the peak or climax of my experience, I realized a great scene was about to unfold within myself. I actually shook and shuddered at what I felt. A tremendous earthquake feeling was building up in me. There was a tremendous force, and I came and saw a glorious beauty of space unfold before me, of light, color, and of song and music, and not only of one thing good and beautiful, but of a oneness in fellowship, a wanting to belong to this greatness of beauty and goodness that unfolded before my eyes, and that I felt. Suddenly, I could see my family handing me great love. It seemed to be pouring out of their hearts. I cried, not bitter tears, but tears of beauty and joy. A beautiful organ was playing in the background, and it seemed as if angels were singing. All of a sudden I was back in eternity. There was music and beauty. Peace and happiness, tranquillity – could not possibly describe my feelings. My heart was filled with joy that was overwhelming. Just a beauty and peace that I have never known. At this point, I felt that time was thousands of years ago, thousands of years from now, and now (Unger, 1965).

The effects of the use of hallucinogens in a religious context show us that part of the basis of the religious ecstasy must involve the interaction of belief systems with the brain's chemistry. I hasten to add that this is not all of what constitutes religious experience – only one component of it. It is also important to emphasize the obvious fact that, in the modern era, use of hallucinogens to achieve religious ecstasy is the exception rather than the rule. In addition, most people who have experienced religious ecstasy have done so without drugs. They often say that the experience was given to them as a gift. Nevertheless, when you look at their histories you find that they engage in consistent religious practices and rituals, they were listening to music, they were walking in the mountains or con-templating a beautiful scene or face, and so forth. From a neuroscientific point of view, it is possible to suppose that these sorts of experiences – as well as persistent performance of religious rituals and private devotional practices – can prime the religion circuit to make it more amenable to activation and production of ecstatic experiences. This, of course, is a bold claim: Engaging in religious practices such as prayer, meditation, reading scriptural texts, listening to sacred music, and so forth can all prime the religion circuit in such a way as to make the experience of religious ecstasy more likely in your life.

The neurologic basis of this claim, however, is simple. The religion circuit is chemically regulated, and neurochemical activity levels throughout the brain are influenced by Mind, beliefs, emotions, cognitions, cognitive practices, and so forth. Thus, it would not be surprising to find that manipulating brain levels of selected neurochemicals in selected brain sites would yield religious experiences. It should not be too controversial to claim that chemically activating the religion circuit produces religious experiences in susceptible individuals that are quite similar to religious experiences induced by other means such as devotional practices, ascetical practices, traditional religious practices, and so forth.

Entheogens and Religious Experiences

What, then, are the most salient features of chemically induced religious experiences? Walter Pahnke summarized them in 1967 (see also Chapter 1). Pahnke was a psychologist who studied ecstatic religious states induced by LSD in a group of Boston theological students. According to Pahnke, each experience of religious ecstasy is characterized by the following several properties:

1. "Unity is a sense of cosmic oneness achieved through positive ego-transcendence...

2. Transcendence of time and space means that the subject feels beyond past, present and future and beyond ordinary three-dimensional space in a realm of eternity or infinity...

3. Deeply felt positive mood contains the elements of joy, blessedness, peace and love to an overwhelming degree of intensity, often accompanied by tears...

4. Sense of sacredness is a non-rational, intuitive, hushed, palpitant response of awe and wonder in the presence of inspiring realities. The main elements are awe, humility and reverence, but the terms of traditional theology or religion need not necessarily be used in the description.

5. The noetic quality, as named by William James, is a feeling of insight or illumination that is felt on an intuitive, non-rational level and has a tremendous force of certainty and reality. This knowledge is not an increase in facts, but is a gain of insight about such things as philosophy of life or sense of values.

6. Paradoxicality refers to the logical contradictions that become apparent if descriptions are strictly analyzed. A person may realize that he is experiencing, for example, an "identity of opposites," yet it seems to make sense at the time, and even afterwards.

7. Alleged ineffability means that the experience is felt to be beyond words, non-verbal, impossible to describe, yet most persons who insist on the ineffability do in fact make elaborate attempts to communicate the experience.

8. Transiency means that the experience does not last in its full intensity, but instead passes into an afterglow and remains as a memory.

9. Persisting positive changes in attitudes and behavior are toward self, others, life and the experience itself (Pahnke, 1967).

Now virtually all mystical experiences and ecstatic religious experiences, whether induced by chemicals or via more traditional techniques (actually, chemical techniques may be quite traditional as they were practiced by ancestral human populations), share these aforementioned properties. More run-of-the-mill religious experiences likewise involve quite a few of these properties, although certainly not all of them. In sum, the phenomenological properties of chemically induced religious experiences share many features with religious experiences not induced by these chemicals – sometimes known as "entheogens." We can be relatively confident then that entheogens produce religious experiences by activating the same brain circuit that normally handles religious experiences – else how would one obtain such similar phenomenological features? The formal similarities in the cognitive, experiential, and phenomenological features obtained by both chemically induced religious experiences and non–chemically induced experiences suggest that both sets of experiences are tapping the same brain circuit. That brain circuit must crucially involve dopaminergic (DA) and serotoninergic neurochemical systems.

Role of Serotonin and Dopamine in Production of Religious Experiences

There are several lines of evidence that indicate a crucial role for the serotoninergic and DA systems in religious experiences. There are consistent correlations between genes that code for DA or serotoninergic activity and various measures of spirituality and religiousness. For example, an association was found between hypnotic susceptibility and the catechol-O-methyltransferase (COMT) polymorphism (Lichtenberg, Bachner-Melman, Gritsenko, & Ebstein, 2000). Hypnotic susceptibility, in turn, is associated with a range of religiosity measures. COMT is an enzyme that has a crucial role in the metabolism of dopamine and norepinephrine (the catecholamines) by inactivating them in the synaptic cleft. I will have more to say about COMT later in this chapter. Borg, Andrée, Soderstrom, & Farde (2003) reported a significant association between the forebrain binding potential of 5-HT1A receptors and "Self-transcendence" as measured by the temperament and character inventory (Cloninger, 1994). Disorders of excessive DA and reduced serotoninergic functioning, such as schizophrenia and obsessive-compulsive disorder (OCD), are often associated with increases in religiosity (Abramowitz, Huppert, Cohen, Tolin, & Cahill, 2002; Brewerton, 1994; Saver & Rabin, 1997; Siddle et al., 2002; Tek & Ulug, 2001; Wilson, 1998). Antipsychotic agents that block DA actions at the level of the limbic system and agents that increase central serotonin activity result in reductions in religious ideation/behaviors and a resolution of religious delusions in these patients. Hallucinatory agents that purportedly enhance religious or mystical experiences do so by reducing central serotoninergic activity and enhancing central dopamine transmission.

Back in 1965, Serafetinides (1965) demonstrated that the site of action of LSD was the temporal lobe. When he gave LSD to epileptics with intact temporal lobes, they experienced the usual hallucinogenic effects.

When, however, he gave LSD to epileptics who had had their temporal lobe (on the right) excised to control seizure activity, the drug had no effect.

Further evidence that hallucinogens work via inhibiting serotoninergic activity and enhancing DA activity in the frontotemporal regions is the finding that the site of pharmacologic action of LSD and perhaps other hallucinogens is the 5-HT2A receptor (Aghajanian & Marek, 1999; Nichols, 2004). The gene that codes for the 5-HT2A receptor is located at 13q14–q21 and appears to be expressed from the maternal allele through polymorphic imprinting of the gene. I mentioned the phenomenon of imprinting in Chapter 2 on the divided Self. Imprinting can be understood as a form of genetic conflict that ultimately leads to a divided consciousness. It is not surprising, then, that entheogens operate on these imprinted genes. If religion acts against divided consciousness, it must affect these sorts of receptors. The gene and the receptor itself are abundantly expressed in the prefrontal cortex (PFC) (Dean, 2003; Kato et al., 1996). Many of the new generation of antipsychotics target this receptor; thus it may also be implicated in pathogenesis of schizophrenia. Indeed, linkage and genetic association studies have pointed to polymorphisms in the gene as a contributing factor to schizophrenic symptomology (Dean, 2003). We have seen that religiousness is elevated in some patients with schizophrenia and that patients with schizophrenia evidence temporal and prefrontal dysfunction.

Many religious behaviors and basic religious cognitive processes must be mediated by the prefrontal lobes (see Chapter 5 and McNamara, 2002, for review), and prefrontal system functioning, in turn, is strongly influenced by serotoninergic and DA activity (Fuster, 2008; Goldman-Rakic, 1987). DA activity, particularly limbic–prefrontal activity, functions to signal "significant" or salient stimuli (Schultz et al., 1995); thus, if limbic DA activity is increased because of an entheogen, a religious practice, or other factors, incoming information will more likely be tagged as overly significant and a greater number of events will be experienced as "highly significant."

Obviously the key structures in mediation of dopamine's role in religiosity are the frontal lobes. The PFC constitutes approximately one-third of human cortex and is the last part of the human brain to become fully myelinated in ontogeny, with maturation occurring in late child-hood/early adolescence (Huttenlocher & Dabholkar, 1997). The PFC receives projections from the mediodorsal nucleus and gives rise to pri-mary motor cortex, as well as premotor, supplementary motor, and the dorsal and orbital sectors of the prefrontal (proper) lobes. All of these PFC areas send inhibitory efferents onto their sites of termination in other areas of the brain and spinal cord, thus suggesting a supervisory or regu-lative role for the PFC.

Impairment in DA and serotoninergic functioning in temporal and prefrontal cortical sites in humans is functionally implicated in virtu-ally every major neuropsychiatric disorder, including depression (Stark-stein & Robinson, 1991), schizophrenia (Lewis, Cruz, Eggan, & Erickson, 2004), OCD (Tek & Ulug, 2001), bipolar disorder (Haznedar et al., 2005), Parkinson disease (Starkstein & Merello, 2002), Huntington disease (Troster & Woods, 2003), the disinhibitory impulsivity syndromes (Berlin, Rolls, & Iversen, 2005), the addictions (Winstanley, Theobald, Dalley, Cardinal, & Robbins, 2006), and several others (e.g., memory retrieval dysfunction and the dementias (Cummings & Mega, 2003). The fron-totemporal region clearly mediates something distinctively human and related to the executive Self given that all of these syndromes share a common pathophysiology and a common final causal pathway in their negative impact on that Self.

Neurochemistry of Frontal Lobes

The frontal lobes are densely innervated by DA fibers originating in the ventral tegmental area (VTA) and the substantia nigra (SN). The nigro-striatal system indirectly influences the frontal lobes through the basal ganglia. The mesocortical system originates in the VTA and terminates in the ventral striatum, amygdala, nucleus accumbens, and the frontal lobes. This latter mesocortical system is crucially important for understanding human behavior as its stimulation appears to be intrinsically rewarding. All drugs/substances of addiction, for example, appear to derive their addicting properties by their abilities to potently stimulate this frontal DA system. Dopamine neurons of the VTA and SN have long been associated with the reward and pleasure systems of the brain. Virtually all of the known addictions (including cocaine, heroin, amphetamines, alcohol, food, and sex) exert their addictive actions, in part, by prolonging the influence of dopamine on target neurons (Wise, 2005). VTA DA neuron responses appear to be necessary to facilitate formation of associations between stimuli that predict reward and behavioral responses that obtain reward (Schultz et al., 1995). The orbitofrontal cortex integrates the most complex level of associations of reinforcement with both stimuli and responses (Rolls, 2004). In summary, stimulation of DA terminals in the mesolimbic-frontal systems constitutes the substrate for a most potent reward/reinforcing system.

The neurochemistry of the DA systems of the frontal lobes is shaped by a number of genes and genetic polymorphisms distinct to human beings. The gene that codes for COMT, which is involved in cortical dopamine catabolism, is particularly interesting. Statistically significant associations of COMT genotype variations with prefrontal cognitive function have been confirmed (Egan et al., 2001; Joober et al., 2002; Malhotra et al., 2002). In humans, the COMT gene contains polymorphisms in its coding sequence that are linked to functional brain and behavior phenotypes relevant for religious experience. Ott, Reuter, Hennig, & Vaitl (2005), for example, reported a significant interaction effect between the 5-HT2A and the COMT genes such that hypnotic absorption scores were highest in subjects homozygous for the TT-genotype of 5-HT2A as well as for the VAL/VAL genotype of COMT. Given that the trait absorption/ hypnotic susceptibility is correlated with measures of religiousness (Batson et al., 1993, pp. 112–113), it seems likely that these genes have influenced variation in levels of religiosity across individuals.

These considerations and the data reviewed in this chapter and in Chapter 5 all suggest that a specific set of neurochemical circuits mediate and regulate the religion circuit in the brain. As previously discussed, the most important neurotransmitter systems for the religion circuit are the dopamine and serotonin transmitters. The neurochemistry of the religion circuit must, therefore, be regulated by genes that code for metabolic pathways involved in the production, maintenance, and breakdown of serotonin and dopamine. I have mentioned at least two of these so far:

the COMT and 5-HT2A genes. I have also pointed out that these genes interact in individuals to produce behavioral traits (e.g., absorption) that are relevant for religion.

There are a number of recent behavioral genetic findings that are consistent with the idea that serotoninergic and DA circuits in prefrontal and temporal lobes shape religious experiences (Goberman & Coelho, 2002). A polymorphism on the dopamine receptor gene, DRD4, as well as the VMAT2 (also called SLC18A2) gene has been found to be significantly associated with intensity of spirituality and score on a "self-transcendence" personality scale (Comings, Gonzales, Saucier, Johnson, & MacMurray, 2000; Hamer, 2004). The VMAT2 gene codes for products that participate in the manufacture of serotonin and dopamine. Thus, the meager literature on genetics of religiosity once again implicates the dopamine and serotonin neurotransmitter systems in mediation of religious experiences and behaviors.

Provisional Model of Neurochemical Regulation of Religious Experiences

Pulling all of the above facts together suggests that one path to religious experience might be as follows (after Pahnke, 1967; Wildman & McNamara, 2008): When a religious experience begins with a reduction in intentionality or a turning over of the will to God, this reduction in intentionality is transient in normal religious experiences but is prolonged in entheogenic experiences. After the suspension of intentionality, there comes a flood of images and affects that resolves into a process of attempts at meaning and then finally insight and gratitude/joy. Now, of course, not all religious experiences contain all of these elements, but I contend that many do and that this modeling of religious experiences as a dynamic process can help us link religious experiences more readily with brain sites and processes.

At the neurochemical level, the reduction in agency/intentionality is mediated by a reduction in serotoninergic activity in the prefrontal and anterior temporal cortices, thus transiently inhibiting prefrontal/temporal cortical function. There is a transient diminution in prefrontal dopamine activity that corresponds to suspension of intentional states at the onset of a religious experience. In entheogenic experiences LSD, psilocybin/DMT (dimethyltryptamine), binds to 5-HT2A receptors in prefrontal and temporal lobes and blocks other serotonin (5-HT) receptors as well (Cooper, Bloom, & Roth, 2003; Nichols, 2004; Serafetinides, 1965). Serotonin is known to exert tonic inhibitory effects on DA neurons (Cools, Stefanova, Barker, Robbins, & Owen 2002; Daw, Kakade, & Dayan, 2002; Giacomelli, Palmery, Romanelli, Cheng, & Silvestrini, 1998; Millan, Lejeune, & Gobert, 2000; Vollenweider, 1998), particularly in the limbic system, and thus removal of the inhibitory 5-HT influence enhances DA activity resulting in religious and hallucinatory experiences (Carlsson, Waters, & Carlsson, 1999; Giacomelli et al., 1998; Iqbal & van Praag, 1995; Tomic & Joksimovic, 2000; Vollenweider, 1998). Gradually the inhibition of PFC wanes, and the combination of high limbic activity in the limbic system and the coming back online of the PFC yield a process of learning and insight. The anterior temporal lobes are densely interconnected with both the limbic system and the prefrontal lobes. The prefrontal lobes are in mutual inhibitory balance with the temporal lobes. Thus, the removal of the inhibition on the temporal lobes (with the drug-induced inhibition of the frontal lobes) as well as the DA stimulation enhancing activity levels in the limbic system yield a hyperactive temporal lobe. As the PFC comes back on line it slowly reestablishes the mutual inhibitory balance and normal activity levels with the temporal lobes. We have seen in Chapter 4 that interactions between the PFC and the temporal lobe are associated with hyperreligiosity.

Both DA and serotoninergic systems converge on the frontal lobes. We have seen that 5-HT2A receptors are abundantly expressed in PFC and that stimulation of these receptors inhibits prefrontal function (and perhaps DA activity in the PFC only) while simultaneously enhancing limbic DA activity. When the physiologic changes are extreme, this condition mimics psychosis. Religious practices appear to be able to enhance both limbic and prefrontal systems but only after an initial and transient inhibition of prefrontal function. Prefrontal activity slowly returns to normal levels and thus, in interaction with limbic and temporal sites, contributes to the phenomenology of the religious experience.

7 Self-Transformation as a Key Function of Performance of Religious Practices

Yen Hui: What is fasting of the heart?

Confucius: The goal of fasting is inner unity. This means hearing, but not with the ear; hearing, but not with the understanding; hearing with the spirit, with your whole being.... The hearing of the spirit is not limited to any one faculty, to the ear, or to the mind. Hence it demands the emptiness of all the faculties. And when the faculties are empty, then the whole being listens.

– Tzu, 1965, pp. 75–76

Unless a grain of wheat falls into the earth and dies, it remains alone, but if it dies it bears much fruit. He who loves his life loses it but he who hates his life in this world will keep it to life eternal.

– John 12:24–25

Introduction

In previous chapters I reviewed a considerable range of evidence concerning neural mediation of the sense of Self as well as neural and neurochemical mediation of religious experiences. It so happens that there is considerable overlap in the neuroanatomy of Self and of religious experience. Both rely heavily on limbic and right-sided anterior temporal and prefrontal networks. Now on the one hand, it should not be too surprising that Self and religious experience share the same neural networks, as it is the Self that experiences, and thus religious experience requires a Self for there to be religious experience at all. On the other hand, all other kinds of experiences, such as aesthetic delight, social interaction, romantic intimacy, scientific discovery, calculation, mental planning, and so forth – all of these also require a Self for them to "happen" at all; yet there is not the same degree of overlap in anatomy of Self and each of these sorts of experiences.

The striking degree of overlap between the anatomy of Self and of religious experience may be functional. It may be that religious experience functions to facilitate something that the Self needs or does. Interlocking neural groups that handle religion-related material with neural groups that handle Self-related material may mechanically facilitate the psychic or cognitive operations associated with each. Just as writing and expressive speech centers overlap near Broca's region in the left inferior prefrontal region for presumably functional reasons, so too do Self and religion overlap in right temporal prefrontal regions.

We should not, however, read too much into the overlapping neural instantiations or representations of religion and Self. After all, there are many cognitive skills that seem to be related functionally and computationally but are not instantiated in overlapping neural regions (e.g., high-level visual analyses are accomplished in both the occipital cortices and in inferior temporal lobes). Whatever the significance of overlapping neuroanatomy of Self and religion, I will argue in this chapter that Self and religious behaviors and experiences are functionally related. Many religious practices function to facilitate transformation and growth of the Self – specifically by reducing the discrepancy between the current Self and an ideal Self and by enhancing prefrontal executive functions. Enhanced prefrontal executive functions create a sense of a unified Self, an ideal Self with a strong sense of agency and Will.

This unified ideal Self, although fought for by so many ordinary people down through the ages, is also the Self that so many philosophers and scientists have attacked as illusory. A whole academic industry "of de-bunkers" of the substantive nature of the Self continue to churn out articles that argue in various convoluted ways that the Self does not exist. In one sense, they are correct; there is no homunculus sitting in the brain pulling the strings that control behavior. It is easy, furthermore, to demonstrate that consciousness is often fractionated and not unified. Nevertheless, we can and do experience our Selves as a unity, and there is little doubt that all of the world's religions believe that there is a unified sense of Self and that the Self is central to the religious enterprise. Even those traditions in Buddhism that assert that the Mind and the Self are illusory nevertheless devote enormous amounts of energies to developing practices that can extinguish the desires that they believe define the Self. If the Self is illusory as these Buddhists claim, then it is nevertheless quite a powerful "illusion."

I think that the debunkers of the centralized Self, postmodernists and Buddhist philosophers, have pointed to an essential set of insights on the executive Self: that it is not a thing but a process, that it is fragile, that it is transient and always in flux, and so forth. When it attaches itself to unworthy objects, slavery is the result. When, however, it lets go of these attachments and instead yokes itself up with "God," illumination and freedom are the result. To let go of unworthy attachments, the old Self has to "die," sacrifice its old loves. Unless the old Self dies, the new Self cannot emerge or be born. In any event, the old Self is always dying off and a new Self is always coming into being. If we do not grow, then we do not adapt to changing contexts and challenges. The Self must change in response to the demands it faces over time. Thus, the Self is always in flux. It is therefore both insubstantial and potent, fleeting and substantive, transient and enduring. The Self is all of these things because it is constructed "on the fly"; it is not biologically given to us; it is instead a dynamic cultural achievement. As many social psychologists have repeatedly pointed out concerning the Self, it is socially constructed. One of the sociocultural arenas in which it is constructed is that of religion.

The Self is one key to all of the fundamental functional aspects of religion and it therefore behooves us to examine religious practices that are specifically aimed at the Self. I think it is fair to say that all religions target the Self for transformation, or better, religion seeks to channel transformations of the Self into a prosocial direction by constructing a unified executive form of the Self. The reasons for this are obscure but instructive. I will return to the issue of why religions seek to transform the Self into an executive Self later in this chapter. First I will review the evidence that religious practices function to transform the Self. After reviewing some of this evidence, I will describe potential reasons why religion should be so interested in the Self and in transforming it.

Religious Practices

Religions promote the continuous transformation of the Self by encouraging the use of private religious practices and participation in the central rituals of the religious tradition. What are private religious practices? Examples include (but are not limited to) prayer; meditations; mental exercises involving the imagination; confessing sins before God and forming resolutions and goals concerning better behaviors; reading and studying scriptural texts; taking a daily moral inventory or reviewing behaviors as well as generating resolutions and plans to improve behaviors; private rituals and devotional practices; reading/studying nonscriptural religious texts; praying with beads and other handheld reminders; praying repetitive prayers; and adopting ritual gestures and postures such as kneeling and "making the sign of the cross."

I assume a neutral stance with regard to the possible transcendent source of the urge to engage in religious practices. I further assume that any sociocultural practice that reliably produces a religious experience is a "religious practice." All of the above examples of religious practices produce transient religious experiences. I therefore need to define what a religious experience is, and here I rely on the Wildman and Brothers treatment of the topic (Wildman & Brothers, 1999). For Wildman and Brothers, religious experiences are a subset of a broader range of "ultimacy experiences" (UE) – roughly those experiences that point to ultimate concerns and elicit our most intense cognitive–emotional–spiritual engagement/ commitment. Wildman and Brothers use a number of sources, including first-person accounts, phenomenological analyses, the judgments of experts in religious discernment, neural and psychological correlates, and the wisdom of generations as captured in the theological, ethical, and spiritual literatures, to identify the distinguishing characteristics of UEs. Focusing on the characteristics of religious experiences, they note that such experiences can be discrete (short-term, single instance) experiences or extended (long-term) experiences. Elements of discrete UEs include sensory alterations, self-alterations, a sense of supernatural presence, and cognitive and emotional changes. Elements of extended UEs include existential potency, social engagement, transformation of character, and transformation of beliefs. When experiences are associated with a number of these markers of discrete and/or extended UEs in the context of a socially or normatively defined "religious" practice, and when the experiences are further associated with emotional engagement/commitment as defined by Wildman and Brothers (1999), then we are likely dealing with authentic religious experiences. The essential points here are that what most people would call a religious practice is typically associated with what most people would call a religious experience and that these experiences can be reasonably well defined using the Wildman and Brothers criteria.

Phenomenological Analyses of Religious Experiences

Wildman and I recently utilized both "expert" analyses of narrative reports of religious experiences and rankings of phenomenologic features of religious experiences by the experiencers themselves (Wildman, 2002; Wildman & Brothers, 1999; Wildman & McNamara, 2008). By "expert" analysis, we mean analyses and ratings of narrative reports of religious experiences. Our work has focused on identifying key phenomenological properties of religious experiences so that empirically based theoretical models of the distinctive aspects of religious cognition and behavior could be developed. We had volunteers recount for us a recent religious experience (if they had one), a recent happy experience, and a recent emotionally neutral experience. We then had the volunteers rate their experiences along 21 dimensions of cognitive and phenomenological characteristics such as the extent to which the experience was meaningful, intense, and/or filled with positive or negative emotion; whether it involved an alteration in the time sense, in memory, or in attentional control; and so forth. Note that these phenomenological properties were not chosen by us to study religious experiences. They were put together by Pekala and associates in a "Phenomenology of Consciousness Inventory (PCI)" to study ordinary and nonordinary states of consciousness. The PCI (Pekala, 1991) is a self-report 53-item questionnaire on phenomenological aspects of a selected state of consciousness. The subject is asked to complete the inventory while recalling a previous state of consciousness. The PCI yields a quantitative profile of the contents and quality of personal consciousness along 21 measures, grouped into 12 major dimensions (positive affect, negative affect, altered experience, imagery, attention, self-awareness, altered state of awareness, internal dialogue, rationality, volitional control, memory, and arousal). The PCI has been repeatedly tested and its domain of validity extended in numerous studies since it was first introduced. Pekala provides detailed validity and reliability data on the instrument. After subjects filled out this inventory concerning their experiences, their experiences were transcribed and then subjected to further narrative analyses. We had the experts, postdoctoral and doctoral students in religious studies, rate these same experiences along the same dimensions. We wanted to see if religious experiences were rated any differently from happy or neutral experiences by both the experts and the experiencers themselves. Thus we had ratings from participants themselves about their own experiences as well as expert analyses of those same experiences as narrated by the subjects themselves.

After controlling for the time it took to recall an experience and self-assessed intensity of the experience, we found that, relative to both happy and ordinary experiences, participants rated their religious experiences as significantly more meaningful, with stronger altered states of awareness, increased inwardness of attention, higher amounts of imagery, more internal dialogue, lower volitional control, and more negative affect. Levels of positive affect in religious experiences fell between levels for ordinary and happy experiences.

To make sense of this set of religion-related characteristics, we next had independent raters who were blind to the purposes of our studies identify the order in which each of these elements (altered awareness, internal dialogue, high imagery, etc.) occurred in narratives of religious experiences and in narratives of happy experiences. We thought that if these elements occurred in a reliable sequence in the narratives, then they might indicate a similar sequence of events in the experiences themselves. Independent ratings of both religious and happy narratives revealed that the distinctive features associated with religious experiences did indeed occur in a particular sequence in the religious narratives. The ordering of thematic elements in happy narratives was difficult to judge because counts were so low for all elements but negative and positive affect.

We found, however, that religious experiences begin with specific cognitive content in the form of enhanced levels of imagery and also with negative affect. Next, internal dialogue ensues and attention is directed inwardly. Volitional control is then relaxed, and positive affect increases. Finally, a significant alteration in awareness and perception occurs. Subjects later refer to the effects of this whole process as filled with significance and meaning.

This phenomenology of religious experiences confirms that each religious experience involves a decentering process. The initiating event in religious experience (the event associated with enhanced imagery, negative affect, and inwardly directed attention) appears to be a reduction in intentionality or volitional control. This latter effect is typically an unpleasant experience (thus, the negative affect associated with it). It was consciously registered as a reduction in volitional control by participants in our studies, but it is noticed only after imagery levels are enhanced and attention is directed inward. This reduction in intentionality/volitional control can be either voluntary or drug induced, but it appears to be the event that triggers the decentering process in consciousness. The enhancement of internal attention and dialogue, as well as the alteration in awareness and perception, is correlated with placement of the Self in suppositional space and search of semantic memory for the ideal Self. The final sense of positive affect, insight, and meaningfulness, presumably, reflects successful integration of the old into the new Self.

All of these phenomenological properties of typical religious experiences support the notion that religious practices (insofar as they promote religious experiences) are about transforming the Self. After all, what else can it mean to say that attention is directed inwardly, that volitional control is reduced, that positive and negative affect levels change, or that perception and awareness is altered – unless we mean that all these experiences involve the Self? The Self undergoes a reduction in volitional control, increases in positive affect, and alterations in awareness and perception.

Religious experiences describe transformations of the Self. Now religious experiences can happen "out of the blue," but most of the time they happen to religious people who actively cultivate them with the aid of private and public religious practices. To see this, let's look at an example of the use of religious practices to induce a transformation in the Self.

The Self and Its Transformation in Islamic Mystical Practices

It is generally agreed that one of the major lineages in Islamic forms of mysticism are the Sufis. Their histories and sacred texts are rich in explicit reference to transformation of the Self as the aim of all religious practices. According to the scholar of Islamic mysticism Sara Sviri (2002), the immediate Arabic equivalent for "Self" in Sufi literature is "*nafs.*" "In Sufi psychology *nafs* became, primarily, the designator of a negative, earth-bound fiery entity that needs to be constantly condemned and watched over" (p. 195) or better, the *nafs* needed to be transformed into a better, higher Self to leave egocentricity and selfishness behind.

Interestingly, Sviri (2002) remarks that, for the Sufis, "[i]t is that very culpable nature of man that in the end, when transformed, ennobles him. Static goodness, such as that of angels, ranks inferior to that which man acquires through repentance and effort" (p. 196). It seems to me that the "Felix culpa" of the Christian tradition is similar in spirit to this Sufi sentiment regarding the *nafs*. To actively choose "goodness" over sloth, indolence, egocentricity, and evil is a greater vocation than that of the angels presumably because it involves the free and sustained effort of a person who could have done otherwise. In support of the high vocation of humans, the Sufis cite the story that God, when asked why he created human beings, replied, "I was a hidden treasure and wished to be known." You can only really know someone when you choose to do so. I cannot say that "so and so" really appreciates me if "so and so" had no choice about becoming acquainted with me. A person wishes to be chosen, and certainly a lover wishes to be chosen by the beloved.

The concerted effort, then, to get to know God is an effort to overcome the *nafs* so that a new person or Self (one that is capable of discerning and choosing the good over the "apparently" good) will emerge.

Sviri continues: "Sufi authors see the transformation of qualities, tabdil al-akhlaq, as the process whereby a holy man, the friend of God, is forged out of faulty human nature. Significantly, one of the highest ranks in the mystical hierarchy is reserved for the abdal, the 'Substitutes.' These are holy men and women, usually forty in number, without whom the world cannot subsist. The term abdal derives from a verbal root, b d l, that denotes transposition and substitution. Hence, according to the standard explanation, the abdal are so called because whenever one of them dies, God substitutes (buddala) another for him. Yet within Sufi circles an additional explanation circulated: they are so called because they have transformed (baddalu) their base qualities" (p. 196).

In the Sufi tradition, apparently, and in most if not all of the other religious traditions, religious practices are focused on transformation of these base qualities to turn them into gold or a set of higher qualities. When enough such qualities have been transformed, you get a new Self.

Sviri points out: "The idea of the transformation of the self has been understood to rest upon three Qur'anic verses which address *nafs* explicitly. The first verse addresses the *nafs* as 'that which incites to evil' (al-nafs al-ammara bil-su; 12:53); in the second, it is designated 'the *nafs* that blames' (al-nafs al-lawwama; 75:2); and in the third it is described as 'the serene self' (al-nafs al-mutma'inna; 89:27). These three designations, culled from disjoint locations, were seen, when juxtaposed in the foregoing order, as a paradigm for the progressive transformation of the lower self through effort, discipline, introspection, and, ultimately, divine grace, into the desired state of fulfillment" (p. 197).

This progressive transformation of the qualities of the Self are remarkably similar to the dynamic experiential process we (McNamara & Wildman, in preparation) described as illustrative of religious experiences in our study participants. There is an initial enhancement of imagery, negative affect, and internal dialogue (self-blaming and incitement to evil).

After reductions in volitional control and the turn inward, there is alteration in perception and awareness, an increase in positive affect, and a heightened sense of meaning (the serene Self). Presumably, each of these mini-experiences involves a decentering effect and builds over time to issue in a consistent sense that a new Self has emerged and that this Self is serene and joyful. It is crucial, however, to keep the "mini" religious experiences coming, and for this you need to keep prolonged effort and frequent performance of religious practices.

How Do the Sufis Use Religious Practices to Tame and Transfigure the *Nafs*? Sufi Efforts at Decentering and Self-Transformation

Sviri (2002, p. 199) describes a short treatise entitled *Rules of Conduct for Acts of Worship (Adab al-'ibadat)* by Shaqiq al-Balkhi, an eighth-century (second century, according to a Muslim calendar) mystic from Transoxania. Shaqiq describes four progressive stages in the process of transformation of the *nafs*: abstention (zuhd), fear (khawf), longing for paradise (al-shawq ila-l-janna), and love of God (al-mahabba li-llah). Different religious practices are recommended for each particular stage. "The period assigned for each stage is limited to forty days, at the end of which the practices pertaining to it may be abandoned" (p. 199). Most of the recommended religious practices in the first stage are ascetical practices; thus the name abstention. Abstention involves a reduction in food intake so that hunger is experienced. Alternatively, one can opt, as Jesus did, for total fasting for forty days. The effects of abstention are such that God plucks the desire for superfluous things out of the Sufi's heart. The Sufi then is on the road to freedom. The next stage, however, is fear. "The practice here begins with contemplating death and educating the *nafs* to fear God intensely" (Sviri, p. 201). Forty days of soberly and piously cultivating fear of God results in what Shaqiq calls mahaba (or awe). "After forty days, the effect of the inner light of awe becomes apparent on the practitioner's face, and he, too, becomes an object of awe... and reverence" (Sviri, p. 201). Interestingly, Shaqiq points out that the emergence of religious awe produces an emotional upheaval in the psychology of the "seeker." Although he prays constantly, he finds no pleasure in religious practices or in social contact or in the world. In the Christian tradition, this stage is often referred to as the period of dryness or the desert experience. If the seeker persists, however, the emptiness, fear, and restlessness are replaced with a longing for God, and the seeker enters the next stage: longing for paradise. "The practice here is to contemplate the everlasting bliss of paradise and its delights, such as the black-eyed beauties (al-hur al-'in), that await the blessed ones. As earlier, here too: when the practitioner, in earnest commitment, disciplines his self to endure the practice of longing, God rewards him by implanting the light of longing in his heart" (Sviri, pp. 201–202). The practice of longing for paradise seems to be related to the Christian practice of "putting on the mind of Christ," during which the seeker attempts to anchor his consciousness in higher spiritual realities and to see the world *sub species aeternitas*. Results of forty days of cultivating longing for paradise appear to be what Christians call the "gifts of the spirit": gratitude, fearlessness, generosity, sincerity, compassion, detachment, and joyfulness. These gifts of the spirit lead to the next stage: love of God. This is the highest and most noble attainment in the spiritual life. The practice here is to cultivate love of all that God loves and to detest all that God detests. God bestows the following gifts on the seeker: "he becomes beloved, noble, intimate, mature, gentle, composed, and magnanimous, and he refrains from vile deeds" (Sviri, p. 202).

Shaqiq's forty-day effort at self-transformation is remarkably similar to the "spiritual exercises" of Ignatius of Loyola. The Ignatian exercises are based on four "weeks." The first two weeks involve contemplation of one's own sin and cultivation of fear of God and hatred of Satan. The last two weeks are focused on cultivation of love of Jesus and conversion to Jesus' "standard."

Sviri also discusses another Sufi author, Al-Hakim al-Tirmidhi, who wrote a manual of religious practices similar to Shaqiq's. Al-Tirmidhi's work was called *The Ranks of Worshippers According to Their Worship* (Manazil al-'ibad min al-'ibada). al-Tirmidhi, however, outlines seven, rather than four, progressive stages (manazil): repentance (tawba), abstention (zuhd), righting the *nafs* ('adawat al-nafs), love (mahabba), cutting of the base inclination (qat 'al-hawa), fear (khashya), and proximity [to God] (qurba).

Although I will not discuss them here, one sees similar descriptions of the use of ascetical religious practices to move through stages of ascent toward God in both the Christian and Jewish mystical literatures (McGinn, 1994; Scholem, 1941). My point in summarizing Sviri's treatment of some early Sufi texts is to point to how clearly the recommended religious practices are aimed at transforming the Self. From an appetite-ridden, fearful, egocentric *naf*, one is transformed via ascetical practice into a serene, free, autonomous, gift-bestowing, compassionate, and generous individual. The gratitude and joy described by many religious people is surely to be treated with respect and taken seriously as a product that is reliably produced by consistent performance of religious practices.

Role of Executive Cognitive Functions in Religious Self-Transformation

How is the transformation accomplished cognitively and neurologically? One simple and very likely oversimplified answer to this question is that religious practices enhance the acquisition of the so-called executive cognitive functions (ECFs), which support self-regulation and autonomy, among many other qualities in an individual. ECFs refer broadly to cognitive activity involving the planning, initiation, maintenance, and adjustment of nonroutine, goal-directed behaviors. Commonly seen clinical manifestations of ECF deficits include disinhibition, amotivational syndrome, depressive affect, cognitive inflexibility, behavioral rigidity, "theory of mind" impairments (where the individual fails to ascribe intentional states, or attributes of Mind, to others), distractibility, and impaired abstract reasoning. The deficits are mediated by the prefrontal lobes in interaction with the temporal and parietal lobes as well as the basal ganglia. The prefrontal lobes appear to be key in supporting ECFs, so I will focus on prefrontal cortex (PFC) contributions to these functions.

The PFC of the human frontal lobes contains intrinsic reward circuits important in the neurobiology of addiction and specializes in both ECFs and skills of social intelligence more broadly.

Prediction of Reward. As mentioned in previous chapters, the frontal lobes are densely innervated by dopaminergic (DA) fibers originating in the ventral tegmental area (VTA) and the substantia nigra. The nigro-striatal system indirectly influences the frontal lobes through the basal ganglia. The mesocortical system originates in the VTA and terminates in the ventral striatum, amygdala, nucleus accumbens, and frontal lobes. This latter mesocortical system is crucially important for understanding human behavior as its stimulation appears to be intrinsically rewarding. All drugs/substances of addiction, for example, appear to derive their addicting properties by their abilities to potently stimulate this frontal DA system (Koob, 1992; Wise & Bozarth, 1987).

Social Skills. Social intelligence involves the ability to act wisely in social situations and appears to depend on the frontal lobes. Sociocognitive abilities linked to the frontal lobes include perspective taking, interpersonal problem solving, relationship maintenance, moral judgment, and socio-pragmatic communication (Eisenberg & Harris, 1984; Hogarty & Flesher, 1999a, 1999b; Worden, 1998).

ECFs and Religious Practices

The connection between ECFs and religious practices has been made before. With some irony, Rabbit (1997) pointed out how congruent are recent concepts of the ECFs of the frontal lobe with formal theological criteria for commission of a serious sin:

> The minimal functional processes involved in the commission of a mortal sin (taking the Roman Catholic framework) are awareness of the self as the intending perpetrator of the act; recognition of the unpleasant implications of the act for others by possession of a theory of Mind; recognition of its moral repulsiveness by possession of a theory of the Mind of God; an ability to simultaneously represent alternative acts and their possible outcomes in working memory in order efficiently to choose between them; conscious formulation of a well-articulated plan to perform the act successfully; self-initiation and execution of sequences of appropriate actions to consummate this plan during which recognition of personal culpability

> is maintained by continuous self-monitoring; recognition of attainment
> of the vile goal state and an intention to use what has been learned in its
> pursuit to perform it again if opportunity occurs. Clearly, only the central
> executive can sin (Rabbit, 1997, p. 2).

Whether or not a "central executive" exists, ECFs clearly do exist, and people need them to engage in any freely chosen path of behavior. Rabbit's tongue-in-cheek list of ECFs that are required in commission of a mortal sin – namely, self-awareness, empathy, theory of Mind, working memory, planning, self-initiation or Will, goal-directedness, and so forth – are all functions that have been shown to depend on the prefrontal lobes. I will review some of the evidence for this claim next.

Prosocial Behaviors of Empathy and Moral Insight

All religions claim to promote prosocial behavior, and it must be said that improved empathy and moral insight can be acquired via religious practices such as participation in communal services and cultivation of an altruistic orientation. Fundamental to the ability to engage in moral choice, empathy, and prosocial behaviors in general is the ability to delay gratification of one's own impulses. If individuals can derive real benefits (e.g., a larger "return" later) by learning to inhibit current appetitive responses, then natural selection would favor those individuals with the ability to delay gratification of impulses. One of the most disabling impairments associated with traumatic brain injury (which impacts primarily the PFC) is loss of the ability to delay gratification of prepotent or previously rewarded responses (Aharon-Peretz & Tomer, 2007; Schnider & Gutbrod, 1999). Relaxed inhibitory control over appetitive and sexual drives leads to inappropriate social behaviors that prevent the patient from returning to full functional independence. The child's acquisition of the ability to delay gratification of impulses develops in tandem with maturation of the frontal lobes (Samango-Sprouse, 1999). In adults, prefrontal lesions are often associated with ECF deficits and disinhibition of drives and aggression (Benson & Blumer, 1975; Fuster, 2008).

Empathy and Perspective Taking. Some models of moral development posit a central role for the capacity for fellow-feeling, empathy, and sympathy. Empathy, sympathy, and the other social emotions constitute prerequisites for mature moral behavior (Hoffman, 2000) and very likely depend on the frontal lobes (Grattan, Bloomer, Archambault, & Eslinger, 1994; Rankin, 2006). Having a "theory of mind" allows one to impute mental states (thoughts, perceptions, and feelings) not only to oneself, but also to other individuals and thereby to take the perspective of another. This theory of mind ability, to some extent, involves empathy and supports development of sympathy. Humphrey (1983) and others (e.g., Keenan et al., 2005) suggest that theory of mind abilities and this empathic kind of awareness evolved in humans because it was a successful tool for predicting the behavior of others. The best strategists in the human social game would be those who could use a theory of mind to empathize accurately with others and thereby be able to predict what the others would do in any given situation and to detect deception by others. It would be interesting to see how persons high in "religiosity" perform on theory of mind tasks and on detecting deception.

One way to show the role of the frontal lobes in supporting these prosocial behaviors is to investigate neuropsychological correlates of anti-social behavior. "Sociopaths" are by definition antisocial individuals, and the evidence for prefrontal dysfunction in these individuals is accumulating rapidly (Damasio, Tranel, & Damasio, 1990, 1991). Sociopaths typically exhibit an inability to empathize with others, egocentrism, an inability to form lasting personal commitments, and a marked degree of impulsivity. Although they may appear to be charming, they evidence serious deficits in expression of the social emotions (love, shame, guilt, empathy, and remorse). In contrast, they are not intellectually handicapped and are skillful manipulators of others (Davison & Neale, 1994; McCord, 1983). What little evidence exists suggests that sociopathy is associated with orbitofrontal dysfunction (Damasio et al., 1990; Smith, Arnett, & Newman, 1992). Dorsolateral function, however, is preserved and would explain the lack of intellectual deficit in these individuals.

The more violent forms of antisocial behavior are also associated with frontal deficits. In their review of the literature on neuroimaging in violent offenders, Mills and Raine (1994) concluded that frontal lobe dysfunction is associated with violent offending. Raine, Buchsbaum, Stanley, and Lottenberg (1994), for example, found that violent offenders (22 subjects accused of murder) evidenced significantly lower glucose metabolic activation levels in medial and lateral PFC relative to controls. McAllister and Price (1987) found that 60 percent of psychiatric patients with prefrontal cortical pathology displayed disinhibited social behaviors, and 10 percent displayed violent outbursts. Heinrichs (1989) showed that the best predictor of violent behavior in a sample of 45 neuropsychiatric patients was a prefrontal lesion.

Will, Planning, Goal Directedness, Optimism, and Hope. Virtually all patients with evidence of prefrontal dysfunction perform poorly on tests of planning and goal-oriented behaviors (Fuster, 2008). Shallice and Burgess (1991), for example, asked three patients with prefrontal dysfunction caused by head injury to perform a set of tasks designed to mimic the errands a person might have to run on a Saturday morning. The patients were given detailed, written instructions so as to avoid memory problems. All three patients failed to carry out the tasks or experienced great difficulties in their endeavors. Patients with lesions in the supplementary motor area of the PFC evidence significant deficits in initiation of behavior, and lesions in adjacent areas are also associated with deficits in "Will," agency, and voluntary behaviors (Goldberg, 1987; Passingham, 1995). Patients report that although they are capable of responding, they have no will to do so and so remain silent. A simple verbal test of initiation is known as the verbal fluency test. Most patients with evidence of prefrontal dysfunction perform poorly on verbal fluency paradigms.

Resistance to interference is a prerequisite for focused, goal-directed, concentrated mental processing. Goal-directed, purposive cognitive processing is not possible for an individual who is incapable of resisting interference from other competing goals. Retaining information in the short-term memory work space is possible only if that information is not immediately displaced by competing interfering stimuli. Frontal inhibitory processes allow us to ignore irrelevant stimuli and to attend to relevant stimuli (Dagenbach & Carr, 1994; Oscar-Berman, McNamara, & Freedman, 1991). It is crucial for concentration and deliberative thought. No sustained attention to a single train of thought is possible if one's thought is constantly falling prey to distractors. Concentration requires the ability to ignore or screen out distracting and irrelevant information. The bare ability to hold something in one's mind (as in the religious practice of focused meditation) requires the ability to resist displacement of that mental object by some other mental object. Patients with frontal lesions perform poorly on tests (e.g., delayed response tasks, the Stroop) of the ability to resist interference (Oscar-Berman et al., 1991).

Although I know of no direct studies that link hope to frontal systems, there is abundant evidence that links prefrontal dysfunction with loss of hope and depression (Lesser & Chung, 2007; Starkstein & Robinson, 1991). Patients with primary depression perform poorly on tests of frontal function; ECF impairment is evident in these patients. Regional cerebral blood flow studies have demonstrated a reduction in blood flow to frontal systems in depressed patients (Baxter et al., 1989).

Theory of Mind, Attributions of Agency

Agency, voluntary action, and intentionality depend in part on neurocognitive networks in the frontal lobes (Barkley, 1997; Benson & Blumer, 1975; David, Newen & Vogeley, 2008; Fuster, 2008; Passingham, 1995; Sebanz & Prinz, 2006). When human beings postulate a god or pray to a god, they are attributing certain cognitive properties to that god – among them, the property of possessing a "Mind." To be capable, however, of attributing Mind to others, or to a god, the pray-er must possess these properties of Mind him- or herself. The so-called Theory of Mind Module (ToMM; Baron-Cohen, 1995, for review) depends in part on frontal sites (Spreng, Mar, & Kim, 2009). Schjødt et al. (2009) have shown that improvisatory prayer is associated with widespread activation in brain regions that are known to be implicated in theory of mind processing.

Summary

Frontal and temporal interactions are a prerequisite for development of various ECF-related functions that are crucial for self-regulation, goal directedness, and intellectual creativity (Flaherty, 2005). Prosocial behavior, including the ability to produce behaviors appropriate to the social context, depends on frontotemporal interactions and functions. Empathy, fellow-feeling, and compassionate sympathy appear to depend crucially on frontal activation. The list could go on, but I think it is reasonable to conclude from the foregoing review that the frontal and temporal lobes appear to mediate those capacities and functions that uniquely define us as mature and free human persons.

It is not surprising then that human cultures throughout the world and throughout history have developed practices – religious practices – that promote acquisition of ECFs. There is no other way to develop a fully responsible, cooperative, and capable human being. Among these cultural practices, the techniques of choice have been religious practices, but is there any evidence that religious practices actually do facilitate acquisition of ECFs and activate frontal networks? There is consistent evidence that performances of a religious practice activate prefrontal networks among other networks. Besides this neuroimaging and clinical evidence, there is also behavioral evidence that religious practices involve activation of prefrontal networks. Here, I briefly summarize relevant behavioral studies.

Religiosity is associated with better acquisition of ECFs. Watson, Hood, Morris, and Hall (1984) found significant and positive correlations between measures of intrinsic religiosity and empathy. In their review of effects of religiosity on individuals who rate themselves as religious or who participate in religious practices, Beit-Hallahmi and Argyle (1997) found that religiosity (particularly intrinsic religiosity) was associated with increases in subjective happiness, health, mental health, and altruism and decreases in some forms of sexual behaviors as well as rates of suicide relative to nonreligious controls. In their review of effects of religiosity on mental health, Worthington, Kurusu, McCullough, and Sandage (1996) summarized a number of studies relevant to the issue of effects of religious practices on mental functions associated with the frontal lobes. Use of prayer, for example, was correlated with indices of hope and with subjective well-being – at least in religiously committed subjects. Prayer appeared to be a very common coping method for persons in distress whether they described themselves as religious or not. McCullough and Willoughby (2009) reviewed a range of evidence linking religious practices and greater self-control. These authors suggested that religion exerts its beneficent effects on health and well-being by enhancing self-control more generally.

In summary, religious practices are aimed at transforming the Self into a higher, better Self. It does this by cultivating a suite of ECFs, which incidentally involves the activation of the prefrontal lobes. These assertions seem reasonable to me. I realize that the evidence for them is mostly circumstantial. Nonetheless, I find it reasonable to interpret all of the various strands of evidence reviewed as consistent with the idea that religion aims to transfigure the Self.

I now turn to the question of why religion is "interested" in this task.

Why then is religion interested in the Self? The answer to this question should be clear by now. Religion is interested in the Self because it seeks to transform the Self. Why does religion seek to transform the Self?

Many influential theories of religion's functions point to social cooperation and cohesion as its major positive function (e.g., Durkheim, 1912/1954; Girard, 1987; Sosis, 2006). Fewer and perhaps less influential theories of religion's positive function have pointed to individual socialization, integration, and autonomy (e.g., Allport, 1950; Batson et al., 1993; Beit-Hallahmi & Argyle, 1997; Hartmann, 1958). Now of course, these two positions need not be mutually exclusive. It could be that religion functions to promote self-transformation so that social interactions and social cooperation may have a chance of succeeding. Conversely, religion may promote social cooperation to protect individuals' self-transformation. Whatever the case may be, it is clear that social cooperation would be more likely if individuals had some help in learning to see one or the other's perspective about matters in dispute. In addition, social cooperation would be more easily achieved if individuals could be brought to actually care about one another as well as the welfare of more than just immediate kin. Although human beings are born with some capacity for social cooperation and empathy, that capacity needs a lot of care, nurturance, and development if it is to operate to promote social cooperation among individuals outside one's immediate genetic relatives. Religion may encode one set of procedures for creating individuals capable of real, long-term social cooperation that transcends altruism directed toward one's own genetic kin.

I do not believe that religion's interests in the individual are merely about creating civilized, trustworthy, cooperative individuals who can be relied upon to cooperate with others if that cooperation protects long-term (genetic) interests of the individual. Religion certainly is about creating such individuals as such individuals are good for creating humane and working societies. Such trustworthy and cooperative individuals also display the best of the martial virtues, of courage, fearlessness, loyalty to comrades, self-sacrifice, ferocity in battle, and steadfastness under fire, but religion does much more than this.

We have seen that from a neurocognitive point of view, religious practices facilitate self-transformation, in part, because such practices activate the frontal lobes, and this in turns makes it easier for the individual to acquire the ECFs. These ECFs in turn facilitate acquisition of many of the religious virtues and "gifts" so often described in the religious literature. The concrete signs that religious practices are having their intended effects include enhanced moral sensibilities, greater internal freedom, greater self-control, deeper insight into Self and others, empathy and compassion for others – even (fallen) enemies (not present and threatening enemies), generativity, and prosocial behavior in general.

Although all of these behaviors are necessary for the production of cooperative individuals rather than free riders (whether the cooperative group is designed for trade, war, or what have you), they might also be seen as serving another purpose. Greater autonomy, distance from impulses, self-control, attentiveness, and so forth, all point to a new set of perceptual abilities or to enhanced abilities to deploy attentional resources with great control, sustained interest, and to great effect. Just as the evolutionary acquisition of language or of theory of Mind abilities by ancestral human populations revolutionized the cognitive and perceptual abilities of our ancestors, so, too, will the acquisition of newer more sophisticated attentional capacities of the human mind.

There are other reasons why religion would be interested in creating a disciplined, highly autonomous central executive Self. The actions of such an individual would be very difficult to predict. As the Biblical author put it: "The wind bloweth where it listeth, and thou hearest the sound thereof, but canst not tell whence it cometh, and whither it goeth: so is every one that is born of the Spirit" (John 3:8; King James Version). To the extent that an individual is autonomous, internally directed, and free from being driven merely by impulses and appetites, he or she is indeed free. To the extent to which an individual has control over his or her attentional resources, he or she is free because he or she chooses what information will gain entry and what information will engage the attention over time. Religion makes the individual free, and a free man is unpredictable. In a world of predators, unpredictability is a priceless asset. In animals, unpredictability takes the form of protean and utterly erratic forms of behavior. But erratic behavior in humans would simply be self-defeating. Internally guided autonomous behaviors, in contrast, would be unpredictable to someone who has never experienced the same.

Another reason why religion would be interested in creating a centralized executive Self is that such a Self can engage in the process called dissociation or trance. Only a centralized Self can undergo dissociation. Why is dissociation or trance desirable? It facilitates healing and pain control in many individuals (McClenon, 2006). Dissociation also allows for access to unusual abilities such as tremendous physical strength, fearlessness, and audacity. Take, for example, the case of the Norse warriors, the "beserkers." These were warriors who would wear bearskins when preparing for battle, then go into a trance, take on the spirit of the ferocity of the bear, and then enter battle in a frenzied whirl of ferocious killing. Presumably, a dissociative process allowed these warriors to set aside their less ferocious Selves to allow the Bear identity to take possession of them. These warriors were capable of holding off whole armies for hours at a time if the conditions were right (such as a battle on a narrow bridge or the like). Similar stories are told of many other individuals who have faced combat and battle. To enter battle, even the lowliest corporal needs to (to some extent) put aside the everyday pacifist Self to become an efficient and fearsome adversary.

In short, religion creates the cultural platforms for creation of a new centralized executive form of the Self. The benefits of such a Self include enhanced autonomy and attentional control and enhanced ability to inhibit free-rider behavioral strategies as well as enhanced cooperativeness. A central executive Self can also undergo a dissociative process and thereby gain access to unusual abilities of healing and aggression. Religion focuses on self-transformation then for good reasons.

8   Self-Transformation through Spirit Possession

I am crucified with Christ: nevertheless I live; yet not I, but Christ liveth in me: and the life which I now live in the flesh I live by the faith of the Son of God, who loved me, and gave himself for me.

– St. Paul, Gal. 2:20; King James Version

Now we see in a mirror, in darkness; but later we shall see face to face. Now I know in part; but later I shall know as I am known.

– St. Paul, Cor. 13:12

Introduction

One of the most ubiquitous phenomena in the world's religions is "spirit possession" or the taking over of the individual's identity and behavior by a supernatural agent. This "taking over" of the host's identity can be either a positive or a negative experience. When it is positive, as in St. Paul's case, personality is transfigured and the individual seems to be acting more freely and effectively. The "possession" seems to have made St. Paul more effective. St. Paul, after all, is considered by many to be a kind of cofounder of a world religion – Christianity. In all cases of positive possession, the new personality has left behind the old "*nafs*" or lower Self, created a new Self, and been given all of those "gifts of the Spirit" mentioned in Chapter 7. These gifts traditionally include some very fine character traits such as gratitude, generosity, compassion for others, fearlessness, clear strategic sense, joy, and many other qualities. Clearly, any process that can give you these character traits must be transformative indeed and must be considered quite valuable – indeed priceless. That is why this form of possession – St. Paul calls it "putting on the Mind of Christ" (Rom. 12:2) – is something all the devout desire. The negative form of possession, however, was and is an experience of a very different kind. Negative possession is an experience that was and is feared and ranked among the most unfortunate and perilous forms of suffering a human being can undergo.

In both positive and negative forms of spirit possession, the Self comes face to face with a supernatural entity. It is a place or experience where the Self is, for better or worse, transformed by religious forces. Spirit possession, therefore, is a phenomenon that might help us unlock the key to the puzzle of the individual's relationship to God and religion – of the Self and religion. The topic is as complex as religion itself. I cannot hope to do it justice in a single chapter.* My aim will be to look at it from the angle of the cognitive neurosciences and to bring what we have learned about Self and religion in previous chapters to bear on the problem.

As with all of the discussions in this book, I leave the metaphysical status of supernatural agents and forces to the theologians and meta-physicians. Nothing I say here should be construed as contradicting the-ological accounts of possession. Conversely, nothing I should say here should be construed as supporting such accounts. If the self-described "anti-religion" readers wish to use the facts I summarize in this chapter as evidence to disprove theological accounts of the matter, then that of course is their prerogative. My personal opinion is that there is much integrity in that position. In contrast, although a minimalist

---

* I recommend Cohen's (2007) excellent ethnographic and cognitive study of the psy-chologic and cognitive mechanisms underlying spirit possession rituals among an Afro-Brazilian religious group in Belem, northern Brazil. Among the cognitive dynam-ics she investigates as constitutive of possession phenomena are "theory of mind" mechanisms.

or scientific reading of the facts seems to militate against supernatural accounts of these possession phenomena, we should nevertheless remain open-minded about what the subjects themselves (i.e., those who have experienced possession) say about their experiences. We will see, in fact, that there is something uncanny and essentially unfathomable about the supernatural agents that possess an individual in a possession experience.

It is important, furthermore, not to prematurely pathologize all possession experiences. In fact, there is usually little or no evidence for brain or personality disorders in people who report possession experiences (see review in DePalatis, 2006). Sometimes, however, a brain disorder is implicated in the onset of a possession experience, and these cases are invaluable for gaining clues as to brain processes involved in the interactions of Self and a supernatural agent. We will examine some of these cases later in this chapter. For people who are firmly attached to a religious tradition, it may even be the case that use of religious rituals from that tradition to "exorcize" the demon (assuming a negatively valenced possession) is the only thing that helps the individual. It is therefore unethical and unwise to tell a patient who reports intense suffering from a possession experience that exorcism rituals are bunk and that religious tools are useless.

Is possession a dissociative process? Placing a label such as "dissociative identity disorder" (DID) on individuals and their experiences may or may not be helpful, depending on the context. Often labeling the phenomenon a DID merely prevents further analyses or observations of the experiences in question. All too often a label explains nothing. Indeed, as has been noted by many other scholars besides myself, this sort of labeling may prevent us from seeing the phenomenon clearly as it presents itself to our eyes. We need to be careful about premature labeling of these experiences as pathological or even as dissociative. Science, in contrast, must proceed with naming, labeling, classifying, and categorizing the phenomenon presented to us. There is no other way to attain progress. We must proceed, but proceed cautiously and with an open mind. I merely point out what many others before me have pointed out, namely, that the classification process must be done, indeed can only be done correctly, by keeping an open mind about the phenomenon and its sources, origins, and causes.

The modern medical community has by and large treated possession phenomena as identical to or related to dissociative phenomena. The International Statistical Classification of Diseases and Related Health Problems, Tenth Revision (ICD-10; World Health Organization, 2004) has issued a diagnostic category (411.3, Trance and Possession Disorders) that appears to link possession and dissociation (Cardeña, 1992; Lewis-Fernandez, 1992). Dissociation is defined by the *Diagnostic and Statistical Manual of Mental Disorders, Fourth Edition, Text Revision* (DSM–IV–TR; American Psychiatric Association, 2000) as "a disruption in the usually integrated function of consciousness, memory, identity, or perception of the environment" (p. 519). This disruption must not be due to psychoses such as schizophrenia or other disorders and must occur outside social contexts that sanction possession (such as religious rituals). Common "symptoms" of dissociative processes are held to be derealization, depersonalization, and psychogenic amnesia.

Near Universality of Spirit Possession

If possession is fundamentally a dissociative process, then dissociative processes must be considered a near-universal human proclivity or capacity because possession itself is a near-universal phenomenon. The German scholar Traugott Konstantin Oesterreich (1921/1966) surveyed a huge array of cultures from around the world and dating back to antiquity. He found accounts of spirit possession, particularly demonic possession, relatively easy to obtain. Ethnographic surveys of small-scale, traditional societies (e.g., Boddy, 1994; Bourguignon, 1973; Lewis-Fernandez, 1992) have documented possession beliefs in the majority of these cultures. Bourguignon (1973) found that 74 percent of a sample of 488 such societies evidenced possession beliefs, and 52 percent of the cultures exhibited evidence of the use of possession "trance" in religious, social, and healing ceremonies.

One technique that is often used in traditional societies to facilitate spirit possession is masking.

Possession States and Masks

Many religious rituals in traditional societies around the world involve participants donning and wearing a mask. Masks appear to facilitate a possession experience. Donning a mask decenters the person's executive identity and makes it easier for the person to access alternative identities. Transforming into a totem animal, ancestor, or spirit allows the individual to act as if he or she embodies the qualities depicted in the face of the mask (Napier, 1986).

The donning of a mask can trigger a decentering episode by concealing the identity of the wearer, putting on a new face but not just any face. In traditional societies, masks were usually carved or sculpted images of totem animals, mythological figures, ancestors, or gods. When the individual's identity is concealed by the mask, there is a reduction in sense of Self/agency and a decoupling of Self from control over executive functions. The old identity is temporarily bracketed. It no longer exists. Instead the individual acts out the intentions of the deity. Onlookers treat the individual as if he were the god depicted by the mask. Adopting the face of a god meant suppression of your old identity and acquisition of a new supernatural identity with special powers.

The production of these ritual masks was a sacred matter – not just a craft. Among the Dogon, Ibo, Edo, and Abua tribal peoples of central and southern Africa, the mask makers were essentially an institutionalized priestly caste, all members of a family and each of whom had received their training from an elder master carver in the family. The techniques, the religious significance, and the ritual meanings of the masks were passed down through the generations.

Whether sought after or involuntarily suffered, possession states were apparently ubiquitous in ancestral populations and traditional cultures. They still occur across the globe today.

Modern Accounts of Spirit Possession

Adityanjee, Raju, and Khandelwal (1989) document "Possession Syndrome" in India. Gaw, Ding, Levine, and Gaw (1998) described a group of Chinese patients reporting possession in the Hebei Province of China. In these cases the possessing agent was often the spirit of a dead human being, animals, objects, or the energy of the chi itself. Ng (2000) and Ng & Chan (2004) summarized clinical characteristics of fifty-eight separate cases of possession trance that were admitted to a hospital in Singapore over the course of six years. Possession states in Singapore appear to be much like possession states anywhere else – although the names of the supernatural possessing agents differ. In Haiti, possession occurs in both Roman Catholic and in Voodoo contexts. With respect to the Voodoo case, the possessing spirits are called *loa*. These spirits can bring good or bad things to the individual and to the community, so it is important to keep them happy with the appropriate rituals. Rituals include drumming and dancing and are designed to honor the *loa*. In the possession trance the possessed individual takes on the powers of a particular *loa* and can then facilitate healing or harm as the case may be (Bourguignon, 1991). Negative possession also occurs in Haiti; in these cases, the possession experience brings misery to the possessed. These possessed individuals then seek relief from both the Voodoo priests and priestesses and the Catholic priests. We will examine some of these cases later in this chapter.

In Brazil, a syncretistic religion like the Haitian Voodoo called Umbanda exhibits a well-defined set of possession beliefs and practices. Spirits that possess individuals can help or harm individuals and the community. Umbanda religious centers are staffed by trained mediums who are regularly possessed by these spirits and gods, who can then be consulted by attendees for assistance in a variety of health-related and personal matters. Hollan (2000) reported on a set of possession trance rituals in Tana Toraja, Indonesia. This ritual is called ma'maro. All of this seems similar in some respects to the Kung San trance/dance/healing rituals, during which individuals dance until they are possessed by spirit and then suck out evil spirit from the ill person (Katz, 1984). Goldish (2003) provided an in-depth survey of possession and exorcism events in Jewish contexts throughout history. Somer and Saadon (2000) described the possession trance rituals practiced by immigrant Tunisian Jews living in Israel.

What occurs in a possession experience? All of the above-mentioned dissociative phenomena, derealization, depersonalization, and amnesia for the experience itself can occur in possession states. It is interesting that these neuropsychiatric phenomena are much more common in negatively valenced possession. These neuropsychiatric phenomena may indicate a derailed or aberrant decentering process.

The most salient aspect of a possession experience, positive or negative, of course is the replacement of one identity with another. In negatively valenced possession, the true identity is lost, hidden, or submerged under the new identity, whereas in positive states the old identity is still accessible to consciousness and is considered to be subsumed under the new identity. The old identity is enriched by the new one in positive states, and the opposite is true in negative states. In these the old identity is attacked and made to suffer. Things (energy, Will, choice, etc.) are subtracted from it. In positive states, things ("the gifts of the spirit") are added to the old identity until it is "reborn" into a different person. Negative possession more often has a sudden than a slow, insidious onset. In positive states, the experience usually constitutes the cumulative fruit of moral effort – although dramatic conversion experiences can occur as well. In both cases, physical changes in brain and body occur. In negative or demonic possession, the possessed individual not uncommonly exhibits enormous physical strength; speaks in some other language with alterations in tone and prosody; emits grunts, growls, and obscenities; reports nausea and vomiting; exhibits "paranormal" abilities; and exhibits sustained and intense aggression toward the possessed individual and any other person in the vicinity. In positive states, physical strength may not be enhanced, but stamina surely is. There are heightened "theory of mind" abilities, heightened interest in others, and heightened generativity.

Given the horrible suffering involved in demonic possession experiences, we must ask why it occurs at all. The traditional theory, of course, is that demons hate people and they want to torment them. Possession is the best way to do that. Whether or not the supernatural explanation is in any way explanatory, we still need a description of how possession operates and why, from an evolutionary point of view, it should be a common human phenomenon. Is there any benefit to be gained for an individual from a negative possession experience? One possible benefit could be a gain in prestige. This was a person who grappled with demons and survived! Bulbulia (2006) suggested a similar boost in social prestige after recovering from illness or from religious healing. There is some evidence that female "shamans" or religious specialists can gain prestige after displaying both healing abilities and possession–trance abilities. Very likely the same goes for male shamans.

Perhaps there is no particular benefit associated with negative possession. Perhaps possession should instead be considered a by-product of the way the brain/mind operates to construct identity. Negative possession then would represent a breakdown in the normal decentering process. During a decentering process, there is competition among several agentic neurocognitive systems for control over the behavior of the individual. If a primitive aggressive system wins out in the competition for dominant control, the possession state will be negative, but this suggestion is mere speculation at this point. Whatever the case may be, we will need a mechanistic explanation of how one identity can replace another with either catastrophic consequences (negative possession) or beneficent consequences (positive possession) for the individual involved.

To build a mechanistic explanation of possession states, we can examine cases of possession to collect clues as to how the process occurs.

Cases of Well-Documented Possession States

The Exorcist (1973), the film written and produced by William Peter Blatty and directed by William Friedkin, was based on a case of a Catholic exorcism of a teenage boy that had occurred apparently in the 1950s. A fair amount of the material depicted in the film was sensationalized but based on real events. In *Possessed: The True Story of an Exorcism*, the investigative scholar Allen (1993) described his attempts to verify the key events in the case. In an appendix of the book, Allen reprints the diary of a priest who had actually assisted in the exorcism. The boy who suffered the possession came from a family that was not particularly religious, but his aunt had an interest in the "paranormal" and taught the boy to use a Ouija board to contact the spirit world. After the aunt's death, all kinds of inexplicable phenomena began occurring in the house when the boy was present. These "paranormal" events included unexplained noises, shaking and sliding furniture, and objects "flying around the house." The boy's mental health began to deteriorate. Allen reported that unexplained bloody scratches were beginning to appear regularly on his skin. After seeking help from friends, doctors, and other experts, the family consulted a Lutheran minister who recommended they approach a Catholic priest about an exorcism. An initial attempt at exorcism was conducted at a hospital, but the boy was somehow able to dislodge a bedspring from the bed on which he was restrained and slash the priest's arm. Then the family took the boy to St. Louis to visit family, but the paranormal events continued to occur and the boy worsened. The family approached a priest – a member of the Jesuit order – with more experience in exorcism. The scratches that appeared on the boy's body were now witnessed by several observers to form letters spelling words. The priests and family then initiated the exorcism that ended up lasting 34 days. The rituals were performed for several hours on a nightly basis. The boy's voice changed, deepened, and spoke as a demon emitting a stream of obscenities and blasphemies. The boy also reacted violently and needed to be physically restrained during the procedures. The turning point came near Easter, when the boy started to improve. He attributed his improvement to help from a supernatural agent (an angel) that drove the demon out of him.

Comment 1. I was not able to find any more recent investigations of this case. If we can trust the diary and the interviews Allen conducted with people involved in the case, then we have to conclude that possession is a remarkable phenomenon. I have no explanation for the "paranormal" phenomena associated with the case. The unfortunate boy's change in voice, physical strength, personality, and behaviors demonstrate the power of identity to organize physiologic powers and capacities.

The movie *The Exorcism of Emily Rose* (2005) was co-written and directed by Scott Derrickson and produced by Paul Harris Boardman. It was based on the story of Anneliese Michel in Germany. The unfortunate girl died after she refused food and water and after dozens of attempts at exorcism had failed. The German court had ruled that the parents and the priests involved were guilty of negligent homicide. The documentary record for this case is extensive. There were and are published interviews with participants, transcripts of court proceedings, as well as audiotape recordings of the forty-two exorcism sessions. Listening to these audiotapes (a couple of which are available on YouTube) is uncanny, as one hears Anneliese's voice growling, grunting, screaming, and occasionally speaking in several distinct "languages." It is difficult to recall that one is hearing the voice of a young woman and not the voice of an animal. Physicians who examined her and suspected epilepsy prescribed antiseizure medicine that unfortunately did not help. She deteriorated rapidly. Whatever caused her deterioration proceeded rapidly, accompanied by all kinds of paranormal phenomena. Her suffering too proceeded apace. She suffered severe muscle contractions and dystonia, malnutrition, dehydration, and damaged bones and musculature, which was exacerbated by repetitive bouts of kneeling and rising during the exorcism procedures. In response to the exorcism rituals, six different demons made themselves known, but it is not clear that all had been expelled by the rituals. She then apparently received a message from the Blessed Virgin Mary giving her a choice to suffer so that others would come to believe in the reality of the supernatural realm. She chose to suffer for others. On July 1, 1976, she died, officially of starvation, but that diagnosis has been disputed.

Comment 2. There are many seizure disorders that do not respond well to antiseizure medications. In these cases, surgery may be indicated. Anneliese and her parents were apparently never made aware of this possibility. Tourette syndrome is associated with barks, tics, and cries... usually of socially inappropriate obscenities. Tourette syndrome is associated with dysfunction in the circuits of the basal ganglia (which project to the prefrontal cortex). I am not suggesting that Anneliese had Tourette syndrome – merely that basal ganglia disorders can be severely disabling and sometimes are associated with changes in voice and behaviors. Whatever the neurologic vulnerabilities of Anneliese, the neurologic correlates cannot explain all of the paranormal phenomena associated with the case. It is remarkable that the girl was able to turn the horrible experience into something psychologically positive. To hope that others can benefit from one's own suffering is remarkable.

To gain a better view on potential neurologic correlates of possession, consider now the following cases reported by Carrazana, DeToledo, Rivas-Vasquez, Rey, and Wheeler (1999):

> Carrazana, Case 1. This 24-year-old Haitian man had his first generalized tonic-clonic seizure at the age of 17 years during the wake of an uncle. The patient had been sleep deprived during the vigil of the corpse. The seizure was attributed to possession by Ogu (the warrior god), the dead uncle's protecting *loa*. Subsequent seizures and morning myoclonus were explained as harassment by the wandering soul of the uncle. The possession was interpreted as a punishment, for the patient had been disrespectful toward the deceased in the past. He was treated by the local mambo (priest) for 6 years and did not see a physician until coming to the United States. His EEG showed 3- to 4-Hz bursts of generalized spike-wave complex discharges occurring spontaneously and during photic stimulation. In retrospect, the patient had a history of waking myoclonus, which had been ignored. He remained seizure free after treatment with valproic acid (VPA). The likely diagnosis is juvenile myoclonic epilepsy (Carrazana et al., 1999, p. 239).

Comment 3. This and the other Carrazana cases are extremely valuable scientifically as they document clear brain and epileptic pathology associated with possession cases. Case 1 furthermore had evidence of sleep disorder. Both seizure and sleep disorders promote parasomnias (difficulty transitioning from one sleep state into another or from sleep to waking). Decentering involves a state transition from volitional control to reduced/absent control during waking consciousness. If the individual is vulnerable to disorders of state transition, then he or she would likely have problems with decentering as well, making him or her vulnerable to possession experiences if the local cultural context "supports" such experiences.

> Carrazana, Case 2. This 27-year-old Haitian woman, with a history of complex partial and secondarily generalized seizures since adolescence, was the product of a long and difficult delivery, which was attributed to a "grip" in the mother's belly by a loa. At the age of 14 years, she fell in an open fire during a seizure and suffered extensive burns to her arm, leg, and parts of the face and trunk. Burns were treated at a local hospital, but the family brought the patient back to the mambo to treat the "possession." This incident was interpreted by the mambo as possession by "Marinnette." *Marinnette-bwa-chech* is one of the most dreaded *loas*, an agent for underhand dealings and an expert sorceress. Those possessed by this *loa* are said to throw themselves in the fire and stamp about until they put the flames out. The patient had bitemporal independent spikes on EEG. Treatment with antiepileptic drugs (AEDs) has decreased the frequency of seizures (Carrazana et al., 1999, pp. 239–240).

Comment 4. The possession experience in this case was associated with bitemporal spikes. As in the case of hyperreligiosity, the temporal lobes apparently play a key role in possession experiences.

> Carrazana, Case 3. This 36-year-old woman had several years of recurrent complex partial seizures that manifested as a strong sense of fear and epigastric coldness, followed by loss of awareness, utterances of nonsensical phrases, and complex motor automatisms. The local mambo attributed the events to her being taken by "Melle Charlotte," a French *loa*, with the nonsensical speech being interpreted as a foreign language. It is said that during the possession by this spirit, a person will speak perfect French or other languages, even though in life, the person has no knowledge of that language. She continued to have seizures despite the mambo's attempts to conjure the spirit. He explained his failure to the fact that Melle Charlotte is a very particular *loa* who makes only sporadic appearances. She was not treated with AEDs until she left Haiti at the age of 34. An EEG revealed a right anterior temporal focus, and magnetic resonance imaging (MRI) showed right hippocampal atrophy. Seizures improved with carbamazepine (CBZ), although compliance with medication was

a problem, largely because of family interference (Carrazana et al., 1999, p. 240).

Comment 5. This case is particularly interesting, as glossolalia was part of the clinical picture. Also we have localizing information: The electroencephalogram (EEG) revealed a right anterior temporal focus. This is a site also implicated in hyperreligiosity (see Chapter 5 on neurology of religious experiences). The right-sided focus also confirms a special role for right hemispheric sites in expression of religiousness.

> Carrazana, Case 4. This 44-year-old Dominican woman (of Haitian parents) for years has been experiencing partial seizures which she refers to as "la cosa" (the thing). Her seizures, with a sudden overwhelming sensation of emptiness, were attributed to her "good angel" leaving her as the spirit of the dead tried to take hold of her ("me mandaron un muerto"). The sending of the dead, l'envois morts, is a feared Voodoo curse, which is said to affect health and prosperity. The mambo explained the failure of the attacks to respond to his exorcisms to the strong hold of the spirit. EEG showed a right temporal focus, and the MRI was normal. Seizures were controlled with phenytoin (PHT) monotherapy (Carrazana et al., 1999, p. 240).

Comment 6. Once again, we have localizing information that refers to the right temporal lobe as the site of the focus. In addition, in this case the patient was able to report an experience associated with the switch in identities. She felt an emptying out before the onset of the negative possession experience. Decentering is postulated to begin with a defeat of the ego and a reduction in the sense of agency and volition. In this patient, this first step in the decentering process apparently occurs, but then the search process yields only a negative new identity.

> Carrazana, Case 5. This 47-year-old Jamaican woman of Haitian descent with a history of Chiari I malformation, syringomyelia, and arrested hydrocephalus has a long-standing history of complex partial seizures with and without secondary generalization. The patient and her family attributed the seizures to Voodoo spirit possessions, being influenced by the olfactory

hallucination of a burning smell, and a rising epigastric aura "taking over the body." A prolonged postictal psychosis would follow, in which the patient would alternate chanting and wooing with periods of total unresponsiveness. EEG demonstrated independent bitemporal interictal epileptiform discharges. She denied her diagnosis of epilepsy, resisted diagnostic and therapeutic interventions, and insisted that she was possessed by spirits of the dead. On immigrating to the United States, she ultimately became seizure free with PHT monotherapy (Carrazana et al., 1999, p. 240).

Comment 7. Bitemporal foci appear to be associated with more severe phenomenology. It is striking how convinced the patient apparently was that she was possessed by spirits of the dead. We are not told by Carrazana et al. if treatment with antiseizure medicine also treated the delusional beliefs (assuming that the beliefs were delusional).

These cases of negative possession states from Carrazana et al. (1999) are interesting for development of a neurology of possession because where localizing information was available it implicated the anterior temporal lobe on the right side or both temporal lobes. These data are consistent with all of the localizing data we have presented in previous chapters for both religious experience and for the sense of Self. In both cases (Self and religion), the right anterior temporal lobe or both temporal lobes in interaction with prefrontal regions were crucially involved. Although not mentioned in these cases of possession, the prefrontal cortex was also implicated in Self and religious experience.

Decentering and Negative Possession

The phenomenology of the possession experiences in these cases is consistent with what we know of possession experiences in traditional societies more generally. The possessed individual exhibits signs of unusual and persistent illness, immoral behaviors, motor tics, and nonsensical speech patterns. In all cases there is depersonalization and loss of Will and volition during the possession with a new identity emerging and controlling behavior. The loss of volition, the ontological uncertainty regarding the Self, and the emergence of a new Self, of course, are all signs that a decentering process is involved in possession.

Consider Nan (Case 4) from Ward and Beaubrun (1980):

Nan, a 25 year old East Indian woman, experienced her first symptoms at 15 in the form of extended, heavy menstrual bleeding, accompanied by dreams of blood. Nan was taken to an obeahman, who told her she was demon possessed, and attempted to release her by ritual ceremony. Although Nan claims that she did not believe in possessions at that time, she reported that the bleeding lessened, although she felt weak, lazy, inactive, and suffered with headaches and melancholia. At 17, Nan found a serious boyfriend who was several years older than she. Although they engaged in sexual relations, her parents did not approve of the boy and insisted that the relationship end. Nan reports depression and guilt feelings at that time as well as a reluctance to "get involved again." At that time, Nan was treated for a nervous condition, still suffering with headaches and melancholia. Assessing the situation retrospectively, Nan believes she was demon possessed. Nan's condition worsened at the age of 24 in connection with a second boyfriend who proposed marriage. After a serious quarrel, Nan became extremely depressed, and a second demon immediately manifest. She began to shake and tremble, exhibiting alternate fits of laughter and tears, as well as speaking in unknown tongues. She reports subsequent loss of appetite, weakness, visions, and black menstrual flow. Nan believes she is possessed by a demon who loves her and appears as a handsome man at night to seduce her. The demon, called Peter, is also very jealous and does not allow Nan to maintain close relationships with other men. Nan believes the demon lives in her womb. Nan was exorcised at her first visit to the Pentecostal Church and reports three exorcisms in a two month period (p. 204).

Comment 7. In Nan, we see all of the typical characteristics of a negative possession state: loss of self-control, attack on the old Self, a sense of being victimized, physical symptoms, trance states (during which the victim fuses with a demonic identity and speaks in unknown languages), motor tics, and immoral behaviors. Again, these are all signs of a decentering process.

You see this same phenomenology of experiences/symptoms in the totally different cultures of South Asia. Consider the case of Somavati from Castillo (1994):

> Somavati was a 29-year-old woman in Sri Lanka who was possessed by a number of spirits. She was the eldest of a poor farmer belonging to the goyigama (cultivator) caste. In early infancy Somavati was given to her maternal grandmother for adoption. She lived with her grandmother, whom she loved very much, until age seven. Somavati recalled these years with her grandmother as the happiest time of her life. At age seven her father brought her back home. Her forced separation from her grandmother was traumatic for Somavati, and her grandmother also cried and objected to her being taken away. Somavati said, "...father took me away, as if by force" (Obeyesekere, 1977, p. 242). However, Somavati's two younger brothers were growing, and her mother, who was pregnant with a fourth child, needed Somavati to help look after her younger siblings.
>
> From that time onward Somavati's life was "full of difficulties." She had to look after her siblings and was regularly beaten if she did not perform these tasks properly. In order to escape her oppressive family, and against their wishes, she married the first young man who showed any interest in her. As it turned out, he was an alcoholic who also beat her severely on a regular basis with little or no provocation. He often threatened to kill Somavati, and she fervently believed that one day he would indeed kill her.
>
> Somavati stayed with her husband for four years. Her parents found out about Somavati's abusive husband and tried to convince her to divorce her husband and come back to live with them. However, even with the threat of serious injury or death at the hand of her abusive spouse facing her, she preferred to stay with her husband rather than return to her parents.
>
> Nevertheless, her father was insistent, and once again Somavati was forced to return to her parents' household. Her husband informed the police that Somavati was being kept "against her will" by her parents, but

nothing came of it. After five months she was granted a divorce by the Sri Lankan authorities. Obeyesekere comments that "it is likely that the return to her parents reactivated the trauma that resulted from an earlier event – her forceful removal from the security of her grandmother's home" (1977, p. 247).

Twenty months after leaving her husband, still living with her parents, she had little leisure, practically no money, and was completely dependent on her parents. Moreover, her parents had no interest in getting her remarried. It was at the point that she had her first episode of spirit possession.

A neighbor's wife was possessed by the ghost of her dead mother-in-law and Somavati was present at the exorcism ritual. Somavati became possessed by the same ghost. She said, "I suddenly felt as if there was a big weight on my head and then I didn't see anything," and fell down unconscious. She had subsequent attacks which she described as follows: "My hands and feet grow cold; it is as if I don't possess them. Then my body shivers-shivers, and the inside of my body seems to shake...This goes on and on...and if I hear someone talk I get angry. My rage is such that I could even hit my father and mother...this is how the illness starts" (Obeyesekere, 1977, p. 249). She has total amnesia of these episodes.

Three months later Somavati is possessed by the spirit of her now dead grandmother. This spirit is equally hostile toward Somavati's family. Later she is possessed by two more spirits; these are not ghosts of dead persons, but are demons from the Sri Lankan pantheon: Riri Yaka (Blood Demon) and Mahasona (the great demon of the graveyard). It is significant that according to Sinhalese belief these two demons are horribly violent beings, totally malevolent and assaultive. Of the demons in the pantheon, Mahasona is the one associated with physical beating; he hits people and the marks of his hands appear on the back (Castillo, 1994, pp. 146–147).

Comment 8. The investigators who published these latter two cases and others like them argue that there are social and psychodynamic reasons for possession. In situations of oppression and misery, possession may allow you to get help and get out. So the argument goes.

But it is certainly odd to attempt to free yourself from one misery by adopting another set of new and now supernaturalized miseries. In negative possession states there appears to be little or no payoff in terms of prestige accruing to the possessed one. Some prestige will accrue to a healer or exorcist, but we need to know why the individuals themselves become possessed in the first place. Lots of girls and boys grow up in traumatizing circumstances, but few become possessed. A breakdown in the decentering process is a much more likely explanation of negative possession than are psychoanalytically oriented accounts.

Less spectacular cases of possession and exorcism continue to occur and some get documented. van der Hart, Witztum, and Friedman (1993) described the case of a 35-year-old ultra-orthodox Jew named Avraham living in Jerusalem. The possession experience began after the patient witnessed a terrorist bombing in the city and ended with ritual commands to the demon to leave the host. Ferracuti, Sacco, and Lazzari (1996) studied a group of sixteen individuals who evidenced altered states of consciousness during possession and who had participated in Catholic exorcisms in Rome, Italy. The authors noted some commonalities across these possession experiences: There was always a change in the moral character of the individual during a possession experience. Blasphemies were expressed, and the "demon" expressed sexual and aggressive impulses. The possessed persons also had frequent vomiting, coughing, and spitting, accompanied by roars, growls, and barks. Ferracuti et al. (1996) reported that although scores on a dissociative disorders inventory were elevated for this group of individuals, not all of the participants could be classified as having DID. Nor did any of the participants report a significant history of sexual abuse or other trauma – although one "demon" reported that the "body" that he possessed had been sexually abused as a child. All sixteen subjects reported that the exorcisms they received helped – they felt better afterward. Peck (2005) has recently published detailed accounts of two exorcisms that he performed in the late 1970s with outpatient psychiatric patients.

Decentering and Unusual Identity Phenomena

I suggest that the crucial mechanism that predisposes or allows one to become either positively or negatively possessed if the conditions are right is the ability to "decenter." As I have suggested in previous chapters, decentering allows you to attempt to integrate an old identity into a new and more complex identity. Decentering must also involve a decoupling of the implementation of an action from the sense of ownership... that is, a switch in attribution of the "source" of action from one identity to another. Bulbulia (2008) offers a similar explanation for certain aspects of religious cognition. In traditional societies where individuals wanted to induce possession states in themselves, this decentering effect was accomplished, presumably, in multiple ways: through drugs, dance, and ascetical practices and through rituals – including rituals that required the donning and wearing of a mask.

However decentering was accomplished, via a mask, or a drug, or through some other ritual process, when decentering was launched, we can assume that the following cognitive mechanisms were triggered. The old identity was bracketed and decoupled from executive control systems. Intentionality and volition were suspended and placed into abeyance. Then a period of uncertainty and drift would ensue when no well-defined identity was in control of the behavior of the individual. Various identities would compete for access to central executive control resources. If the individual was wearing a mask, the identity depicted in the mask would likely be at an advantage in the competitive process. If ritual processes referred to ancestor spirits, totem animals or gods would then have an advantage. During the period of drift, however, many unusual cognitive phenomena would occur. This period of drift would be similar to the transitional states between sleep states and waking when different physiologic systems would compete for access to conscious awareness.

It is worth mentioning some of the unusual cognitive states that would manifest during the period of transition from one identity to another. One of the most interesting from a cognitive point of view is the phenomenon of the "Double."

Possession and the Double

Traugott Oesterreich (1921/1966), in his massive work on possession, describes a phenomenon referred to as *Verdoppelungserlebnis* (doubling of consciousness), in which the individual really experiences a double awareness of two forms of cognitive content each from the same identity and then two separate identities during spirit possession. In the first phase of this doubling effect, you can get the uncanny experience of the doubling of cognitive aspects of the Self as well as doubling of the entire Self-concept. This experience is known as the experience of the Double.

The experience of meeting one's own double (the Doppelgänger) has been reported throughout recorded history and has most often been described in literature as a profound and dangerous encounter with one's own soul.

In neurology, experience of the Double is treated as identical to or related to the phenomenon of autoscopy (seeing one's Self). Autoscopy "is a complex psychosensory hallucinatory perception of one's own body image projected into external visual space" (Lukianowicz, 1958, quoted in Devinsky, Feldman, Burrowes, & Bromfield, 1989, p. 1080). In both psychiatric and neurologic syndromes, the Double usually appears suddenly, directly in front of, and about an arm's length away from the subject. Most frequently, only the upper torso (face and shoulders) of the Double can be seen. As the subject raises his or her right arm, the Double will raise its left, and so forth. The image is usually not seen in color. Often the subject feels some kind of intense emotional connection with the Double, as if the Double held some special meaning for the subject. Sometimes a sense of resignation and sadness pervades the whole experience, which usually lasts only a few seconds.

Devinsky, Feldman, Burrowes, and Bromfield (1989) have pointed out that autoscopic phenomena are remarkably similar to those that occur in persons with near-death experiences or psychiatric disorders such as various dissociation phenomena and out-of-body experiences. In out-of-body experiences, the body is usually seen or viewed from above, perhaps in a corner of the room. In depersonalization there is a feeling of detachment from one's own body. The subject experiences intense distress and sees him- or herself as split into two entities – one observing the other. Splitting also occurs in multiple personality disorder (MPD) and in schizophrenia.

Although autoscopy is surely related to the phenomenon of psychic splitting, it is distinguished from dissociation in that consciousness is still localized within the subject. In autoscopy, furthermore, some aspect of the body image is projected into space. It is interesting that the Double is usually seen only from the torso up and appears in the form of a mirror-image duplicate of the subject. These facts point to a projection of a memory image (the only place the subject ever sees a mirror image of him- or herself is in the mirror!), rather than a new or constructed image.

In cases where autoscopy is associated with organic lesions, the site of the lesion is usually in the right anterior temporal lobes (Devinsky et al., 1989). At this point (assuming the reader has plowed through the material in previous chapters), we are no longer surprised to see links between phenomena involving aberrations in self-consciousness with the right anterior temporal lobe.

How can we explain the "Double"? The doubling effect can be seen as a prematurely terminated decentering process such that the new identity that the old Self is supposed to integrate into is merely the old identity (no ideal Self is posited or found in a search process). In cases where the old identity binds to old Identity 2, we get an inflated ego fanaticism and narcissism. In doubling cases, the fusion of the two old identities does not occur and we get two Selves.

The trigger for a doubling experience is the same as the trigger for any decentering process. The Self or ego is bracketed, decentered, or decoupled from control over central executive control processes. The ego under these conditions experiences the decoupling as a defeat. We can see these sorts of processes occurring in Dostoevsky's novel *The Double* (Dostoevsky, 1846/1972). In the novel, a Mr. Golyadkin is haunted by his own double. The Double makes his first appearance after Mr. Golyadkin has disgraced himself at a party in State Councillor Berendeyev's house in front of "society" and a woman whose hand he favors. After Mr. Golyadkin is "shown out" of the party, he heads back home in shame and in the snow and rain:

> Although the snow, rain, and all the conditions for which there is not even a name, which prevail when blizzard and tempest rage under the November sky of St. Petersburg, had assailed Mr. Golyadkin, already crushed by his misfortunes, suddenly and all at once, showing him not the slightest mercy, giving him not a moment's respite, piercing him to the marrow, plastering up his eyes, blowing right through him from every direction, driving him off his course and out of his last remaining wits, although all this had crashed down on Mr. Golyadkin, as though purposely joining in league and concert with all his enemies to bring the ruin of his day, his evening and his night to triumphant completeness – in spite of it all, Mr. Golyadkin remained almost insensitive to this last evidence of the malignancy of fate, he had been so shaken and overwhelmed by all that had happened a few minutes earlier in State Councillor Berendeyev's House (Dostoevsky, 1972, p. 166).

It is in this state of extreme shame, defeat, and despair that Dostoevsky has his hero, Mr. Golyadkin (senior), meet for the first time his double, Mr. Golyadkin (junior):

> He stopped dead in the middle of the pavement and stood there motionless as though turned to stone; in those moments he died and disappeared off the face of the earth; then suddenly he would tear himself away from the spot like a madman and run, run without a backward glance, as though trying to escape from some pursuit or an even more terrible disaster... His situation was really one of horror... At last, drained of all strength, Mr. Golyadkin stopped [and] leaned his arms on the parapet of the embankment... at that juncture Mr. Golyadkin had reached such a state of despair, was so harassed and weary, had so drained and exhausted the already feeble remains of this spirit, that he forgot for a short time all about everything... Suddenly... suddenly his whole body quivered, and involuntarily he leapt to one side. He began to look around him with inexplicable anxiety; but there was nobody, nothing particular had happened, and yet... and yet it seemed to him that just now, this very moment somebody had been standing there, close to him, by his side, also leaning on

the parapet and – extraordinary thing! – had even said something to him, something hurried and abrupt, not altogether understandable, but about a matter touching him nearly, something that concerned him (Dostoevsky, 1972, p. 167).

In this passage, we see that the onset of the appearance of the Double is associated with an extreme state of exhaustion of the resources of the ego. Furthermore, we know that what occasioned this state of affairs was not physical illness, emotional loss of a loved one, or any of the normal sources of acute suffering. Instead, the course of the disaster in Mr. Golyadkin's case was extreme loss of face, in the language of psychological shame. Therefore, the ensuing damage was to the ego as a viable entity that left the contents of this ego's history – autobiographical memory – "up for grabs." This is part of the decentering process.

For decentering to be complete, the autobiographical memories associated with Identity 1 must be integrated into Identity 2. If the integration has not yet been accomplished or has been left incomplete, then consciousness is aware of two identities that are nevertheless the same as they share the same set of autobiographical memories.

It is interesting to note in Dostoevsky's story that, just before the appearance of the Double, two important mental events occur in Mr. Golyadkin. The first appears to be a transient amnesia: " . . . he forgot for a short time all about everything." Here we see that there is a period when autobiographical memories are "up for grabs." The second event can be described as a triggering of a kind of primitive physiological alarm and defensive system: "Suddenly . . . suddenly his whole body quivered, and involuntarily he leapt on one side." When the Double appears, he is experienced as being within a certain intimate distance relative to the victim (i.e., close to him), and mirrors the stance of the ego/victim: " . . . somebody had been standing there, close to him, by his side, also leaning on the parapet . . . " The Double is experienced as having a significant message to give to the ego/victim: " . . . had even said something to him, . . . about a matter touching him nearly . . . " These events signal the onset of the new identity's emergence. That new identity may in cases of possession be a demonic identity.

Although Mr. Golyadkin experiences awe, dread, and even horror at the appearance of the Double, there is no sign that the Double is at this point regarded as evil. It is not until Mr. Golyadkin (senior) sits down for a dialogue with Mr. Golyadkin (junior) that the Double begins to take on characteristics we normally associate with a demon. Mr. Golyadkin begins to experience his double as despicable and malevolent. "As for him, he's such a base and ignoble wretch, so mischievous and wanton, so frivolous and sycophantic and groveling, such a Golyadkin!" (Dostoevsky, 1972, p. 212). With the disappearance of his old identity and the subsequent emergence of the shadow-double, Golyadkin passes from the realm of the absurd to the realm of the terrifying.

In Edgar Allan Poe's *William Wilson*, the hero is rejected by his family and placed (or abandoned) in an English boarding school. Shortly thereafter, his double appears. Interestingly, Poe links the appearance of the Double in this case not merely to the "woes" experienced by this hero, but also to his eternal and ancient soul. The appearance of the Double, says the hero, inspires wild and deep memories of time before memory herself was born in the hero's consciousness.

> Todd and Dewhurst (1955) have reviewed the role the Double played as the immortal soul in traditional societies and tribal religions (see also Hallam, 1980). In these cultures, the Double represents the immortal soul of the individual. For the Nagas, the Andamanese, the East Indian Islanders, and the Karo Bataks, the soul is an exact image or replica of the individual. Evidence like this suggests that the Double is inextricably related to the experience of a timeless personality and has long been mythologically conceived as the eternal soul. How then, in a possession experience, does the soul/double take on the form of absolute evil (i.e., become demonic)?

Todd and Dewhurst (1955) quote the German writer Richter (who frequently wrote stories about a Doppelgänger) on his double to the effect that the author looks at his double, who looks back at the author and the two of them, who hold their mutual ego in horror. Whence comes the

horror? In a decentering process, when the integration of the old identity into the new identity fails, there is this moment when the two old
identities exist in logical suppositional space. Each has some capacity
for consciousness so that they are able to contemplate one another with
horror as each knows that nonexistence is imminent.

The Argentinean writer Borges was obsessed with the themes of memory, identity, timelessness, and evil. In his essay on the Catholic writer
Léon Bloy (entitled "The mirror of enigmas," Borges, 1964, pp. 209–212),
Borges follows Bloy's meditations on St. Paul's description of the human
experience of being "on the wrong side of creation." Borges quotes Bloy,
who describes the painful emergence of such a perspective:

> Everything is a symbol, even the most piercing pain. We are dreamers who
> shout in our sleep. We do not know whether the things afflicting us are
> the secret beginning of our ulterior happiness or not. We now see, St. Paul
> maintains, per speculum in aenigmate, literally: "in an enigma by means
> of a mirror" and we shall not see in any other way until the coming of the
> One who is all in flames and who must teach us all things (Borges, 1964,
> p. 211).

This "coming of the One" is the coming of the new Self in the form of the
Creator. Because every act of creation is an excessive act that negates the
old Self, it is apt to be experienced as an absolute evil by the old identity.
That is why the higher Self "comes in flames" from the point of view
of the old Self. That point of view is on the wrong side of creation. The
higher Self represents the best hope for the old identity, but the old Self,
the nafs, does not see this. If the new Self fails to integrate the old Self into
the new life, then you get demonic possession and endless intrapsychic
conflict, but if real integration occurs, then the old Self is transfigured
and you get the rebirth and new life promised by all religions.

Decentering and Normal and Abnormal Religious Experiences

With this discussion of spirit possession and the Double, we conclude our
discussion of disorders relevant to religion and Self. I suggest these disorders (MPD, schizophrenia, the Double, and possession) can be profitably

Table 8.1. Decentering: normal operations and breakdowns

Process/Stage	Religious ritual	MPD	Possession	Fanaticism	Double
1) Decrease agency	Yes	No	Yes	No	Yes
2) Transfer of Self-construct into possible world box	Yes	Yes	No	Yes	Yes
3) Search – Comparison of old Self with target Self	Yes Old vs. ideal Self and supernatural agent	Yes Old Self vs. desired Self	Yes Old Self vs. supernatural agent	No Old Self vs. old Self	No Old Self vs. old Self
4) Binding/integration	Yes	No	Yes	Yes	No

Note: MPD = multiple personality disorder.

interpreted as breakdowns in the decentering process (see Table 8.1). When decentering works the way it is suppose to work (in ritual contexts), you get healthy integration. When it fails at one or more of its stages, you get disorder.

9 God Concepts

> Oh Lord, you are not only that than which a greater cannot be conceived,
> but you are also greater than what can be conceived.
>
> – Anselm in *Proslogion* XV

Introduction

No account of the neurocognition of religious experience would be complete without some account of religious cognition. Central to religious cognition are concepts of supernatural agents and God.

As always, I bracket the issue of the metaphysical status of gods or God. For now I am simply trying to clarify how concepts representing supernatural agents function in the cognitive economy of the Mind. I begin therefore with a summary review of the origins and functions of God concepts.

Origins, Nature, and Functions of "God concepts"

God concepts are concepts about supernatural agents. Supernatural agents are often (although not invariably) beings with Minds like ours but no bodies. Most often the Minds of supernatural agents are more powerful than ours. When there is a high God who rules over lesser spiritual entities in the supernatural realm, this high God often has a mind so powerful that He or She can know virtually everything one is thinking or doing. A high God who is also a "full strategic access agent" knows everything you have ever thought or done or everything you will ever do or think. These "full strategic access agents" again point to the intimate relationships that exist between religion-related matters and the Self. Only in the realm of religion will we find an agent who ostensibly knows the Self so thoroughly and completely.

Where do God concepts come from? One possibility is that supernatural agents actually exist and that our intuitions about them are largely accurate. I set aside that possibility for now and focus on potentially simpler solutions to the problem. Another possibility is that supernatural agent concepts are products of the human Mind gone awry. Boyer (2001) and other cognitively oriented anthropologists and psychologists (Atran, 2002; Barrett, 2000) have helpfully suggested that our conceptions of supernatural agents are constructed out of the inferential machinery that draw on normal folk psychological processing routines concerning actions performed by ordinary agents such as persons and animals. God concepts are said to be "minimally counterintuitive." They depart from everyday ideas about persons only slightly. A god is a person who has no body and who can read your mind in such a way as to know all that there is to know about you. A "hyperactive agency detection device," coupled with the tendency to imagine minimally counterintuitive agents and the innate human tendency to assume that the mental is nonphysical, all lead to the propensity to postulate supernatural agents. Some experimental evidence suggests that subjects are, in fact, better able to remember minimally counterintuitive agents (Barrett, 2000; Boyer, 2001).

As many investigators (e.g., Atran, 2002; Pyysiäinen, 2004; Whitehouse, 2002) have pointed out, the category "minimally counterintuitive agents" does not adequately capture key properties of God concepts. There are many counterintuitive agents (e.g., space aliens or the cartoon character Mickey Mouse) that are not gods, nor are they supernatural in any way. Nor do most counterintuitive agents (e.g., ghosts and other spirit entities) exhibit the powers gods typically exhibit. They are not omniscient or especially powerful, for example.

Boyer and other scholars have pointed out that gods emerge when counterintuitive agents exhibit "full strategic access" to your mind and history. They argue that focusing on this characteristic of the gods, particularly the high gods, will help us find clues as to potential functional roles for gods in human societies. In this account, the interesting thing about gods is that they are distinguished by the fact that they have full strategic access to all the important information about you as a character or a person. In short, it is the relation to your Self that makes a God concept. Your Mind and biography are fully known to them. They also know similar facts about other persons whom you care about. What is more is that the gods can and will use this information to punish wrongdoers. In short, gods are powerful unseen beings who monitor you and your neighbors in terms of moral behavior and other socially important behaviors. I call this theory "the God as policeman" theory. Here the gods are enlisted to police human behaviors to ensure cooperation and to punish free riders. The idea is that if God can read your thoughts, intentions, and desires, you had better not entertain "bad" or uncooperative thoughts, intentions, and desires.

The problem with the policeman theory of the function of God concepts is that it is too narrow a conception of the gods. Some gods care not a whit about human beings – never mind whether they cooperate with one another. They have the ability to know you intimately if they wish, but they may not wish to do so. Many of the Aztec gods, for example, seemed simply to want propitiation. Even if gods are indeed mostly concerned with preventing free riders from exploiting human groups and conversely in producing human beings who follow the rules even when they are not among other human beings, it appears that they have largely failed at the task. Free riders are ubiquitous, and most human beings seem to entertain quite a few thoughts, intentions, and desires that are antisocial in the extreme. God, it seems, is a poor policeman.

Nevertheless, there is little doubt that many gods do exhibit the ability to see and to know all there is to know about you and your neighbors. It is also clear that many gods perform a monitoring and punishing function in many human societies, so there is some truth to the "God as policeman" story. God concepts are also at least partially counterintuitive in the way Boyer argued. Although minds without bodies are not a shocking prospect to most people, they are still nevertheless significantly atypical with respect to our everyday experiences. In short, both the "counter-intuitive agents" account and the "full strategic access" account must be seen as advances in our understanding of the origins and functions of God concepts. These accounts nevertheless have limitations, as summarized earlier. Can these accounts be supplemented or improved upon?

Dream Characters as the Origins of Some God Concepts

I suggest that some of the early anthropologists (e.g., Tylor, Frazer) who pointed to dreams as sources of God and spirit concepts were on the right track. On the face of it, the only other minds in the universe other than humans are animal minds. As reviewed, however, in previous chapters, numerous empirical investigations of various neuropsychiatric disorders such as multiple personality disorder, schizophrenia, bipolar disorder, various forms of epilepsy, and so forth have suggested to some that there may be several Minds or subpersonalities within a single person. The multiplicity of minds within a single person can even be seen in normal, healthy individuals when we dream. My colleagues and I (McNamara, McLaren, Smith, Brown, & Stickgold, 2005) reported that characters or Minds in dreams associated with the rapid eye movement (REM) sleep state were quite different from characters or Minds associated with the non-REM (NREM) sleep state. Characters in REM dreams, including the dreamer, were very often aggressive, whereas characters in the NREM sleep state were found to be friendly toward the dreamer. In the NREM sleep state, furthermore, the dreamer never initiated an aggressive encounter with another character in the dream.

These results concerning social interactions of characters in REM and NREM dreams suggest that characters in dreams can operate independently of the Will of the dreamer. When the dreamer is under attack from some other character, the dreamer never wishes it were so. Instead, the dreamer does everything that he or she can to flee the aggression. Characters in dreams, therefore, are not mere inventions of the dreamer.

They are to some extent independent of the dreamer's Will. Do they therefore satisfy criteria for being mental agents in and of themselves? Or better, are dream characters enough like "persons" that our ancestors reasonably took them to be in some sense "real" and "special" persons?

All of the available evidence suggests that the answer to that question is "yes." Ancestral populations very likely took dream characters to be real and special persons. They were persons who did not have normal bodies or limitations, but they nevertheless had minds. To see why our ancestors' position on the "real-ness" of dream characters is understandable or reasonable, consider the following: If we take a very common dream theme such as the dreamer being chased by a male stranger who intends to hurt the dreamer, we will see that attribution of intentional states and other mental states to the dream character does occur. Let us take the stranger first. He clearly satisfies criteria for possessing Mind or consciousness. He can manipulate his attention. Indeed he keeps his eye on the dreamer and can adjust his chase route to catch the dreamer as she attempts to lose him. The stranger also evidences will and volition when he intends his target and adjusts his actions to get his target. The stranger also evidences awareness of subjective experiences when his rage levels change as a function of the chase. His mood changes from menacing and hate-filled rage to malicious delight and satisfaction when the target is about to be caught. We do not know if the stranger evidences signs of a persisting identity beyond the current dream episode. However this problem can be overcome by examining repeating, recurrent dreams or dream series and by examining dreams as they occur across a single night. It turns out that dream characters can re-appear in recurring dream series and in dream series that occur across a single night when they appear to "remember" previous interactions with the dreamer and adjust their behavior accordingly (McNamara, 2004). Now all of these considerations concerning the mental status of the "stranger" character in a dream also apply, except more strongly in the case of the dreamer herself. The dreamer is a character in the dream, too. She intends to escape. She plans and adjusts her behavior accordingly. She has internal subjective experiences of fear, terror, relief, or despair, depending on the outcome of the chase. In addition, she can access memories that attest to her persisting identity across time periods and beyond the current dream episode.

In short, dream characters (both the dreamer and other characters within a dream) appear to satisfy some of the most stringent criteria philosophers have produced for "personhood." It should not be surprising, therefore, to find that our ancestors treated dream characters as spirit persons and accorded special and sometimes divine status to characters in dreams.

Metzinger (2006) disagrees with the idea that dream characters satisfy criteria normally associated with personhood. Instead, he argues that phenomenal dream content is associated with an inability on the part of the dreamer to focus attention. Nor does the dreamer exhibit any capacity for rational mental concept formation.

Metzinger may be mistaken, however. Dream characters regularly act rationally, and some even verbalize their thinking processes. Take, for example, the following dream (Schneider & Domhoff, 1999):

Alta: a detailed dreamer: #86 (4/18/86)

I'm at the library doing something about furniture in a reading room that bears no resemblance to anything in the new or old buildings – it's a very quiet, isolated room with big windows (or a window-wall) that look out over a lot of blue sky and a clean, green landscape with white buildings. The room is in shade. There's a magazine rack to be moved or sold, the furniture has been changed somewhat in function. I look around and find the magazines are now just arranged on top of a cabinet, in the old-style red-edged holders. There's not a lot of furniture here at all, and I don't actually see any tables for reading, or anything much in the way of people using the room, but I know it's a reading room like the old one, for magazines and newspapers. I think it has a parquet floor.

I'm leaving, and Lisa is with me. We're going to get something to eat together, and she's driving. We're going into an old neighborhood and it's dark and the feel of the place is that I've gone back in time to Grandmom's neighborhood. Lisa says something, responding to me, that is very typically Pleasing-type, and I react amused, and comment on it. She doesn't know about this, so I explain a bit and also make clear that there's nothing wrong with it, it's just that it's so recognizable. [What she said was in response to me expressing some kind of discomfort and she offered ways to help, but I don't know what it was that I'd said.] We get where we're going, which is a kind of drug/grocery store, small, old-timey, and I live there, or at least I keep my groceries there. I have an ice chest and something else and I'm looking at a couple of large chocolate cakes, sheet size, with chocolate frosting and nuts on top, they're probably more ice than cake. I don't remember how I got them, but I wonder what I can do with them besides eat them all at once like a glutton. I have an inspiration: I'll keep them and have them at a party! No, 2 parties! Considering how big they are, they'll do very well – even cut in half they'll serve a lot of people. I can freeze them until then. I'll cut them in half, and they'll fit in the ice chest better since they're a little too big the way they are. I open the lid and see that the ice is mostly melted. Oh dear, I can't put cake in there. Even wrapped up the best possible way, it won't prevent it from getting soaked eventually. I'll have to think of something else. Meanwhile I notice that my space is being a bit further limited by the produce/cold case that's been shoved further forward and now forms a part of my area – I remark to Lisa that what's in it isn't mine after all, but the store people probably just didn't think how awkward that is.

Clearly this dreamer can perform rational problem solving when faced with a mundane problem such as finding space in a freezer and then use results of this problem solving to adjust his or her behavior. What is lacking is insight as to the overall significance of the situation to which the dreamer is reacting. Nevertheless, the dreamer thinks through a problem and comes up with rational solutions to the problem. Note that this dream was picked at random after engaging in a search of the online databank of dreams (www.dreambank.net). On the database's search page we entered the phrase "think of something," and this yielded five dreams with greater than fifty words; we randomly chose this specimen dream. There are numerous instances of episodes like this in dreams (Schneider & Domhoff, 1999).

There are plenty of other dream accounts in which the dreamer not only solves this sort of low-level planning problem but even engages in creative problem solving (see Barrett, 2007). Metzinger's concerns regarding the cognitive status of the dreamer, although legitimate, seem misplaced. Metzinger also appears to be skeptical as to whether dreams exhibit a first-person perspective (i.e., subjectivity). Metzinger claims that dreamers are unable to experience themselves as agents. I really do not understand why Metzinger believes this about the dreamer. The hallmark experience of everyone who has experienced a dream is that they are in the dream as a character and they are experiencing something and try-ing to do something. That something could be intending or trying to escape, to move forward, or to deflect aggression, and so on. Dreamers also routinely feel and express emotions; they desire, they believe, they intend, and they act. Metzinger's position does not seem to be consonant with the facts concerning dreams and dream characters. Dream characters express thoughts, feelings, desires, emotions, sensations, and every other type of mental state. The cognitive neurosciences have demonstrated beyond reasonable doubt that the REM dreaming state is accompanied by high levels of brain activation in selected areas of the forebrain (see review essays in Volume I of Barrett & McNamara, 2007). When those areas of the brain are activated in waking life, you get the full panoply of intentional states, and there is no reason to believe that activating those same brain regions during the dreaming state will not also induce inten-tional mental activity and other subjective states such as emotions and desires.

Whatever the philosophical status of dream characters as full-fledged mental agents, our ancestors certainly treated them as such. It may even be said that dream characters were just as important emotionally to per-sons in those days as were other waking characters.

Dreams in Traditional Societies

Most premodern traditional peoples regarded most dreams as arenas for interaction with the spirit world. Thus, Michael Harner (1972) reports that the South American Jívaro consider dreams to reveal a truer spir-itual reality behind the illusory images people perceive in waking life. The Zuni and Quiché Maya traditions studied by Barbara Tedlock (1987) see dream images as communications from ancestors, spirits, or divini-ties. The Tikopia (Firth, 2001) in Polynesia see dreams as opportunities for visitation of spirits to the dreamer. Perhaps most commonly among premodern peoples, dream images are explained as the experiences and perceptions of the dreamer's soul as it wanders outside the body (e.g., T. Gregor, 1981; T. A. Gregor, 1981 on Amazonia; Lohmann, 2003a, 2003b, 2003c on Oceania; and Tonkinson, 1974, on Aboriginal Australia).

To become a spiritual specialist or diviner among the Temne peoples you must demonstrate expertise in interacting with spirit beings in dreams (Shaw, 1992). Temne diviners derived their abilities from an initial dream or nightmare in which they meet some supernatural agent that then serves as a source of power and prestige for the dreamer. The diviner attempts to gain favors and power from subsequent encounters in his dreams with his patron spirit and other spirits in the "dream town" or ro-mere. The diviner then asserts authority as a spiritual specialist to interpret the dreams of others and to predict fortune or misfortune for these others.

The Yansi from the Democratic Republic of Congo begin each day with a discussion of the dreams of the night. Those who share especially compelling dreams are accorded more attention and consideration. The sharing of a compelling dream has material consequences for the individual and others extending widely through the society. Dreaming in Yansi society, for example, appears to be integral to the Yansi witchcraft–sorcery–medicine complex. In his studies of the Toraja (wet rice farmers who live in hamlets throughout the central highlands of South Sulawesi, Indonesia), Hollan (2003) reported that the Toraja, despite being Christianized, still encounter ancestor spirits (nene') and other spiritual beings (deata) in their dreams. Robbins (2003) studied the ways in which dream sharing allowed Melanesians to channel charismatic leaders into roles that benefited rather than threatened tribal political stability. He notes that "Throughout Melanesia, people are regularly thought to have contact with supernatural beings, and in the eyes of those around them these contacts endow them, at least momentarily, with exceptional powers to foretell the future, heal others and so on" (p. 23). Robbins then notes that " . . . it is in dreams that Melanesians most regularly come into contact with supernaturals and with supernaturally given knowledge that may afford them extraordinary powers" (p. 23).

Drawing on the work of Keesing (1982), Boyer (2001) notes that "The Kwaio concept of spirit-ancestor (adalo) illustrates ... the mundane business of representing religious agents in practical contexts and interacting with them. The Kwaio live in the Solomon Islands; most of their religious activities ... involve dealing with the ancestors, especially the spirits of deceased members of their own clans, as well as more dangerous wild spirits. Interaction with these adalo ... is a constant feature of Kwaio life. As Keesing points out, young children need no explicit instruction to represent the ancestors as an invisible and powerful presence, since they see people interact with the adalo in so many circumstances of everyday life ... people 'meet' the ancestors in dreams. Most people are particularly familiar with and fond of one particular adalo, generally the spirit of a close relative, and maintain frequent contact with that spirit" (p. 138).

Not only do people derive God concepts from dreams, they may even derive religious ritual institutions and practices from dreams. The African Ingessana peoples, for example, use dream images and events to create religious rituals.

Summary of the Dream Origins of God Concepts

These examples of how traditional peoples meet and interact with spirit beings, including spirit ancestors, could be multiplied indefinitely. These examples and data from other similar societies support my contention that dreams shape the generation and concept of spirit beings. The sharing of dreams that involved interaction with a spirit being very likely enhanced the prestige of the dreamer. Dreams – even visitations from the spirit world – are thought to be involuntary experiences. They cannot be faked; thus they are often considered reliable information about the dreamer. Traditional people are not gullible. They understand that people can lie about or embellish the content of a dream, but this did not mean that dreams themselves were unreliable.

Nor do traditional peoples "confuse" dream images with reality. Schweder and LeVine (1975) and Shweder (1982) studied the development of dream concepts among Hausa children. It turns out that Hausa ten-year-olds, like Western adults, tend to adopt a negative assessment of dreams claiming that they are unreal and generated solely by the mind. Hausa adults then step in and show the children that dreams give them access to an external, objective realm of the wandering soul. The children then reject their former "realist" positions and instead adopt an interpretation of dreams more consonant with their tribal beliefs. Dreams are emotionally compelling experiences and they were valued as a primary place of spiritual encounter in ancestral populations.

In summary, one clear origin for God concepts among traditional peoples is the dream. Both ancestral figures and nonancestral supernatural agents appear in dreams and are reverenced in daily life. The spirit beings that appear in dreams can be either positively or negatively disposed toward the dreamers – that is, both evil and good supernatural beings appear in dreams. Interactions with these spirit persons/gods in dreams confer status on the dreamer and can often establish one's status as a spiritual specialist in the tribe or group.

Dream characters, therefore, have a prima facie case to be considered as the cognitive source for supernatural beings. People in traditional societies treat them as such, and it is likely that ancestral populations also treated them as such. Dreams, furthermore, do not give rise to an indiscriminate variety of agents. Mickey Mouse does not appear with any frequency in children's dreams, for example. Instead, animals, strangers/unknown adults, and family members (dead or alive) frequently appear in children's dreams (Foulkes, 1982; Van de Castle, 1994).

Are dream characters "minimally counterintuitive"? From the point of view of waking consciousness they are, as they do not have bodies but they do have minds. In contrast, I doubt that ancestral populations were puzzled by dream characters in any way. After all, it was not clear that they themselves had a body when they were dreaming! The two realms, the dream world and the waking world, were complementary and different but equally real, and thus the spirits we meet in the dream realm are real. They have an impact on the waking world, influencing healing potential, personal power and status, and knowledge stores more generally.

Can dream characters be considered to be like the gods who have "full strategic access" to our minds and memories? Yes. Most dream characters seem to know what the dreamer is thinking or intending. It is difficult to deceive a dream character about one's (assuming now that you are the dreamer) intentions. If we assume with modern neuroscience that all characters in a dream are in some way produced by the same Mind/brain, then it should not be surprising that all the dream characters in a dream display this godlike quality of knowing the minds of all other characters in a dream.

If we suppose then that supernatural agent concepts are generated by the dreaming mind with cognitive mechanisms available to the dreaming Mind/brain, then what follows for religious cognition, religious language, and religious rituals? The memorability, complexity, and vividness of God concepts may not be due merely to their counterintuitive properties. Dream images have an innate emotional charge, high memorability, vividness, and complexity properties, and these alone might help account for the impact of God concepts on other cognitive and behavioral systems.

Decentering and Dream Entities

Most importantly for our purposes, the fact that God concepts come out of the wealth of dream characters produced each night by every human being as far as we can tell helps us to understand why both negative and positive supernatural agents are frequently implicated in the range of clinical disorders involving derangements of the decentering process. Where do alter identities come from when they appear in a psychosis or in a dissociative disorder? The adoption of grandiose divine identities by manic patients and schizophrenics, and the possession by spirit beings during both positive and negative possession and dissociative states, all can be related to the accessing of one or more of these highly charged dream characters when decentering is underway. Many "alters," "subpersonalities," and God concepts, I suggest, come from dreams.

Because some God concepts come from highly charged dream images/characters, they prolong the decentering process when it is triggered. Decentering continues until the original identity or some other competing identity wins out in the competition to control executive functions of the Mind/brain. If a highly charged God concept is a competitor identity, the original Self finds it harder to integrate into a higher Self and regain control of executive functions. Thus, the whole process is prolonged. Ultimately, however, when the Self "competes" with the God image for control over executive cognitive functions, the God image does not supplant the original identity or Self. Instead, the Self is yoked up to the God image, and this has the effect of enriching the Self by enhancing the Self's control over executive functions. The yoking-up process, however, takes some time during each decentering episode. This "God-related" prolongation of the decentering process shapes the key features of religious language, ritual, and experience.

I turn next to a consideration of religious language.

10 Religious Language

And when you pray, do not keep on babbling like pagans, for they think
they will be heard because of their many words. Do not be like them, for
your Father knows what you need before you ask him.

– Matt. 6:7–8

Introduction

Although prayer is one of the constants of religion, the practice of praying varies tremendously in form and content (repetitive mantras, praise,
petition, worship, thanksgiving, etc.) (Geertz, 2008). When people pray
or when they engage in religious ceremonies or rituals, they talk in a more
formalized style of language. There is also a generalized displacement of
agency from the pray-er or from the people in the congregation and onto
the deity. This displacement process is marked in the language used in
religious rituals. We will review those specialized characteristics of religious language later in this chapter, but first we must ask why religious
language is associated with special forms of language and language use.

One reason why religious language is peculiar is that the addressee of
religious language (God) is special. How do you talk to God? Most people
have never seen God or a god and even if they had the superior status of
God would require special forms of address. In any case, for most people,

language addressed to a god entails speaking to an invisible interlocutor who may or may not respond clearly.

Keane's 1997 review of religious language very ably summarized the special issues and questions raised by religious language:

> By what means can we, and in what manner ought we, talk with invisible interlocutors? How can we get them to respond? How should we talk about them? By what marks do we know that some words originate from divine sources? Are these words true, fitting, efficacious, or compelling in some special way? These questions touch on more general problems concerning the relations among performance, text, and context. They also involve the relations among experience, concrete practices, and what is culturally construed to lie beyond ordinary experience, whether that be in the past, the future, at a spatial distance, or across an ontological divide. The problems of communication between this world and another, or of handling authoritative words derived from distant sources, are critical to many religious practices: Not only do they impose special semiotic difficulties on human practitioners, but their language must sometimes contend with the fact that the very presence of the deity, spirits, or ancestors cannot be taken for granted (Keane, 1997, p. 48).

Although Keane argued that no single set of formal or pragmatic features is diagnostic of religious as opposed to other marked uses of language, he nevertheless agreed with DuBois (1986), who listed the following linguistic features as characteristic of religious language: " . . . marked voice quality, greater fluency relative to colloquial speech, stylized and restricted intonational contours, gestalt knowledge (speakers often learn texts as a whole and cannot recite them in parts), personal volition disclaimer (crediting a traditional source for one's words), avoidance of first and second person pronouns, and mediation through several speakers" (Keane, 1997, pp. 52–53).

Now why should religious language exhibit just these features? Du Bois (1986) argues that these features tend to shift the source and control of speech from the individual to some other more superior agent or God. Other markers that shift the focus from the individual to God are the use of archaic elements (including words and grammatical forms that speakers believe to be archaic), elements borrowed from other languages, and solemn use of repetitive chants, declamations, and petition. In short, the speaker's or the ritual participant's volitional agency in the discourse is reduced while the presence of God is increased.

All of this indicates that, during a religious act involving religious language such as prayer or ritual celebration, the individual sets aside his or her own identity to interact with or participate in the identity of the spirit or God. As mentioned in previous chapters, I call this process of the reduction in Self and the enhancement of an alternative identity, in this case God, "decentering."

Religious language appears both to mark the onset of the decentering process and to facilitate it. What is more important is that the ritual and religious language facilitates the search and integration process whereby the old Self integrates into a higher Self or God. When, for example, the traditional Xavante peoples narrate their dreams, they alter their pronoun use, voice quality, and language style to facilitate identification with the spirit being encountered in the dream (Graham, 1995). Use of glossolalic style utterances also seems to facilitate onset of decentering. The individual who engages in glossolalia describes a lack of voluntary control over the vocalizations. Self-consciousness is reduced so that the spirit can speak, and the fusion of the old identity with the god can be facilitated.

Speech Acts and Decentering

Several authors (Bell, 1997; Rappaport, 1999; Tambiah, 1979; Werlen, 1984) have pointed out that many forms of religious ritual, including the Christian Mass, are characterized by use of a very formal style of language with all of the characteristics just mentioned. Crucial to the creation of the formal religious style is the use of special types of speech acts. The mention of speech acts requires a short digression.

In the 1940s, Austin pointed out that language does not merely consist of statements about reality, but that people could use words to create realities, as in the utterance, "I baptize you . . . " or "I now declare you man and wife." Here we have two of the most central sacraments of the

Christian faith accomplished – at least in the earthly realm by use of speech acts. Austin (1975) called such utterances "performatives."

Liturgy, even the key rite involving "The Eucharistic Prayer," can be seen as a performance of an action – a thing done as the early ritual theorists described Greek tragedy. In this sense, liturgy involves an enactment of intentions with participants setting aside their proximate intentions and God accomplishing a different intention during the ritual. Intentions are directed to something in the real world. In religious rituals, individual intentions are suspended in deference to God's intentions or will. Religious language enacts and reveals the suspension and displacement of intentional states during religious rituals.

Ritual is "people's work." During religious rituals, participants do something together that cannot be done by each participant alone. They therefore need to align their intentional states accordingly. As Rappaport (1989) pointed out, when people pray, sing, or perform other communicative actions together, they signal that they are subsuming their own intentional states temporarily and aligning those states with the intentions of others. The ritual language registers this fact via use of the first-person plural form or "we" utterances in prayer and song.

Although there is this signaling to others who are present during the ritual, the primary communicative act is directed toward the deity. Religious language and ritual center on communication with God. When addressing God, we are confronted with all of those questions summarized earlier. How do you communicate with an invisible and powerful agent?

You do so carefully, deferentially, and with respect. Thus the language needs to be formal, serious, and deferential. The participants therefore utilize the following types of speech acts: confessions of faith, praying, petitioning, promising, praising, and blessing.

God also uses speech acts during rituals. Participants listen to God speak during rituals because they want to draw close to the deity. They may even want to identify with the deity. The participants want to be subsumed into the deity. Thus, the language needs to help the participant "see" and become the deity. The ritual specialist who represents the deity must therefore actualize the deity's presence by speaking like the deity. The language must be powerful and definitive. This is where "declarative" or "directive" speech acts come in. Declarations manifest/enact/accomplish an action with the utterance of the word. When God speaks, participants listen and respond.

God speaks through the priest or ritual specialist. These speech acts include blessing (e.g., "I bless you in the name of the Father...," consecrating ("I consecrate you to the Lord"), commanding (e.g., "take and eat, this is my body..."), and baptizing (e.g., "I baptize you in the name of the Father...").

In summary, religious language has distinctive linguistic characteristics including formal styles, reductions in first-person pronoun use and elevation of third-person pronoun use, and an abundance of speech acts used in both private and public ritual contexts. Use of religious language both facilitates entry into the decentering process and prolongs the decentering process so that the individual's identity is subsumed into that of the deity.

Language, therefore, is shaped by and shapes the decentering process. Before concluding my discussion of religious language, however, I wish to mention one other form of religious language that is influenced by the decentering process – that is, narrative.

Decentering and Narrative

Narrative is a temporal ordering of a series of events involving a challenge, a climax, and a resolution. Narratives are composed of a plot or plots with goals and subgoals of an agent who strives to achieve these goals in the context of a setting and a plot. Typically, what drives the story line is conflict between the agent and other actors concerning their goals.

Invariably the agent or the "hero" suffers a setback or a defeat. Even when he does not suffer a defeat, he is typically blocked in successful pursuit of his goals. This temporary defeat of the hero constitutes the challenge the hero must face and overcome. The hero's attempt to overcome obstacles and defeat leads to a climax wherein the hero either wins or loses. If he wins, he grows spiritually; if he loses – well, we are not told anything about what happens to the hero who is defeated.

In any case, the hero always suffers a setback in a narrative; there is always a conflict or a challenge that needs to be faced and resolved. This setback or defeat of the hero implies a reduction in agency and volition on the part of the hero. The ego suffers a defeat and agency is temporarily reduced. This reduction in agency triggers a decentering process. As always, the decentering process can result in a diminution or an enhancement of the moral character of the individual, and that is what all narratives are ultimately about.

Narratives are particularly good vehicles for revealing character traits or dispositions of the actors depicted in the story: How does each actor respond when faced with a struggle or conflict? Narratives depict a triggering of a decentering process and reactions of individuals to that decentering process. Thus narratives reveal character. Persons can therefore form their personal identities, in part, via construction of autobiographical narratives or life stories (Gallagher, 2003; Schectman, 1996). Ricoeur (1992) argues that in narrative a character is either an agent who does things to others or he undergoes a reduction in agency. I suggest that the value of stories for human beings lies in the fact that they depict how a person might react to that critical decentering process after he suffers an ego defeat. Some of the best stories invented by mankind are the myths that inform all religious traditions and that help structure the rituals at the center of these traditions. It is to rituals we next turn.

11 Ritual

> Look at nothing in defiance of ritual, listen to nothing in defiance of ritual, speak of nothing in defiance of ritual, never stir hand or foot in defiance of ritual.
>
> – Confucius, *The Analects or Lunyu* 12.1

Introduction

Many religion scholars believe that religious rituals are a major source of the world's religions (i.e., that religion is rooted in ritual). Whether this is the case, there is little doubt that attaining a better understanding of religious rituals may give us a better understanding of religion in general. In recent years, anthropological and cognitive approaches to ritual behaviors and ritual form have registered some remarkable advances (Bloch, 1974; Humphrey & Laidlaw, 1994; Lawson & McCauley, 1990; Liénard & Boyer, 2006; McCauley & Lawson, 2002; Rappaport, 1999; Seaquist, 2006). I will try to build on these advances by systematically examining psychological and cognitive effects of ritual behavior on the individual.

To forecast my conclusions regarding the nature and functions of ritual, I find that, with respect to its effects on the individual, religious rituals often involve a reduction in agency/volition. The individual sets aside his

212

or her own immediate intentions and instead performs actions stipulated by others – such as gods and ancestors, long ago. Religious rituals also constrain the decentering process in such a way as to facilitate selection of a new more powerful Self. In nonreligious contexts, this reduction in agency and its associated communal actions during ritualistic activities has the overall effect of enhancing cooperative social interactions and reducing the potential for aggression within the group. An example of these sorts of effects is the case of cross-cultural politeness conventions in social interactions. To observe politeness conventions, you put aside your agenda for a moment and perform a ritual display that signals your willingness to consider the other's comfort or point of view.

Religious rituals are associated with a similar reduction in agency and then a displacement of intentional states onto the deity – in short, a decentering process. This ritualistically constrained decentering process facilitates identification with the deity or a higher more powerful Self. The effects of decentering in religious ritual contexts, except perhaps in the case of ecstatic cults, tend to be salutary: Temporal cognition is altered encouraging reflection, emotional processing is altered in favor of emotions that "elevate" or link up the self with the deity, and attentional and executive functions are enhanced improving self-regulation.

In ancestral and traditional societies the effects of religious rituals differ as a function of sex. In boys and men the social function of some rituals (e.g., initiation rites) appears to enhance the capacity for controlled forms of aggression towards other groups. Executive functions, strategic thinking, and self-regulation are enhanced in service to heightened aggressive instincts. For men, therefore, religious rituals (at least ancestral rituals) functioned to produce "warriors." In women, too, religious rituals enhance in-group cooperation and out-group enmity.

In the modern world in the West there has been a centuries long, concerted attack on Christian religious traditions of the West. Religious rituals in the West, therefore, have been altered or, in the cases of some Protestant sects, entirely jettisoned. As a consequence, therefore, ritual effects on individuals are less noticeable than they once were.

With respect to cognitive effects of ritual, I argue that religious rituals enhance key aspects of temporal cognition as well as the related cognitive process known as "historical consciousness." I link historical consciousness up with ancestral forms of religiosity that were centered on family and clan lineages and ancestor worship. Respect for clan lineage traditions and the ways things were done in the past encourages imitation of past behaviors (mimesis), and when combined with decentering, historical consciousness enhances a religiously inspired set of craft traditions and technical intelligences.

I turn now to the evidence for each of these arguments concerning ritual.

Characteristics of Rituals that Need to Be Explained

A survey of recent work on formal features of rituals reveals their key characteristics, and it is these characteristics that any theory of ritual needs to explain. Rappaport (1999) suggested that rituals involve "the performance of more or less invariant sequences of formal acts and utterances not entirely encoded by the performers" (Rappaport, 1999, p. 24). Liénard and Boyer (2006, p. 815) recently proposed that ritualized behaviors are characterized by compulsion (one must perform the particular sequence), rigidity (it must be performed the right way), redundancy (the same actions are often repeated inside the ritual), and goal demotion (the actions are divorced from their usual goals). Humphrey and Laidlaw (1994) emphasized a process similar to Liénard and Boyer's concept of goal demotion. Humphrey and Laidlaw pointed out that the normal relationship that develops between an actor's intentional states and his or her motor acts is altered in rituals. Instead of performing one's own intended actions during a ritual, one performs actions stipulated by others – others who devised the actions long ago – sometimes centuries ago. Ritualized acts in liturgical traditions appear as already formed by others, almost like an object or tool. The individual must then use the tools appropriately.

Whitehouse (2004) suggested that religion's key rituals might be usefully classified into two broad subgroups depending on the accent they place on verbal versus nonverbal procedural displays. Religions in the doctrinal mode rely on verbal expression, are highly repetitive, spread by proselytization, and can occur over wide areas. Religions in the imagistic mode prefer use of visual symbols and iconic imagery. Reliance on imagery reduces the need for verbal exegesis. The high memorability of visual displays means that rituals in these religions need not be performed frequently. In contrast, these rituals and religions are hard to spread because they tend to occur only locally. Whitehouse tentatively suggested that the contrast between imagistic and doctrinal modes of religiosity is mediated by differing forms of memory: flashbulb memories for the former and semantic memory for the latter.

Lawson and McCauley (1990) derive performative aspects of ritual form not from underlying memory systems but from the degree to which the supernatural agent or God is the central actor or agent in the ceremony. McCauley and Lawson (2002) note that in religious rituals God or a supernatural being may act as the doer of an action (and thus appear in the agent slot of a ritual representational sentence) or the receiver of an action, and thus would appear in the patient slot of the main clause in the sentence. The centrality of a ritual will correspond to how deeply the supernatural being is embedded in a sentential clause. They also argue that "special agent rituals" (those in which the relevant supernatural being is the agent of the action) are reversible but nonrepeatable: There are rituals that can reverse the results of these rituals (for a marriage ceremony there is, in principle, a divorce ceremony), but in general there is no need to repeat these rituals because, when they have effected a result, that result is fairly permanent. Special patient rituals, in contrast, are repeatable but nonreversible. Similarly, special agent rituals tend to be performed less often than special patient rituals because they need not be repeated, and they tend to be associated with greater sensory stimulation. Some of these predictions of the ritual form theory have been supported empirically (Barrett & Lawson, 2001).

Although these classification and theoretical efforts to capture variability in religious ritual forms are laudable, they do not answer the question of the functions of ritual. Ritual form theories are nevertheless advances as they point to potential avenues to explore to identify functional correlates of ritual.

Neurobiology of Ritual

Virtually nothing is known about neurobiologic mediation of rituals, religious or otherwise. Behavioral rituals (in this case stereotyped and repetitive behaviors) can be associated with obsessive–compulsive disorder (OCD). OCD is known to be associated with abnormally elevated activity in the orbitofrontal cortex. The orbitofrontal cortex helps to regulate the emotional limbic system and is in turn influenced by dopamine.

In rats, ritualization is accomplished via enhancing forebrain dopamine to very high levels. As the level of dopamine in the system increases, a smaller number and variety of behaviors are emitted until only one or two stereotyped displays are emitted over and over again (Tucker & Williamson, 1984). Depletion of central dopamine stores prevents this sort of ritualization of behaviors.

With respect to functional behaviors, it seems clear from the animal literature that ritualization of behaviors tends to act as a signal that the animal will not attack another animal, that the animal is interested in cooperating (e.g., in a sexual act), and so forth. Interestingly, ritualization seems to facilitate the evolution of signaling production and comprehension/receiving behaviors (Bradbury & Vehrenkamp, 1998, pp. 499–500). In any ritualization process, a set or sequence of behaviors that are reliably associated with a biologically significant event or process is selected and then reduced to a more simple form. If, for example, the set of behaviors in question involves sixteen identifiable subcomponent processes, then ritualization will reduce the sixteen to eight such subcomponents. Next, these eight fundamental components will then be exaggerated and repeated during a signaling display. Over time and with repetition, the animal learns to reduce the variability in expression of the display such that the display becomes a stereotype. Finally, the set of stereotypic behaviors that has been used to signal one thing becomes emancipated from this original signaling context and is then used to signal something related but more abstract. In this manner, ritualization serves to facilitate communication of very abstract information between two animals.

We have seen in previous chapters that central dopamine, particularly dopamine in prefrontal cortex, may play a key role in support of religiosity. It may be that the links between dopamine and religiosity begin with dopamine's role in selection of behaviors for output given a social context and in restriction of the range of behaviors to a single type given a social context. The role of dopamine in production of a single, high-profile behavior that is emitted over and over highlights dopamine's role in the production of information. The emission of a redundant and repetitive signal reduces uncertainty in messages transmitted between a sender and a receiver and thus increases the information content of the signal.

When attempting to engage in an aggressive contest of strength, it is beneficial for an animal to signal aggressive intent. The receiver therefore is given a choice: engage or disengage. If the two animals fight, ritual behaviors will enhance the strength of each as aggressive attacks unfold as a stereotyped sequence of behaviors that deliver very deadly and damaging blows to an opponent. Ritual behaviors can also signal disengagement, deference, and submission.

So too with human beings. Rituals can signal and deliver both aggressive blows and signals of disengagement, submission, or even cooperation. The latter set of signals is exemplified in rituals concerning social deference and honor. These signals are embedded in politeness rituals across a wide range of cultures.

Ritual and Politeness Theory

Politeness rituals signal nonaggressive intent and are therefore absolutely critical to social cohesion and cooperation. Without them, society would fall apart and force would rule all (Fukada & Asato, 2004). As Confucius argued, rituals are the very bedrock of society. You can quickly learn how to live and operate in a foreign society by looking at the cultural rules, norms, and rituals that exist to preserve honor, "face," and reputation. Brown and Levinson (1987; see also Ide, 1989) argue that every member of a society has face, or social reputation/prestige, which evolutionary psychologists might call a measure of "resource holding potential."

If reputation is lost then social standing is lost and the individual is excluded from society. In ancestral conditions, such exclusion could well have meant a death sentence.

"Face" then must at all costs be preserved. When an individual acts in a way that could endanger the "face" or reputation of another, strategies must kick in to preserve the face of that other person. If they do not then the other person may resort to aggression to preserve face. Use of a politeness strategy to minimize the risk of any person losing face thus helps to ensure peace and concord among people in social interactions.

According to Brown and Levinson, there are two types of face. One is negative face, which concerns freedom from personal restriction and insult. The other is positive face, which is more purely related to social reputation and the desire to be appreciated or approved of by other members of a society.

Brown and Levinson suggest several possible strategies to prevent or alleviate a face-threatening act and the aggression that might result from such an act. One strategy is to simply not perform the face-threatening act. But that strategy is usually not available as it would mean that the individual cannot obtain what he seeks to obtain, so some sort of act needs to be implemented. The task is to reduce its face-threatening possibilities. Here is where politeness strategies come in.

The riskier the individual or speaker perceives his face-threatening act to be, the greater the number of face-saving strategies he will want and need to employ, including of course the politeness strategies. According to Brown and Levinson, the individual assesses the degree of riskiness of the face-threatening act (x) he is contemplating committing by computing: the social distance between the speaker (S) and the hearer (H), a measure of the power that the hearer has over the speaker, and the absolute ranking of impositions in the particular culture.

Riskiness of face-threatening act (x) = Distance (S,H) + Power (H,S)

+ Rank of imposition (x)

If the hearer has greater social standing, power, or prestige than the speaker, then riskiness will increase. As x increases so too will an individual's level of politeness. This politeness theory is important for ritual theory because politeness is a ritual act. The politeness theory predicts that as riskiness of a face-threatening act increases, so too will ritual gestures increase . . . in this case, politeness rituals.

Ritual gestures, such as politeness strategies, then are linked to people's attempts to get along with one another, to control aggression, and to cooperate with one another. Politeness rituals and other social gestures certainly facilitate social cooperation, but apparently they were not enough as religious rituals have also been a constant part of the history of human cultures. Religious rituals accomplish what the politeness rituals accomplish, but they do much more because they employ the process of decentering.

Religious Ritual and Decentering

Rappaport's (1999) treatment of ritual is particularly helpful for understanding the role of decentering in religious rituals. As mentioned earlier in this chapter, Rappaport (1999) defined ritual as "acts and utterances not encoded by the performers themselves." Rituals, in other words, were not invented by the people who participate in ritual. Instead, rituals are handed down by elders, ancestors, or gods. Rituals, in short, come from the past, and participants in a ritual are linking themselves to an order (as inscribed in the acts and utterances of the ritual) that is inherited from the past.

The fact that participants perform acts in a ritual that were not formulated by themselves suggests that participants temporarily suspend their own identities, including their volitional and intentional states (except, of course, the supraordinate intention of performing the ritual itself). This observation is similar to the observations made by Humphrey and Laidlaw (1994) regarding the "ritual stance" or "ritual commitment" and Liénard and Boyer's (2006) concept of "goal demotion" during ritualized behaviors. I suggest that the temporary suspension of ongoing volitional states in favor of performance of someone else's action sequences must involve a kind of decentering process. The Self's subordinate aims are suppressed in favor of ritual action to pursue the Self's supraordinate aims of fulfilling ritual obligations. There is nothing mysterious here. To fulfill long-range goals, you have to accomplish intermediate goals. The only difference here is that the intermediate actions are not formulated by the Self; thus the Self is temporarily demoted or decentered. In ancestral societies, people very likely used additional means besides performance of ritual acts to facilitate decentering. These were things such as putting on masks, speaking in the voice of the god, ingesting mind-altering substances, depriving oneself of sleep, and so forth.

When decentering is triggered, the ritual itself takes over control of the behavior of the individual. The participant effectively puts himself into the hands of the ritual. Here ritual constitutes a safe holding place for the individual's identity. When things go right, religious ritual takes this identity, transfigures it, and then "hands it back" to the individual who is enriched by the process. The ritual takes Identity 1 (Self) and yokes that identity up to Identity 2 (God). Ritual uses several procedural techniques to accomplish this yoking-up of Self to an ideal Self and ultimately to God.

One way that ritual accomplishes the yoking of Self to God is by focusing the attention of the ritual participant on the deity as present in the ritual. Rappaport (1989) argued that ritual conveys (to both participants and to God) both "self-referential" messages (the "current physical, psychic or social states" of participants) and "canonical messages." Canonical messages are often delivered by speech acts of ritual performers (see Chapter 10 on religious language) on behalf of God and are often contained in things such as sacred texts, prayers, incantations, and pronouncements. The participant hears these canonical messages given in the voice of God and then is encouraged to identify with those messages, to speak them, and to internalize them. The sense of Self (of the participant) is reduced, and the sense of the deity is made more real as the deity speaks and acts in the ritual. Various devices are used to facilitate construction of a relationship between the participant and the deity. In highly emotional, ecstatic, and visual rituals, the participant is encouraged to identify with the deity. In more mundane, doctrinal forms of rituals, the participant is encouraged to form a bond with the deity but not to become the deity. In both cases the decentering process ends with the elevation or transfiguration of the Self via the acquisition of divine qualities.

Because rituals, in their performative capacity, facilitate decentering, those states become indexical signs (an indexical sign is an index of some other event; e.g., smoke indicates fire, a footprint indicates a person has passed by). In contrast to symbols and icons, indexical signs are a very reliable means of conveying accurate information about the persons in the ritual (i.e., that they are attempting to adhere to and accept a certain transcendent order). To the extent that a participant identifies with the deity and takes on divine qualities, he or she will be considered more trustworthy, powerful, admirable, prestigious, and so forth. Those divine qualities include all of the major "gifts of the spirit" mentioned in previous chapters such as fearlessness, self-control, steadfastness, insight, compassion, and joy. These character traits then become lasting indexical signs and proof positive of the individual's commitment to the religious group.

Rituals affect the sexes differently in traditional societies. In traditional and tribal societies, men specialized in hunting and warfare. Women could be as fierce, warlike, and bloodthirsty as men, but men tended to do the fighting. Boys, therefore, had to learn to become effective fighters and warriors. Religion was a crucial tool used to turn boys into men and warriors. The primary means by which boys were turned into warriors were the famous initiation rites. As far as I can tell, these rites were every bit as challenging, bloody, and terrifying as the original ethnographies reported. In his early study of warfare among "primitive" tribal cultures, Davie (1929) notes: "Since war is a matter of supreme importance in savage life it permeates every phase of the group's interests and mores, and the aid of religion among other things is called in during the training of the warrior" (p. 240).

Ritual Sacrifice

There is often some sacrifice associated with the rituals, such as circumcision, amputation of a finger, or knocking out a tooth. Prehistoric rock art throughout the world testifies to some of these ritual sacrifices. Reversed handprints with clear, amputated digits are not uncommon even in cave art of the Upper Paleolithic period. The sacrifice and training for war begins quite early. The Gallas peoples of Northeast Africa amputate the nipples and breasts of boys soon after birth, "... believing that no warrior who possesses them can possibly be brave" (Davie, p. 239). Boys in traditional societies around the world are trained to sacrifice and suffer. They spend hours in frozen rivers to inure themselves to cold; they are expected to endure long treks into the wilderness and are often left alone to fend for themselves. On Tud Island of the Torres Straits, the boys and young men drink the sweat of renowned warriors and eat the blood-soaked refuse from the clothes and skins of great warriors to imbibe their strength and courage.

Given the deadly ubiquity of war across all human cultures and periods as well as the great prestige accorded to the warrior by men and women of the tribe, it is no wonder that religious rituals were recruited to turn boys into warriors. Davie reports: "Among the Dieri and other kindred tribes of Central Australia, the next ceremony after circumcision is one called Wilyaru. The boy is directed to close his eyes. One of the old men then binds the arm of another old man pretty tightly with string, and with a sharp piece of flint lances the vein about an inch from the elbow, causing an instant stream of blood, which is allowed to play over the young man until he is covered with it, and the old man is exhausted. Another then takes his place, and so on until the young man becomes quite still from the quantity of blood adhering to him. The reason given for this practice is that it infuses courage into the young man, and also shows him that the sight of blood is nothing, so that should he receive a wound in warfare he may account it as a matter of no moment. The next stage in the ceremony is that the young man is told to lie down on his face, when one or two young men cut from three to twelve gashes on the nape of his neck with a sharp piece of flint. These, when healed into raised scars, denote that the person bearing them has passed through the Wilyaru" (pp. 238–239). The shaman or priest (along with leaders among the warriors) typically carries out the initiation rituals, and the gods of war are invariably invoked to witness the rituals. The boys are urged to identify themselves with the war god and to learn fearlessness. "Another excellent example of the relation of religion to war is the Omaha ceremony of cutting the hair, by which the boy was consecrated to the thunder god, who thenceforth became the arbiter of life and death to the man. The hair which was cut off was laid away in a sacred case, in care of the thunder priest" (Davie, p. 240). In so-called primitive societies, after the ceremonies and prayers of the initiation ritual are over, the boy is given a new name and a weapon. Then he is instructed in the myths, religious rituals, and mores of the tribe. He is told what his duties will be; these duties are typically to uphold the traditions of the tribe and to war on behalf of the tribe.

These forms of ritual sacrifice all involved the initiate – the boy who would become a warrior, but many religions have practiced much more bloody and elaborate forms of sacrifice, including human sacrifice. Human and animal sacrifice has been documented as part of the religious ceremonies of virtually every known culture down through history. What could such sacrifice possibly mean or indicate? The priests and shamans who presided over these sacrifices saw the victims as substitutes for people in the community. To restore balance, to atone for the sins of the people of the community, blood had to be spilled. It was important that the victim be innocent of the crimes committed by people of the community.

From the point of view of the individual psyche, this sort of victim sacrifice must have had profound effects. It is impossible to observe the dismemberment of even a chicken or bird without some discomfort – even for the most practiced of executioners. Did sacrificial blood trigger a decentering process in the individual, or did sacrifice require a decentering process on the part of onlookers for it to have its intended effects at all? If you cannot sacrifice your old Self in a decentering process, perhaps witnessing the sacrificing of another would help. This decentering theory seems too facile an explanation for so bloody a phenomenon. Ritual sacrifice remains a mystery to me – yet it is clearly fundamental to religion.

Cognitive and Emotional Functions of Ritual

Religious rituals, I suggest, also promote "historical consciousness" and appreciation of "tradition." Ritual facilitates appreciation of the past in two ways: As discussed earlier in this chapter, ritual involves the performance of actions that were created by beings (ancestors, gods, etc.) in the past. Ritual, therefore, involves a repetition of things past and a bringing back to life of past events. All of this promotes a view of oneself as situated against an uncanny, vast, and meaningful past. At the microcognitive level, ritual also has an enormous impact on rates of cognitive processing as I explain next.

Religious Rituals, Temporal Cognition, and Historical Consciousness

Religious ritual involves performance of highly formalized action sequences not devised or "encoded by the participants themselves," as Rappaport (1999) and others (e.g., Humphrey & Laidlaw, 1994) have remarked. Performance (or witnessing the performance) of the stipulated action sequences requires suspension of, or displacement of, the immediate intentional states of participants, and therefore yields a series of cognitively empty time intervals for the participants. The experience of empty intervals during the performance of apparently "meaningless acts," as well as the reference to, or imitation of, past actions of the ancestors or the gods, alters temporal processing frames and sense of time of participants and initiates a cognitive shift toward an experience of atemporality or timelessness. Ritual actions thus constrain temporal processing routines into either of two routes toward the experience of "timelessness." These processing routines, in turn, have profound effects on a number of fundamental cognitive processes. The shift in temporal processing parameters during ritual can be modeled in a number of ways. If we use Glicksohn's (2001) multiplicative function for apparent duration:

$$T \text{ (apparent duration)} = N \times S,$$

where N = number of subjective time pulses/units, S = size or length of subjective time unit, the number of subjective time units progressively increases, and the size of the subjective time unit decreases until it is confined to the present moment and the participant moves toward an experience of timelessness. Conversely, as the number of subjective time units progressively decreases while their size increases, time slows down and at the limit enters an eternal frame of reference. In the former case, subjective time speeds up and rituals tend to conform to Whitehouse's (2002, 2004) imagistic mode of religiosity. In the latter case, time slows down and ritual form conforms to doctrinal modes of religiosity. In both cases, at the limit of the function, temporal processing breaks down and yields the experience of timelessness.

Timelessness, in turn, yields two further forms of consciousness – a sense of being outside time and a sense of the meaning of time and history. The ritual then "invites" the participant to contemplate and commit to a timeless order referenced (in symbols, texts, images, myths, etc.) by the ritual. By their participation in a ritual display, participants also to some extent display commitment to its "reference" – this timeless order. This commitment is a "hard to fake" signal of commitment to a given outcome and order.

In addition to being costly signals, rituals help the individual to link his or her personal goals into a hierarchy of values that are linked to a transcendent order.

Interestingly, Rappaport (1989) points out that the "canonical messages" of the ritual when the god speaks directly or indirectly are most often not "indexical," but rather are "symbolic." These symbols give the self-referential messages their meaning by specifying that they are linked to a transcendent order or to what it is that the ritual achieves (e.g., a marriage or an initiation). It is the canonical messages that define the nature of the order and the god that the ritual participant seeks to identify with. The sacred order transcends the present moment, so the participant becomes aware of the past and the future and then likely ponders their meanings. The ritual participant is asked, invited, or urged to commit to and identify with not just the god but to the world history and order ordained by the gods.

In performing a ritual, Rappaport (1989) argues, a person accepts the canonical scheme governing the ritual and agrees to be bound by the obligations to the timeless order the ritual references. Crucially, this acceptance to be bound by the timeless order referenced by the ritual is not only something performers do in performing a ritual, but also something they indexically convey to others, who can from then on consider them persons who have accepted that order.

History, Tradition, and Lineage

The forms of temporal consciousness produced by ritual also concern eschatology or the meaning of history. It involves a reflection on the past, particularly the past that concerns the individual in question. For our ancestors, that past would have included the familial and clan lineage. This familial and clan lineage may be one origin of the totem animal.

A totem is typically an animal or a spiritual substance that is believed to watch over and protect the interests of generations of a clan or lineage. Totemistic beliefs and practices have been documented throughout much of the world and appear, along with ancestor worship, to be some of the early or root forms of religion. Indeed, totemism may be considered a form of ancestor worship as the totem animal or spirit was considered the progenitor and primary ancestor of the clan and lineage that it protected. Steadman and Palmer (2008) point out that "the most complex development of totemism known in the world is among the Australian Aboriginal peoples" (p. 73).

Basing themselves on Elkin's (1964) ethnographic observations, Steadman and Palmer (2008) note that "The 'clan' rituals performed by the Australians are mainly of three kinds (1) those involving the initiation of new cult members, 2) rituals that reenact the doings of the ancestral hero . . . and 3) magical rituals said to promote or increase the fertility of the totem animal or plant – the alleged 'codescendants' of the cult members – and perhaps even the fertility of the cult members themselves" (p. 78). Steadman and Palmer argue that the effect of such totemistic rituals is to identify those individuals who are your kin and to whom you should direct your altruistic activities. The worship of ancestors and the establishment of lineage-based ritual traditions increase the reproductive success of descendents of a particular ancestor.

Traditional religion, therefore, reflects a particularly long-term reproductive strategy – it focuses on transmitting genes not just to one's children but to one's great-grandchildren and their grandchildren as well!

The reverence for tradition and for history reflects the wisdom of invest-
ing in one's distant kin and descendents.

We now have excellent genetic evidence for the remarkable effectiveness of religious traditions and religious identity in facilitating transmittal
of genes down the generations. Take the case of the priestly Kohanim traditions within Judaism. Jewish tradition, based on the Torah, holds that
the Kohanim are direct descendants of Aaron, the brother of Moses and
the original Kohen. The line of the Kohanim is patrilineal: It has been
passed from father to son without interruption from Aaron, for 3,300
years, or more than 100 generations. Genetic analyses of Y chromosome
transmission patterns in Kohanim and non-Kohanim subjects revealed
that a particular marker was detected in 98.5 percent of the Kohanim,
and in a significantly lower percentage of non-Kohanim. A second set of
genetic markers that became known as the Cohen Modal Haplotype also
reliably picked out Kohanim versus non-Kohanim (Skorecki et al., 1997).

Ritual Decentering and Technical Intelligence

The reverence for tradition in premodern societies and among ancestral
populations may also be seen in the making of tools and crafts. Stone
tool making was handled by families and passed down through the generations in these families. The extreme influence of tradition on the evolution of stone tool technologies is seen in the faithfulness with which
tool types were reproduced from generation to generation. Paleolithic
stone technologies like the Oldowan and earlier Acheulean were associated with virtually identical tool kits that persisted for centuries. It is no
exaggeration to say that tool manufacturing was associated with craft traditions and religious traditions that persisted for hundreds of thousands
of years. The later Acheulean core forms that emerged ca. 500,000 before
the Paleolithic period were more innovative but nevertheless remained
distinctively "Acheulean" for tens of thousands of years.

Craftsmen learned the skill at the feet of a master, usually a relative,
and in the presence of the gods. As each tool was made, the gods were
invoked and the craftsmen went into an altered state of consciousness or,
more likely, a decentered state. The aim was to have the god or totem spirit

(rather than the individual craftsman) make the tool or the weapon. The residual effects of these ancient religious ways of creating a tool, weapon, or object is seen in testimonies by artists, engineers, and writers that a kind of muse took over and created the piece him- or herself with the artist just serving as a vehicle for transmission of the idea.

According to the Tukulor weavers in Africa, weaving has its origins in the spirit world, whence the craft was acquired by an ancestor and handed down to man in the time of myth. The weavers attribute their skill and their designs to knowledge acquired from jinn of the forest. Stout (2002) studied adze makers of the village of Langda in Indonesian Irian Jaya. He found that adze-making skill is acquired through a period of apprenticeship at the feet of a master that may last five years or more. Stout shows that "Adze production is itself a social phenomenon, defined as much by personal and group relations, social norms, and mythic significance as by specific reduction strategies and technical terminology" (Stout, 2002, p. 693). Religious ritual permeated the lives of traditional peoples and likely permeated the lives of ancestral populations. Given the integration of stone tool–making technologies into the religious rituals of the tribe, it is reasonable to assume that ritual influenced the development of technical intelligence in human beings.

The effects of religious rituals on early hominids and early human beings, therefore, must have been tremendous. These rituals created craftsmen and warriors, they created reverence for traditional ways and a sense of the past, they healed, and they enhanced group cohesion. Ritual was and is central to human life.

12 Life-Span Development of Religiosity and the Self

When I was a child, I spake as a child, I understood as a child, I thought as a child: but when I became a man, I put away childish things. For now we see through a glass, darkly; but then face to face: now I know in part; but then shall I know even as also I am known.

– St. Paul, 1 Cor. 13:11; King James Version

Introduction

We know quite a bit about the development of the Self and quite a bit about the development of religiosity, but we know very little about the development of religiosity in relation to the Self. Although there are many studies of religiousness and spirituality in children (e.g., Allport, 1950; Elkind, 1970; Goldman, 1964; Hyde, 1990; Rosengren, Johnson, & Harris, 2000; Tamminen, 1991) and several descriptive "stage models" (e.g., Fowler, 1991; Oser & Reich, 1990a, 1990b) about the development of aspects of religiosity such as "faith development" and "religious judgment," there are no systematic research data available, as far as I know, about the impact of the development of religiousness on the development of the Self. A few psychoanalytically oriented scholars (Coles, 1990; Rizzuto, 1991) have discussed the relationship of the development of God concepts to the development of a mature sense of Self, and these (along with the aforementioned studies on religious stages and cognition in children) have made it clear that religion and Self are tightly bound together in development. It is clear, therefore, that there is a relationship between Self and religiousness during development, but the nature of that relationship is unclear.

I have been arguing throughout this book that one of the functions of religiousness is to facilitate construction of an executive Self. If that argument is correct, then we would expect to see that construction of a strong sense of Self would more easily occur in children who are introduced to religion than in children not introduced to religion. As I have made clear, however, in earlier chapters, I am not suggesting that religion is the only way you can construct an executive Self. I am merely suggesting that it is one way and perhaps the preferred way for ancestral populations.

If my argument about religiousness and the Self is correct, then children who are able to use religious tools and ideology to construct their identity may be at an advantage in building an executive Self in certain respects relative to children who are prevented from using religious tools. There are indirect data that seem to support that claim. If we assume that impulse control and related self-regulatory functions are functions of the executive Self, then it becomes clear that religiosity enhances self-control in children and adolescents. Religiosity in children, for example, has been demonstrated to predict better school performance and lower levels of drinking, drug use, delinquency, and early sexual behavior (Donahue & Benson, 1995; National Center on Addiction and Substance Abuse [NCASA], 2001; Regnerus, 2007; Schmeltzer, 2002; Smith, 2003; Weaver et al., 1998). Bartkowski, Xu, and Levine (2007), for example, examined the links of parents' religiousness and their children's self-control and impulsivity among nearly 17,000 children (95 percent of whom were first-graders) from the Early Childhood Longitudinal Study. Bartkowski et al. found that parents who frequently attended church and who discussed religion in the home rated their children as having higher self-control and lower impulsiveness. The children of religious parents were also rated by their teachers as higher in self-control and lower in impulsiveness than children whose parents were less religious. These associations were obtained even when controlling for children's gender, ethnicity, and grade in school; parents' gender, employment status, age, and educational level; family income levels; a variety of family structure variables; and several other potential confounds.

In contrast, we should not be blind to potential dangers of inculcating toxic forms of religiosity in children's minds. Toxic forms of religiosity in my view include forms that teach the child to hate members of out-groups, mistrust their senses, denigrate the sciences, and instill purely punitive images of the deity. Religion is not always good for the child, but my reading of the available literature suggests that it usually is. In any case, we know so little about the impact of development of religiosity on sense of Self in children that all of the conclusions I reach in this chapter will need to be considered tentative at best. Nevertheless, it is necessary to evaluate whatever evidence exists with respect to the issues of Self and religion that I have been dealing with throughout this book. I begin with a question that one might have thought would have been settled long ago but appears to be far from settled at all. Do children need to be taught to be religious or are they born that way?

Acquisition of Religiousness

A 5-year-old little girl who has received no overt instruction about God or religion holds up a toy telephone to her mom and says, "God wants to tell you that he loves you very much and wants to talk with you every day...." The mom almost fearfully takes the toy telephone from the child and says, "Hello," but hears nothing but static and air in the phone's earpiece. This story is not at all unusual as any parent can tell you. Kids as young as 2 years old know about and can talk about God. They know about invisible beings that watch over them and those near them. Most importantly, they express consistent beliefs that a God created the natural world. Where do kids get these kinds of beliefs if their parents are not instructing them about God?

Presumably kids combine basic innate capacities to posit intentional states to visible and invisible beings and then, when exposed to an environment that occasionally references a powerful invisible being called

God, they use their innate cognitive capacities to generate thoughts and talk about God. Genes may also make a contribution.

Genetics of Religiousness

In a recent analysis of more than 500 identical and nonidentical twins, a group of investigators led by Laura Koenig, McGue, Krueger, and Bouchard (2005) at the University of Minnesota found that, during the transition from adolescence to adulthood, genetic factors increase in importance in determining level of religiosity whereas shared environmental factors decrease. In short, certain genes turn on during the adolescent period and influence religious interests and behaviors. There were other suggestive findings in the study: Consistent with the idea that genes influence religiosity levels, identical twins evidence similar patterns of religious interests and behaviors over time, whereas the nonidentical twins diverged as they got older.

Genes then clearly influence dispositions to be religious, but does this mean that there is a "God gene"? Debates about a "God gene" flared up when Dr. Dean Hamer (2004), chief of the Section on Gene Structure and Regulation at the National Institutes of Health, reported that people's ability to believe in a higher spiritual force was correlated with activity in the gene VMAT2. This gene codes for products that participate in the manufacture of serotonin and dopamine. We have already seen that serotonin and dopamine levels in the brain circuits determine the shape of the religious experience available to the individual. It is no wonder then that genes that regulate the manufacture of these neurotransmitters would be related to scores on a "spirituality" inventory.

Natural Born Theists?

If serotonin and dopamine levels in the appropriate brain circuit influence levels of religiosity in children and in adults, then it would not be surprising to find manifestations of religiosity in children. We know that the structures of the religion-related brain circuit (amygdala, frontal and anterior temporal) are already in place and communicating with one another by the age of 2 – although they are far from being fully developed at this early age. Very carefully designed experiments with children of various ages have consistently shown that children naturally suppose that a world of objects and forces is governed by teleological entities and that God exists and is watching over them.

A landmark experiment by Barrett, Richert, and Driesenga (2001) illustrates this predisposition to posit an omniscient God to explain the natural world. These investigators gave 3- to 5-year-olds so-called "false-belief tasks" – tests that putatively measure children's theory-of-mind abilities; that is, the ability to understand that other people have thoughts and intentions and that some of these thoughts may be mistaken regarding important events in the world. Theory-of-mind abilities normally appear at approximately 3 years of age. In adults and very likely in children as well, theory-of-mind abilities depend on the amygdala and the orbitofrontal cortex – two crucial structures in the religion circuit.

To do "theory-of-mind" processing, children must construct a model or theory or guess what is going on in the mind of others when they see these people behave inappropriately in the world. Children were shown a cracker box, asked what they believed it contained, allowed to peek inside and see the actual contents (pebbles), and then asked the test question, "What would someone (who had not been shown the pebbles) believe was inside the cracker box?" As is typical in such studies, Barrett et al. (2001) found that 3-year-olds failed the test, giving "pebbles" as the answer. In contrast, an increasing percentage of 4- and 5-year-olds passed, saying "crackers" – an answer recognizing the fallibility of beliefs. Interestingly, however, a different pattern emerged when these children were asked what God would believe. At all ages tested, children treated God as all-knowing, even when they clearly understood that earthly agents would have a false belief. Similar results have now also been obtained with Yucatec Mayan children (Atran, 2002; Knight, Sousa, Barrett, & Atran, 2004).

Keleman and her colleagues (e.g., DiYanni & Kelemen, 2005) have documented very early forms of teleological reasoning in children, with children assuming that a god created most of what they see. Similarly,

Evans (2000) demonstrated a creationist bias in children, even in secular households.

Children appear to use God concepts quite early in their development and often in the absence of any instruction from parents or other adults. I have argued that one source of God concepts is dreams. I now wish to suggest that a major source of God concepts for children comes from their dreams.

Dreaming in Childhood

In landmark longitudinal studies of the development of dreaming in children, Foulkes, Petrik, and Scott (1978) and Foulkes (1982, 1999) showed that children's dreams are characterized by relatively poor narrative structure and high levels of scenes of static images...typically of animals or people.

In the studies by Foulke, dream recall rates, not surprisingly, were predicted by age. Preschoolers reported dreams on only approximately 15 percent of awakenings, and the narratives were not actively self-oriented. Adolescents, in contrast, reported dreams on upwards of 80 percent of awakenings. Parents are invariably surprised when they hear the low dream recall rates reported by Foulkes. So, Resnick, Stickgold, Rittenhouse, and Hobson (1994) reinvestigated the issue. They had parents collect dream memories from their 4- to 10-year-old children. Before falling asleep, children were encouraged to remember their dreams. Parents awakened their children 15 minutes earlier than their usual wake-up time and asked for dream reports. Children as young as 4 and 5 years old were able to report their dreams in more than half of the awakenings. In addition, Resnick et al. reported that children's dreams were not lacking in narrative or particularly high in passive victimization.

There are obvious design limitations to this study, such as its demand characteristics...children want to please their parents, so they may be inventing dreams. In contrast, parents were convinced that their children were reporting real dreams, and the narratives apparently exhibited typical dream characteristics. If we assume that the truth about children's dreams lies somewhere between the Foulkes studies and studies such as those of Resnick et al., then we can conclude that the dream life of young children begins as soon as they can report on them and that victimization themes while present are not ubiquitous and that animals appear as characters in nearly every dream.

Strauch's (2005) longitudinal data set on children's dream content changes confirms this general picture. Dream recall rates increase as the child gets older, with boys lagging behind girls until middle childhood, when they catch up with girls. Dreams in both girls and boys become more realistic and complex, with the dreamer taking a more active role in the dream scenario and interacting with other dream characters more frequently.

I could identify only one study of dreaming in children that directly mentions supernatural beings. Adams (2005) identified and analyzed dreams of children that reportedly contained spoken content or auditory messages. She reported that Christian, Muslim, and secular or unaffiliated children had auditory message dreams with similar themes. Their dreams brought divine messages that gave them reassurance, predictions of future events, life directions, and guidance on mundane stresses, such as homework and peer conflicts.

The Special Role of "Supernatural Agents" and Monsters in Children's Nightmares

Preschool and older children who report dreams also report imaginary friends and fear of imaginary beings such as ghosts, monsters, and beings in the dark. It was originally believed that as children got older, nonhuman agents began to disappear from children's dreams. This supposition was based on the fact that fear of imaginary beings tends to decrease with age across the childhood years.

Bauer (1976) studied the nighttime fears of 4- to 6-, 6- to 8-, and 10- to 12-year-old children ($N = 54$). Seventy-four percent of the 4- to 6-year-olds, 53% of the 6- to 8-year-olds, but only 5% of the 10- to 12-year-olds reported fears of ghosts and monsters. These age-related differences were also reflected in the description of scary dreams reported by the younger and older children. The younger children reported that appearances of monsters caused their fear, whereas the older children imputed harmful actions to the monsters. In both age groups, however, supernatural agents and scary monsters were the objects of children's fears – although fear of imaginary beings was less likely in the older groups than in the younger children.

Taken together, the studies conducted by developmental psychologists on the development of religious ideas in children suggest that God concepts are available to and are used extensively by children as young as 4 years old – perhaps even younger if we can believe the dreams children share with adults. What could possibly be the evolutionary background to an early appearance of God experiences in children?

Evolution of Childhood

Humans are unique relative to other animals in that we exhibit a developmental period of "childhood" inserted between the developmental periods of "infancy" and "puberty." How and why did childhood evolve?

Childhood is defined by specialists via several developmental characteristics, including a slowing and stabilization of the rate of growth relative to the period of infancy, dependence on older people for food, propensity for play, and immature motor control. Brain growth peaks at about seven years (Cabana, Jolicouer, & Michaud, 1993), with a small increase occurring later at puberty (Durston et al., 2001; Sowell, Thompson, Tessner, & Toga, 2001). Myelination of neurons and some neuronal and synaptic proliferation continue into adulthood (Bjorklund & Pellegrini, 2002; Taupin & Gage, 2002).

Childhood commences with the end of nursing and the beginning of a different kind of dependency on adults or older individuals. Specifically, dependency on the mother lessens (but does not cease), and dependency on other adults increases. Anthropological data suggest that most children in premodern societies were/are weaned before their third birthday (Sellen & Smay, 2001), with supplemental foods introduced early, usually within the first six months (e.g., Dupras, Schwarcz, & Fairgrieve, 2001; Waterlow, Ashworth, & Griffiths, 1980; Winikoff, Durongdej, & Cerf,

1988). Thus, other adults besides the mother must step in to provide the child with food when the child is approximately 3–4 years old.

The two most important of these older adults from an evolutionary point of view was the grandparent (usually grandmother) and the father. The switch in child care responsibilities from the mother to other adults (and perhaps older siblings of the child) meant that the mother could now devote more of her resources to having another child. The evolutionary value of childhood, therefore, lay in the mother's freedom to initiate a new pregnancy because she could pass care of the current child to trusted others. Doing so enhanced the mother's reproductive fitness without increasing the costs to her infant or older children.

These trusted others who care for the child are highly skilled in providing specially prepared foods that are high in energy and nutrients until self-care becomes possible, and in various hunter–gatherer societies this is what is done (Blurton Jones, 1993; Estioko-Griffin, 1986; Hewlett, 1991). Summarizing the data from many human societies, J. B. Lancaster and C. S. Lancaster (1983) called this type of child care and feeding "the hominid adaptation," for no other primate or mammal is so actively involved in these ways in providing for the young. For humans, early weaning (by three years) reduces the birth interval and allows the mother to successfully produce two offspring in the time it takes chimpanzees and orangutans to successfully rear one. Thus, we see childhood as a suite of adaptations that enhances maternal reproductive fitness.

Cognitive and Psychological Growth of the Child

In what has come to be known as the "five to seven year shift" (Sameroff & Haith, 1996), new learning and behavioral capabilities emerge, including development of so-called higher-order theory-of-mind abilities, in which children can understand that person X thinks that person Y is thinking that Z and so forth. These theory-of-mind abilities development in concert and partially depend on the amazing capacity for language learning evident in children. When children learn languages, they learn them without tremendous effort or instruction. Surely the learning of language constitutes one of the great cognitive achievements of childhood.

Play, Religion, and Self

Religion tends to be a serious matter – even for children – yet children spend a lot of time just playing around. The childhood period, in fact, is characterized by abundant amounts of play. Pretend play, in particular, is favored and appears to be a uniquely human form of play. All forms of play (pretend, rough and tumble, etc.) emerge in toddlerhood, peak in the childhood/juvenile period, and fall off rapidly as sexual maturity is approached. Religious development appears to follow an opposite course. It emerges slowly in the childhood/juvenile period but then peaks during adolescence and then flowers in adulthood up to and including old age. Whereas play predominates in childhood and is nonserious, religion predominates in adolescence and adulthood and is a serious business.

Development of the Sense of Self in Children

Another area in which the child is doing an enormous amount of developmental work is in the development of the sense of Self or identity. The Self-concept, including the dream ego, is therefore correspondingly weak. Children have a fragile sense of Self – or at least a sense of a fluid and developing Self. There is obviously no way to get anything like a clear picture of the impact of religiousness on development of the Self in children without first looking more carefully into how the Self develops in children.

I cannot possibly summarize the vast literature on the development of Self in children. I am interested here in a more modest look at the sense of the strength of ego or Self... intimations of the development of an executive Self – that thing, ability, construct, ability, or social process that allows children to regulate their impulses and their goals.

Loevinger, Wessler, and Redmore (1970) and Loevinger (1976) used a sentence completion procedure to gather data on the development of what I would call ego strength. She and her colleagues (Loevinger et al., 1970) utilized 36 sentence stems such as "The thing I like about myself is...," "What gets me into trouble is...," "I am...," and so forth. After testing hundreds of subjects, Loevinger et al. devised a coding system based on thousands of responses for each stem. The responses were classified into separate categories that seemed to reflect stable personality traits or modes of responding. Loevinger then noticed that these modes were characteristically associated with different age groups and so probably reflected distinct stages in the development of the sense of Self.

The general picture that emerges from Loevinger's analyses of self-development might best be illustrated with a description of typical response modes associated with the "I am . . . " stem. Impulsive personalities (classified as I-2) do not reflect on their responses but tend to provide short, simple, and uninformative responses such as "I am nice" or "I am tall." These young children tend to dichotomize all events into good and evil categories and do not consider the complexities of social life. They are concerned only with themselves rather than the world. At the next stage of ego development ("delta" transitional) the individual seems to become more aware of the world around him or her but has no sense of the complexities of the world. There is an ego there but it is small, weak, and fragile. It needs to be protected. The child is suspicious, self-protective, and opportunistic. He or she eschews responsibility and is preoccupied with staying out of trouble. His or her humor is often hostile and rejecting. The next (I-3) stage of development involves a broad socializing trend. The child turns toward the world but often in a conformist way. He describes himself only in socially acceptable terms. He or she uses a kind of self-deprecating and ingratiating humor: for example, "I am a big mouth" or "I am such a . . . " He or she uses broad, sweeping generalizations to describe others and relies on formulistic and stereotyped responses in social interactions. His or her focus concerning Self is concrete and oriented toward his or her physical appearance.

The next stage (I-3/4) involves a series of responses that are transitional between conformism and the I-4 stage: "conscientious." The I-3/4 transitional stage is characterized by self-criticism and self-consciousness. The child's view of the world and him- or herself is now richer and more nuanced, but negative reactions to Self predominate. The Self is strong enough to reflect some complexity and to undergo some attacks but not strong enough to see the self-attacks as harsh and unjustified. No simple straightforward responses are given to the "I am . . . " stem. Instead, one gets responses such as "I am . . . not like anyone else." The next stage, I-4, is dubbed "conscientious." There is a rich inner life and true conceptual complexity. The child has a strong sense of responsibility and has developed a moral sense and standards of excellence. There is a general awareness and orientation toward long-term goals and a restlessness and impatience to reach them. The I-4/5 transitional stage is characterized by complex responses. The child provides nuanced and contradictory descriptions of self. The teenager tries on all sorts of new identities and is happy with none of them. There is a tendency to try to justify all of one's responses. The I-5 "autonomy" stage is usually not reached until adulthood and is characterized by the ability to balance dimensions of personality that seem to be in conflict. The individual cultivates a rich array of preferences, inclinations, and behaviors but may not be able to integrate, and thus be enriched by, all these options. The last stage (I-6) is characterized by "integration." Here the individual, presumably a young adult, harmoniously balances opposing tendencies within him- or herself. He or she enjoys a rich internal life but is oriented to the world and sees service to others as his greatest concern.

Summary of the Transition from Childhood to Executive Self

In summary, early childhood is characterized for the child by a switch in dependency from the mother to the father and/or other adults and by an enormous investment of time and energy into learning very advanced cognitive skills including theory-of-mind skills, language skills, and personal memory skills and (most importantly) developing a sense of Self or identity. The ego or sense of Self in childhood is fragile . . . but Loevinger and associates describe a process of self-development that eventuates in conscientiousness and integration – or a central executive Self that can balance and mediate between opposing points of view and conflicting desires.

The transition from the maternal to the paternal sphere, from breast-feeding to eating solid food provided by other adults besides the mother, must involve a huge psychological adjustment for the child. As has often been pointed out, the mother shares half her genes with her child, whereas the father (given paternity uncertainty) may not. The father had to be made to believe that the child was his. The child could help to do this by developing cognitive and emotional specializations to relate to the psychology of the potential father. These specializations likely involved signaling genetic fitness and genetic likeness as well as emitting signals that elicited love and care from the father. Presumably the acquisition of theory-of-mind abilities, language skills, and a "sense of Self" facilitated father–child and adult–child interactions more broadly.

The acquisition of theory-of-mind skills must have created mental opportunities for the child that allowed for prediction and manipulation of the adults around him. These skills also must have involved a dawning realization that all kinds of mental agents were "out there" and that these mental agents carry a variety of intentions toward the child. Among these intentional agents must have been imaginary nonhuman agents, and these agents populated both the imagination and the child's dream life.

Similarly, the development of language skills also likely facilitated interactions with adults besides the mother. The mother will feed the child whether or not he or she speaks to the mother. Speaking of course helps, but the mother does not require extra coaxing to feed her offspring. She will do so instinctively. The father, in contrast, does require extra coaxing, and language must have helped the child in this respect. Language also gave the child access to other adults. With language, the child can interact with anyone. Without language, his effective interactions are confined to the mother, whereas all other interactions will be labored and difficult.

Finally, the sense of Self greatly enhances the child's ability to socially interact with all kinds of others. The three great developmental achievements of childhood – "theory of mind," language, and "the sense of Self" – all have as their apparent aim the enhancement of the ability of the child to interact socially with others, particularly adult others. The enhanced ability to interact with others was vital to the child's survival, given his or her dependence on these others for food. How would religiousness fit in here? I suggest that religiousness facilitated development of the sense of Self and that the "Self" was particularly important vis-à-vis interactions with the father and other male adults. If early emerging signs of a strong sense of Self signaled strength and fitness, the child was likely to retain the goodwill of the males in the tribe; this could make all the difference in survival during rough times.

Freud and many other scholars have pointed out that most gods are male and have explained the predominance of male gods as rooted ultimately in emotionally charged interactions with the father. They may have been partially correct, but it was not so much that children turned their fathers and other male adults into gods out of some sublimation process, but rather that children used religiousness to create and fashion a thing we call the Self so as to influence the behavior of adults, particularly dangerous adult males.

Adolescence

We have seen in previous chapters that the primary neurocognitive networks that subserve religiosity are in the frontal and temporal lobes. When a child reaches adolescence, his or her frontal and temporal lobes come fully "on-line." These cortical sites become more fully myelinated so that communication with them and between them is more efficient and reliable. Not surprisingly, therefore, religiosity levels generally increase in adolescents, particularly in those with even minimal exposure to religious ideas. In all but modern secular societies, adolescents evidence an interest in religious topics and rites and, as we have seen in previous chapters, often have to undergo religious initiation rites to become full members of the community or tribe.

Adolescent rites of passage are found in 70 percent of the world's societies and occur in cultures as diverse as Australian hunter–gatherers, African agriculturalists, and American industrialists (Lutkehaus & Roscoe, 1995). Interestingly, during these religious rites, music plays a central role. Adolescent interest in music is universal (Alcorta, 2006).

In traditional cultures, rites of initiation turned a child into an adult, and they were always religious ceremonies. Gods, ancestors, or some other supernatural agents were invariably involved in the ceremonies. One of the things that the initiate is instructed in is the religious myths, rituals, or doctrines of the community (Schlegel & Barry, 1991). In addition, puberty rites usually involve some intense – even harrowing – challenge or ordeal for boys who are to become men, particularly in societies that have seen war. Because most human societies have experienced war, most human societies have had harrowing initiation rites for boys. Religion was the only force that could produce a man and a warrior out of a boy.

These initiation rites also likely facilitated development of executive cognitive functions (ECFs), as ECFs are known to come fully on-line in most individuals during adolescence. ECFs allow for inhibition of impulses, delay of gratification of wishes, and thus accurate planning for long-term future rewards versus impulsive indulgence in immediate short-term and more salient rewards.

ECFs typically develop across childhood and then plateau after puberty. Brocki and Bohlin (2004) assessed a variety of ECFs in children and adolescents and then conducted dimensional analyses on performance scores. The dimension interpreted as Speed/Arousal seemed to be the first one to reach maturity, with the most active period of development occurring around the age of 8. The "withholding" dimension of inhibition matured around age 10, along with the first developmental spurt on a "Fluency" factor. The second developmental spurt on Working memory/Fluency continued into adolescence. Levin et al. (1991) found an increased ability to inhibit responses with increasing age on the go/no-go test of impulsivity in a normal sample. Impulsive errors (commissions) declined steadily up to adolescence and then plateaued out. Luciana, Conklin, Hooper, and Yarger (2005) asserted a similar pattern of steady improvement and then a leveling off after puberty for planning and working memory tasks.

These neuropsychologic results are consistent with a host of recent neuroimaging studies of the developing brain (reviewed in Blakemore, den Ouden, Choudhury, & Frith, 2007 and Paus et al., 2001). Both gray- and white-matter volumes increase in most brain regions until puberty. After puberty, gray-matter volumes do not change significantly, whereas white-matter volumes continue to increase. Giedd and coworkers (1999) observed a linear increase in gray-matter volume in the parietal and frontal regions between 4 years of age and the approximate age of onset for puberty. In girls, the asymptote for these anatomical developments was at 10.2 years in the parietal cortex and 11.0 years in the frontal cortex. For boys, the asymptotic ages were 11.8 years and 12.1 years for the two respective areas.

The maturation in adolescence of the brain circuits (frontal and temporal lobes) that normally mediate ECFs, the Self, and religious experiences is consistent with the claim that I have made in these book regarding the impact of religiousness on the development of the executive Self. That impact is seen in stark relief in adolescence. The brain development is of course a prerequisite for development of Self, ECFs, and religiousness. Interestingly, it is during adolescence when schizophrenia makes its appearance. Schizophrenia is an adolescent-onset disease and involves dysfunction precisely within the temporal and prefrontal cortices. These brain regions do not develop normally in adolescence. One of the most common delusions associated with schizophrenia is religious delusions. Up to 70 percent of persons with schizophrenia experience auditory hallucinations involving the voice of God or some other supernatural agent, and 90 percent experience delusions at some point in the course of their illness. These delusions very often involve religious themes. Rarely, the patient may hear supernatural or demonic voices that command the patient to harm him- or herself or others.

Transition to Adulthood

In any case, under normal conditions, brain regions implicated in religiosity in adults become fully operational in adolescence, and expressions of religiosity, music, poetry, and sexuality flourish together during this period. With the onset of young adulthood, however, the dorsolateral prefrontal lobes become fully myelinated and they send inhibitory fibers down onto orbitofrontal and anterior temporal regions. This inhibition of orbitofrontal and anterior temporal cortex allows for adult-appropriate behaviors, inhibition of sexual impulses, and inhibition of the religion-related regions more generally. The individual now settles on a life course. He or she ceases his search for a purpose or mission. He or she leaves the realm of lush myth, luxuriant sexual imagery, and ecstatic musical and mystical experiences and gradually learns to ignore the promptings and lures of the religious realm. Instead, these realms are to a certain extent tamed under the suppressive and inhibitory powers of the newly developed prefrontal networks that come fully on-line in young adulthood. Under special conditions of ritual, drugs, or devotional practices, the religion-related brain circuits (e.g., amygdala, orbitofrontal, and anterior temporal) will overwhelm dorsal prefrontal inhibitory powers for small amounts of time during adult life, but the circuit will need to wait until old age before the prefrontal networks begin to relax their "grip" and their suppressive powers dissolve. When that happens, the religion circuit will reemerge – except this time in the context of the wisdom of decades of experience that comes with old age.

Old Age

Individuals with the highest levels of religious intelligence and religious commitment tend to be elderly individuals. This was especially the case in ancient and premodern societies. The elders knew best how to tell the religious stories and to perform the religious rituals.

Why are elders often the carriers of religious tradition? Perhaps one proximate factor is that the religion-related brain circuit is released from the inhibition under which it is put during young and middle adulthood. Why has Mother Nature allowed a re-emergence of the full-blown religion in old age? What good does it do?

As discussed earlier in this chapter, humans have a unique life history. We have a juvenile period that is 1.4 times longer than that of chimpanzees and a mean adult life span that is 2.5 times longer than that of chimpanzees. The reason that humans have a long life span relative to that of the other primates is because of the assistance of males and grandparents in providing food to the young and of older men and women in rearing the young. Among human beings, elders participate in child care, and this has allowed for a prolonged juvenile period and the huge growth of the human brain. One possibility is that Mother Nature wants the very wise to instruct the very young. To be really wise, however, you need religion.

13 The Evolution of Self and Religion

Every man who has reached even his intellectual teens begins to suspect that life is no farce; that it is not genteel comedy even; that it flowers and fructifies on the contrary out of the profoundest tragic depths of the essential dearth in which its subject's roots are plunged. The natural inheritance of anyone who is capable of spiritual life is an unsubdued forest where the wolf howls and the obscene bird of night chatters.

– Henry James, Sr., 1866, p. 75

Introduction

I have presented evidence in this book that amygdalar, prefrontal, and anterior temporal networks, particularly on the right side, mediate religious experience and core aspects of the sense of Self. The anatomical overlap between religion and Self could be merely fortuitous or it could be functional. I have argued that religion, among many other things, functions, in fact, to construct an executive Self – an autonomous, self-regulating, mature individual. Among its myriad functions, religion can be considered a biocultural system that facilitates maturation of autonomous individual, each of whom is capable of experiencing a unified sense of Self. To that extent, then, religion is an engine that enhances consciousness and self-consciousness in particular.

In previous chapters, I have argued that a unified sense of Self, an "executive" Self, is valuable from an evolutionary point of view for the following reasons: 1) a unified Self may be more effective in pursuing behavioral goals than a disunified, conflicted Self, 2) a unified Self may be more effective at signaling intent (e.g., to cooperate) to others than a disunified Self, 3) a unified Self may be more effective than a disunified Self in evading predators, 4) a unified executive Self would be more effective in combat and war than a disunified Self, and 5) a unified Self would more effectively focus a variety of Mind/brain capacities on a single problem than would a less centralized or disunified Self.

A unified executive Self could also function as a signaling device or system. Constructing a unified Self is difficult and presumably metabolically costly. It takes years to construct. It requires work to keep it functioning. Maintaining a centralized executive Self would require, at a minimum, suppression of competing desires and tendencies; thus, it would require increased inhibitory capacities and, by implication, enhanced cellular capacity in the orbitofrontal, dorsolateral, and anterior temporal lobes – brain sites known to specialize in inhibitory control of other regions (Bjorklund & Harnishfeger, 1995; Dagenbach & Carr, 1994; Dempster & Brainerd, 1995; Starkstein & Robinson, 1999). Because it is costly to construct the Self, the centralized Self could function as a "costly signal" to others.* The more highly committed, the more work one has put into creating such a Self, the greater the stake in the religious group, and therefore the greater the hostility to threats to the group's well-being. Like the peacock's tail that signals genetic fitness because it can develop and maintain such a costly ornament, the Self too can be considered a kind of costly ornament that signals the capacity for prolonged use of metabolic resources and effort under adverse conditions – and thus genetic fitness. I suggest that religion constructs this centralized executive Self. It may be that one reason that religion evolved and evolved in the way it did was to bring to birth this unified sense of Self, this unified self-consciousness known as the "executive" Self.

---

* An anonymous reviewer of this work pointed out that this theory would predict greater out-group hostility among those persons least able to defect from their tradition.

I want, in this chapter, to draw out some implications of this view on religion's role vis-à-vis the executive Self for the evolution of religion itself. I begin by summarizing some of the debates and data on the evolution of religion.

Evolution of Religion

Debates on the evolutionary status of religion have taken on a hugely controversial character with some authors prematurely proclaiming religion an unfortunate by-product of more useful cognitive capacities of the human mind. Other investigators have pointed out that the debates on the evolutionary status of religion are far from over.

The stakes are huge. The outcome of this debate will influence how religion is regarded in civil society for decades to come. If religion is regarded as a dangerous by-product of other cognitive functions (i.e., as a delusion or as a kind of trance or "spell"), then it makes sense to pass legislation limiting its expression as many communist countries did in the past. If religion is regarded as a classical biological adaptation then it very likely has a significant function for individuals and for human society more generally. In that case, the argument that religion should receive legislative protections would be bolstered. Everyone in society, therefore, has a stake in the outcome of these debates.

Is Religiousness an Adaptation?

One major question concerning the evolutionary history of religion is whether any aspect of religiousness can be considered an adaptation.

To qualify as an adaptation, most evolutionary biologists and evolutionary psychologists would say that the trait in question would need to exhibit evidence that it was designed to solve a fitness-related problem for ancestral populations. Evidence of design in the human context, in turn, could entail: 1) universality across cultures, 2) relative effortlessness of acquisition of the trait (the trait is not learned via laborious study), and 3) an associated "biology," which refers to a consistent set of physiologic systems that reliably support, mediate, and produce the trait or behavior in question (see Harris & McNamara, 2008). A "biology" of a human trait that functions as an adaptation would, in turn, likely include 1) a genetic component as evidenced by gene–behavior correlations and heritability studies, 2) a brain component as evidenced by classical neuropsychology and neuroimaging studies, and 3) a chemistry component as evidenced by pharmacologic studies.

When we examine the biologic basis of religiousness we are presumably examining the proximate mechanisms by which religiousness is realized. Details on the proximate mechanisms of an adaptive trait, in turn, can give us vital clues as to both the function and design complexity of the trait.

It is important to note that the design of a trait does not have to be "optimal" from an engineering perspective to qualify as an adaptation. Often sexual selection drives functional traits into seemingly maladaptive or wasteful spaces (like the secondary sexual organs). Instead, the trait has to be designed reasonably well to solve a problem faced by ancestral populations.

It is reasonable to suppose that religion is an adaptation. The practice of religious rituals and belief in supernatural agents occurs in virtually all human cultures (Brown, 1991; Murdock, 1965). When Murdock chose a sample of 186 societies to represent the full range of human experience in various types of societies, religious rituals and beliefs in supernatural agents occurred in all of them (Johnson, 2005; Murdock & White, 1969). Children do not need to be force-fed religiousness to posit supernatural beliefs. They do so spontaneously. I have argued in previous chapters that one source of these supernatural agent concepts is the experience of beings, animals, relatives, and unfamiliar characters in dreams. Children eventually spontaneously posit an omniscient supernatural agent. Developmental psychologists have found that children spontaneously ascribe omniscience to God – He can see all, can know all, and cannot be fooled by standard theory of mind and false belief tasks (Barrett, Richert, & Driesenga, 2001; Bering & Bjorklund, 2004; Kelemen, 2004). Religiousness is partly heritable. D'Onofrio, Eaves, Murrelle, Maes, & Spilka (1999) Koenig and Bouchard (2006) have reviewed the literature on the heritability of religiousness and found that religiousness exhibits a moderate to high heritability coefficient ($h^2 = 0.28$–0.72; the 0.72 heritability coefficient refers to religious fundamentalists). Religiousness "has" a biology. It is associated with a consistent set of processing systems in the brain. The serotoninergic and dopaminergic systems of the prefrontal and temporal lobes appear to be key nodes in a widely distributed neural network that supports religious experiences and behaviors. Drugs that address this neural network (i.e., that enhance dopamine transmission and decrease serotonin transmission) can induce religious experiences in persons who are well disposed to religiousness or spirituality. Drugs that block dopamine transmission can reduce religiously tinted delusions in various psychiatric populations (Nichols & Chemel, 2006). Disorders that affect this brain circuit also affect religiousness. In short, religiousness appears to be associated with a complex set of cognitive systems and supporting brain circuits that are dedicated to processing information related to religion and Self.

Taking these various strands of evidence together, as well as all of the evidence presented in this book, we can conclude that religiousness, insofar as it concerns the Self, exhibits design complexity and therefore could be adaptive.

For those scientists like me who think that all this evidence supports some variant of an adaptationist position, the questions shift to what part of religiousness is actually adaptive and what functions might religiousness enact? My answer is that religion's impact on the problems associated with the Self, Will, or consciousness is adaptive. Some investigators suggest that the aspect of religiousness that was "selected" over evolutionary history was the capacity for trance, placebo responding, or altered states of consciousness. The capacity for trance, placebo responding, and altered states of consciousness, of course, would yield both health benefits and arational or even irrational belief states over time. I have argued that the capacity for trance and related states are all capacities of the Self or more precisely of the divided Self, so we must take the Self into account when discussing the evolutionary history of religion. Other theorists suggest that the aspect of religiousness that was selected over evolutionary history was its ability, primarily via ritual displays and other "costly signals," to solve the free-rider problem (in which unscrupulous individuals exploit the benefits of group cooperation without paying any of the costs of that cooperation) and thereby promote cooperation among individuals within early human groups. I have pointed out that religion first solves cooperative dilemmas within the individual and that that step is a prerequisite for creating the cognitive powers to suppress free-rider behavioral strategies, thus allowing the individual to signal prosocial intentions such as the willingness and capacity to cooperate with others.

Other theorists who tilt toward some kind of adaptationist position emphasize both costly signaling theory as well as gene–culture interactions to explain particular associations of religiosity, such as its ability to promote character strengths, its ability to protect against death-related fears, its ability to generate life meanings, its ability to address attachment needs, its links with the sources and phenomenology of dreams, and its similarities to special perceptual capacities of the aesthetic sense. Again, all of these latter capacities are capacities of the Self, so the Self needs to be brought into the discussion.

If it is reasonable to entertain the possibility that religiousness is an adaptation, what does that imply for the evaluation of religion itself? First, it suggests that when authors dismiss religion as a dangerous delusion, they are probably wrong to do so. Indeed, if religion is an adaptation, it likely is not a delusion or an illusion. That does not mean that some adaptations cannot eventuate in delusional beliefs (such as incorrigible optimism in the face of bleak facts), only that they are less likely to do so ... most adaptations produce fairly reliable estimates of reality or fairly effective and functional behavioral systems.

Instead, if religion is an adaptation, it suggests that religion solved some problem for our ancestors and may be solving some problem for humanity even today. Religion has for centuries generated public rituals and dogmatic traditions that have presided over millions of births, weddings, and deaths. Established religions and their attendant rituals and dogmatic traditions are the result of centuries of work by nature and flawed human beings. They are a collaboration between nature and humanity. They are often not pretty, but they are always, like nature itself, protean, wild, elaborate, and functional.

The Cultural Evolution of Religion

If we proceed with the "religion as an adaptation" premise, a number of tasks suggest themselves. First, because religion is both a generator of cultural artifacts and is shaped by culture itself, we will need to embed the theory of religion within a broader "evolution of culture" scholarship (Boyd & Richerson, 1996; Boyd, Richerson, Borgerhoff-Mulder, & Durham, 1997; Cavalli-Sforza, 1998; O'Brien & Lyman, 2000; O'Brien, Darwent, & Lyman, 2001; O'Brien et al., 2002; Shennan, 2002; Shennan & Wilkinson, 2001).

Boyd et al. (1997) summarized extant models of cultural evolution. These models reduce to three major alternatives. One model involves only vertical transmission of cultural elements from one generation to the next and that inherited information is transmitted via social learning of children from elders. Another model proposes the exact opposite of the first. With culture, no vertical transmission occurs – instead, all cultural information is transmitted horizontally in a sort of epidemiologic spread of cultural units. Intermediate models of cultural evolution propose a mix of vertically and horizontally transmitted units of information.

To decide between these models of cultural, in this case religious, evolution, we will need to look at the expression of religious experience across cultures and through the archaeological and historical records. It is vitally important to identify elements that are vertically transmitted and differentiate them from elements that are horizontally transmitted because each form of transmission has its own laws, tendencies, dynamics, and functional effects. Religion very likely exhibits both vertical transmission and horizontal transmission of religious ideologies and practices. What is crucial, of course, is differentiating the two: Which elements are vertically transmitted and which are horizontally transmitted? Are rituals, for example, vertically transmitted and conserved across generations, while ideologies are horizontally transmitted? Cladistic methodology is used to analyze phylogenetic relationships in lineages that are recognized by the presence of shared and derived (advanced) characteristics. When cladistic methodology is supplemented with the advanced statistical tools of "phylogenetic analysis," you get precise and powerful techniques for identifying vertical versus horizontal forms of transmission and reconstructing evolutionary history. These techniques have now been successfully used in the cultural arena (e.g., see the essays in Mace, Holden, & Shennan, 2006).

Scholars of ritual and religious practices have now amassed a huge amount of data on the historical development of ritual practices and on ritual practices in premodern human groups. There may be, therefore, enough data to reconstruct the evolutionary history of ritual practices in certain human lineages.

If we can construct a phylogeny of some ritual practices in some cultural groups, then it may be possible to determine what those ritual practices are correlated with over time. If there are, for example, enough data available on the history of religious ritual practices in various cultural groups defined by a language family the phylogeny of which is known and enough historical data available on various forms of healing practices or cooperative enterprises (e.g., farming or herding), it may be possible to assess change in ritual practices against change in these other forms of human activity. By superimposing phenotypic features (e.g., ritual practices) over accepted language phylogenies, one can reconstruct the history of evolutionary change in ritual practices as well as potential correlated change in health or in cooperative practices. Thus, hypotheses about potential adaptive functions of key aspects of religiousness may be tested quantitatively using these sorts of methods. With these sorts of methods, one could also potentially assess whether some aspect of religiousness (e.g., ritual practices) fit criteria for an adaptation or an exaptation. An adaptation involves the modification of a phenotypic feature (e.g., a particular ritual practice) that accompanies or parallels an evolutionary acquisition of a function (new healing practices or new forms of cooperation). However, in exaptation, the feature originates first rather than in parallel and only later is co-opted for the function in question. In short, because phylogenetic analysis involves quantitative reconstruction and analysis of histories of shared and derived traits, it provides powerful methods for identification of potential adaptive functions of religion.

To my knowledge, no phylogenetic analyses of religious cultural evolution have yet been published. Instead, we have intriguing cross-cultural analyses of religion in relation to key functional variables.

Evolution of the Self

As many scholars have pointed out, the Self is a social and cultural construct. It emerges out of the social interactions that children and young adults undergo throughout their lives. It is maintained and updated within the social context of the adult. Whereas the Self is certainly rooted in genetically shaped biologic potencies, these biologic roots are in turn manifested in and shaped by social and cultural interactions. The brain regions that mediate various component processes of the Self are also influenced by social processes. I have argued throughout this book that the Self is a construct with functional antecedents and effects. It is an accomplishment of the individual and his or her social milieu. It is influenced by mechanisms of social prestige – the more prestige it accumulates, the greater its fitness. Construction of an executive Self is an arduous process that requires years of effort. The effort signals fitness, and the existence of a unified sense of Self, in the past, must have been a signal of power and prestige. In the past, construction of the Self also required the help of religion. This is still true for most of the world's population who use religion for personal ends. Indeed, construction of a unified consciousness may have been one of religion's prime functional aims. Whether that is the case, there can be little doubt that the executive Self has an evolutionary history bound up with the evolutionary history of religion.

The evolutionary roots of the Self have been examined via the window of "self-awareness" or the ability to monitor one's own bodily or mental state. Self-awareness appears to be a relatively recent evolutionary innovation dependent upon complex brain structures and thus limited to the great apes (e.g., Gallup, 1970) and dolphins (Marino, 2006). In previous chapters I have presented evidence that self-awareness is mediated by right prefrontal and anterior temporal cortical networks. For example, neurologic patients with damage in the right hemisphere typically exhibit symptoms of "neglect." They fail to attend to one-half of their bodies or their attentional space; they are sometimes unaware of any illness at all (anosognosia); they may neglect one particular body region or part (asomatognosia); or they may be unable to recognize themselves in a mirror (autoprosopagnosia) (see Keenan et al., 2005). Right prefrontal lesions also may be associated with inability to efficiently retrieve autobiographical memories. One way the executive Self is constructed is via editing of autobiographical memories. In general, autobiographical memory is constructed by retrieving a set of memories/episodes that can match the current self-model and its goals (Conway & Pleydell-Pearce, 2000). Memory is, to some extent, in service to the Self and its goals.

Where did this ability to use memory to construct an executive Self come from? In evolutionary history, prospects for agile use of cognitive systems to construct an executive Self very likely improved when human beings acquired language. Crow (2000) points out that Buehler argued that the structure of language has, at its core, a deictic origin of the "I, here, and now" and that language is built around this origin. In effect, just as is the case with religion, Self and language also appear to have co-evolved, with each shaping and influencing the further evolution of the other.

Crow (2000) argued that the evolutionary acquisition of language created a cerebral torque such that:

> [t]he anatomical disposition of the torque along the anteroposterior axis allows the motor and sensory engrams in Broca's and Wernicke's area respectively to interact with differing polarities with the corresponding areas of heteromodal association cortex in the non-dominant hemisphere. Thus language is conceived as a bihemispheric phenomenon with a deictic focus in Broca's area and its relationship on the one hand to the internal word of thoughts in the right dorsolateral prefrontal cortex and on the other hand to the external world of perceived speech in Wernicke's area. In this way can be conceptualised the critical role of the self in the origin of language and the phenomena of psychosis (Crow, 2000).

Crow's hypothesis on the cerebral torque points to another source of the sense of Self – inner speech. Formulation of language plans begins in the prefrontal lobes and in the right prefrontal cortex in particular. This capacity for inner speech contributes to the sense of Self, and it allows for manipulation of autobiographical memories in such a way as to fit a narrative about the Self that facilitates development of an executive, "in control," Self construct.

In summary, the evolution of Self-awareness appears to be dependent upon large and complex brains given that self-awareness is found only in apes, humans, and dolphins. In humans, however, self-awareness also evolved into what we now call a centralized executive Self. Instead of just a passive awareness of Self, the executive Self claims that it has agency and can guide behavioral goals of the individual. The first boost to this centralized executive Self likely came from rudiments of ritual among early humans and among Neanderthals. A second boost also came from acquisition of left-lateralized language capacity, as the central executive Self could now draw upon the representational resources of the "I" and the grammatical resources of the sentence-level grammar with its subject and object verbal transformations. Language resources also facilitated the transformation of autobiographical memory processing into a process that could be used to help build a narrativized picture of the Self – an executive Self or what was called the "agent intellect" by Aristotle and the medieval philosophers – that was doing things and pursuing appropriate goals. Clearly, then, the acquisition of a full-blown grammar and language by early humans had a major impact on the evolution of a central executive Self with a unified consciousness. The left lateralization of language in most people also had an effect on the anatomical systems implicated in Self.

Both the Self and religiousness appear to be selectively mediated by amygdala and anterior cortical networks in the right hemisphere. The right hemisphere was likely favored by the Self (and religiousness) because the left anterior cortical networks were dedicated to language functions, leaving only the right hemisphere to handle other complex functions like Self-consciousness. In addition, as mentioned earlier in this book, the right-sided anterior networks are known to be implicated in powerful inhibitory and regulatory control functions over a diverse set of other brain regions. Thus, right-sided anterior cortical networks are in an ideal position to act as a central executive Self.

In the model of "mosaic evolution" (Barton & Harvey, 2000; Hollo-way, 1968), evolutionary forces can act on individual interconnected neu-ral circuits that mediate specialized behavioral capacities without altering overall brain size. In this model, individual circuits can change in size in relative independence of changes in overall brain size. I suggest that the Self and religion are associated with a distinct functional circuit involving the amygdala, the prefrontal lobes, and the anterior temporal region. I also suggest that this circuit evolved in a mosaic fashion. Presumably the circuit originally supported ritualization of behaviors in primates. The cir-cuit was then co-opted for use in other signaling functions. Because Self and religion are relatively recent evolutionary innovations, there seems to be little prospect for testing this idea. In contrast, it is possible that the key nodes in the circuit (right-sided amygdala, prefrontal and anterior temporal regions) became an integrated circuit only recently in evolu-tionary time and that that integration might have been associated with the acquisition of language.

Alternatively, such a religion/Self brain circuit could have been inte-grated functionally by a single genetic event. The "developmental con-straints" model of brain evolution (Finlay & Darlington, 1995; Finlay, Darlington, & Nicastro, 2001) postulates that a single mechanism (e.g., genes regulating prenatal neocortical development) act to produce a gen-eralized effect on the absolute size of all brain regions. Genetic changes, for example, could prolong the division of progenitor cells that give birth to neocortical neurons (Rakic, 1995), which would subsequently increase the size of the forebrain generally. Finlay and Darlington analyzed the covariances among the absolute size of 12 brain regions across 131 species of mammals and found that a single factor accounted for 96 percent of the variance, thereby supporting the single developmental mechanism the-ory of brain evolution. Finlay and Darlington's methods and conclusions, however, have been criticized by a number of authors (see commentaries in Finlay et al., 2001); thus, the theory remains controversial.

Summary Regarding Evolution of Self and Religion

Whatever the correct evolutionary history of religion and Self turns out to be, the story is a remarkable one. A unified sense of Self, a unified consciousness, is quite an achievement for human beings. It freed us from slavery to impulse and from ineffective and divided goal states. That does not mean that we never experience divided and conflicting desires. It merely means that we have the ability to take conflicting desires and states and synthesize them into a new unity that benefits the individual. The benefits to the group or community are also clear. Cooperation is well-nigh impossible if you have a collection of individuals all of whom are riven with internal conflict.

I suggest that religion was one of the forces (indeed a primary force) that created the executive Self. Since its appearance among archaic humans, each subsequent historical epoch has created its own version of the executive Self, and each cultural group has created its own version of the executive Self. The executive Self is a social Self and is a master of social cooperation, but it also looks to its own goals to guide its behavior. Religion uses the decentering process to help transform the Self and to resolve internal conflict. The process is ongoing, involving constant growth and ever greater internal freedom and external cooperation. The executive Self is more than just a psychological and cultural construct that heals inner divisions and allows for greater social cooperation; it is also a highly sophisticated and very delicate cognitive system that is capable of handling greater computational and information-processing demands than any comparable system based on divided consciousness. It is unlikely that technical or computational intelligences of human beings could have evolved as far as they have if the executive Self, the "agent intellect," had never been developed by our ancestors. Our ancestors used religion to do so. Religion remains the best available means to continue to benefit from the intelligences generated by that Self – your Self.

References

Abramowitz, J. S., Huppert, J. D., Cohen, A. B., Tolin, D. F., & Cahill, S. P. (2002). Religious obsessions and compulsions in a non-clinical sample: The Penn Inventory of Scrupulosity (PIOS). *Behaviour Research and Therapy, 40*(7), 825–838.

Adams, K. (2005). Voices in my dream: Children's interpretation of auditory messages in divine dreams. *Dreaming, 15*, 3.

Adityanjee, Raju, G. S. P., & Khandelwal, S. K. (1989). Current status of multiple personality disorder in India. *American Journal of Psychiatry, 146*(12), 1607–1610.

Adler, C. M., McDonough-Ryan, P., Sax, K. W., Holland, S. K., Arndt, S., & Strakowski, S. M. (2000). fMRI of neuronal activation with symptom provocation in unmedicated patients with obsessive compulsive disorder. *Journal of Psychiatry Research, 34*(4–5), 317–324.

Adolphs, R., Russell, J. A., & Tranel, D. (1999). A role for the human amygdala in recognizing emotional arousal from unpleasant stimuli. *Psychological Science, 10*, 167–171.

Adolphs, R., Tranel, D., Damasio, H., & Damasio, A. (1994). Impaired recognition of emotion in facial expressions following bilateral damage to the human amygdala. *Nature, 372*, 669–672.

Aghajanian, G. K., & Marek, G. J. (1999). Serotonin, via 5-HT2A receptors, increases EPSCs in layer V pyramidal cells of prefrontal cortex by an asynchronous mode of glutamate release. *Brain Research, 825*, 161–171.

Aharon-Peretz, J., & Tomer, R. (2007). Traumatic brain injury. In B. L. Miller & J. L. Cummings (Eds.), *The human frontal lobes: Functions and disorders* (2nd ed., pp. 540–551). New York: The Guilford Press.

Alcorta, C. S. (2006). Religion and the life course: Is adolescence an "experience expectant" period for religious transmission? In P. McNamara (Ed.), *Where God and science meet: How brain and evolutionary studies alter our understanding of religion: Vol. 2: The neurology of religious experience* (pp. 55–80). Westport, CT and London: Praeger Publishers.

al-Hakim al-Tirmidhi. (1980). *Kitab manazil al-ibad min al ibada*. A. A. al-Saih (Ed.). Cairo.

Allen, T. B. (1993). *Possessed: The true story of an exorcism*. New York: Doubleday.

Allport, G. W. (1950). *The individual and his religion*. New York: Macmillan.

American Psychiatric Association (2000). *Diagnostic and statistical manual of mental disorders, Fourth Edition, Text Revision (DSM-IV-TR)*. Washington, DC: American Psychiatric Association.

Aquinas, T. (1954). *Aristotle's De Anima in the version of William of Moerbeke and the commentary of St. Thomas Aquinas* (K. Foster & S. Humphries, trans.). New Haven, CT: Yale University Press.

Aquinas, T. (1993). *Aquinas: Selected philosophical writings* (T. McDermott, trans., pp. 176–183). Oxford: Oxford University Press.

Atran, S. (2002). *In gods we trust: The evolutionary landscape of religion*. Oxford: Oxford University Press.

Austin, J. L. (1975). *How to do things with words*. Cambridge, MA: Harvard University Press.

Azari, N. P., Missimer, J., & Seitz, R. J. (2005). Religious experience and emotion: Evidence for distinctive cognitive neural patterns. *International Journal for the Psychology of Religion, 15*(4), 263–281.

Azari, N. P., Nickel, J. P., Wunderlich, G., Niedeggen, M., Hefter, H., Tellmann, L., et al. (2001). Neural correlates of religious experience. *European Journal of Neuroscience, 13*, 1649–1652.

Barkley, R. A. (1997). Behavioral inhibition, sustained attention, and executive functions: Constructing a unifying theory of ADHD. *Psychological Bulletin, 121*(1), 65–94.

Baron-Cohen, S. (1995). *Mindblindness*. Cambridge, MA: The MIT Press.

Barrett, D. (2007). An evolutionary theory of dreams and problem-solving. In D. Barrett & P. McNamara (Eds.), *The new science of dreaming: Vol. 3: Cultural and theoretical perspectives* (pp. 133–153). Westport, CT and London: Praeger Publishers.

Barrett, D., & McNamara, P. (Eds.). (2007). *The new science of dreaming* (3 vols.). Westport, CT and London: Praeger Publishers.

Barrett, J. L. (2000). Exploring the natural foundations of religion. *Trends in Cognitive Sciences, 4*(1), 29–34.

Barrett, J. L., & Lawson, E. T. (2001). Ritual intuitions: Cognitive contributions to judgments of ritual efficacy. *Journal of Cognition and Culture, 1*(2), 183–201.

Barrett, J. L., Richert, R. A., & Driesenga, A. (2001). God's beliefs versus mother's: The development of nonhuman agent concepts. *Child Development, 72*(1), 50–65.

Bartkowski, J. P., Xu, X., & Levine, M. L. (2007). Religion and child development: Evidence from the early childhood longitudinal study. *Social Science Research, 37*(1), 18–36.

Barton, R. A., & Harvey, P. H. (2000). Mosaic evolution of brain structure in mammals. *Nature, 405,* 1055–1058.

Batson, C. D., Shoenrade, P., & Ventis, W. L. (1993). *Religion and the individual: A social-psychological perspective.* New York: Oxford University Press.

Bauer, D. H. (1976). An exploratory study of developmental changes in children's fears. *Journal of Child Psychology and Psychiatry, 17,* 69–74.

Baxter, L. R., Schwartz, J. M., Phelps, M. E., Mazziotta, J. C., Guze, B. H., Selin, C. E., et al. (1989). Reduction of prefrontal cortex glucose metabolism common to three types of depression. *Archives of General Psychiatry, 46,* 253–260.

Bear, D. M., & Fedio, P. (1977). Quantitative analysis of interictal behavior in temporal lobe epilepsy. *Archives of Neurology, 34*(8), 454–467.

Beauregard, M., & O'Leary, D. (2007). *The spiritual brain: A neuroscientist's case for the existence of the soul.* San Francisco: HarperCollins.

Beauregard, M., & Paquette, V. (2006). Neural correlates of a mystical experience in Carmelite nuns. *Neuroscience Letters, 405,* 186–190.

Beit-Hallahmi, B., & Argyle, M. (1997). *The psychology of religious behavior, belief, and experience.* New York: Routledge.

Bell, C. (1997). *Ritual: Perspectives and dimensions.* New York: Oxford University Press.

Benson, D. F., & Blumer, D. (1975). *Psychiatric aspects of neurological disease (Seminars in psychiatry).* New York: Grune and Stratton.

Berdyaev, N. (1949). The crisis of the human person: Some personalist interpretations (J. B. Coates, Ed.). London, New York, and Toronto: Longman's, Green and Company.

Bering, J. M., & Bjorklund, D. F. (2004). The natural emergence of reasoning about the afterlife as a developmental regularity. *Developmental Psychology, 40*(2), 217–233.

Berlin, H. A., Rolls, E. T., & Iversen, S. D. (2005). Borderline personality disorder, impulsivity, and the orbitofrontal cortex. *American Journal of Psychiatry, 162,* 2360–2373.

Berridge, C. W., Espana, R. A., & Stalnaker, T. A. (2003). Stress and coping: Asymmetry of dopamine efferents within the prefrontal cortex. In K. Hugdahl & R. J. Davidson (Eds.), *The asymmetrical brain* (pp. 69–104). Cambridge, MA: The MIT Press.

Bjorklund, D. F., & Harnishfeger, K. K. (1995). The evolution of inhibition mechanisms and their role in human cognition and behavior. In F. N. Dempster & C. J. Brainerd (Eds.), *Interference and inhibition in cognition* (pp. 141–173). New York: Academic Press.

Bjorklund, D. F., & Pellegrini, A. D. (2002). *The origins of human nature: Evolutionary developmental psychology.* Washington, DC: American Psychological Association.

Blakemore, S. J., den Ouden, H., Choudhury, S., & Frith, C. (2007). Adolescent development of the neural circuitry for thinking about intentions. *Social Cognitive and Affective Neuroscience, 2*(2), 130–139.

Bloch, M. (1974). Symbols, song, dance, and features of articulation: Is religion an extreme form of traditional authority? *European Journal of Sociology, 15,* 55–81.

Blurton Jones, N. G. (1993). The lives of hunter-gatherer children: Effects of parental behavior and parental reproductive strategy. In M. E. Pererira & L. A. Fairbanks (Eds.), *Juvenile primates: Life history, development, and behavior* (pp. 309–326). New York: Oxford University Press.

Boardman, P. H. (producer) & Derrickson, S. (director). (2005). *The exorcism of Emily Rose* [Motion picture]. United States: Sony.

Boddy, J. (1994). Spirit possession revisited: Beyond instrumentality. *Annual Review of Anthropology, 23,* 407–434.

Borg, J., Andrée, B., Soderstrom, H., & Farde, L. (2003). The serotonin system and spiritual experience. *American Journal of Psychiatry, 160,* 1965–1969.

Borges, J. L. (1964). The mirror of enigmas. In D. A. Yates & J. E. Irby (Eds.), *Labyrinths: Selected stories and other writings* (pp. 209–212). New York: New Directions.

Bourguignon, E. (Ed.). (1973). *Religion, altered states of consciousness and social change.* Columbus: The Ohio State University Press.

Bourguignon, E. (1991). *Possession.* Long Grove, IL: Waveland Press.

Boyd, R., & Richerson, P. J. (1996). Why culture is common, but cultural evolution is rare. *Proceedings of the British Academy, 88,* 77–93.

Boyd, R., Richerson, P. J., Borgerhoff-Mulder, M., & Durham, W. H. (1997). Are cultural phylogenies possible? In P. Weingart, P. J. Richerson, S. D. Mitchell, & S. Maasen (Eds.), *Human by nature: Between biology and the social sciences* (pp. 355–386). Mahwah, NJ: Lawrence Erlbaum Associates.

Boyer, P. (2001). *Religion explained: The evolutionary origins of religious thought.* New York: Basic Books.

Boyer, P., & Liénard, P. (2006). Why ritualized behavior? Precaution systems and action parsing in developmental, pathological and cultural rituals. *Behavioral and Brain Sciences, 29*(6), 595.

Boyer, P., & Liénard, P. (2008). Ritual behavior in obsessive and normal individuals: Moderating anxiety and reorganizing the flow of action. *Current Directions in Psychological Science, 17*(4), 291.

Bradbury, J. W., & Vehrenkamp, S. L. (1998). *Principles of animal communication.* Sunderland, MA: Sinauer Associates.

Brewerton, T. (1994). Hyperreligiosity in psychotic disorders. *Journal of Nervous and Mental Disease, 182*(5), 302–304.

Brocki, K., & Bohlin, G. (2004). Executive functions in children age 6–13: A dimensional and developmental study. *Archives of General Psychiatry, 49*, 728–738.

Brown, D. E. (1991). *Human universals.* Philadelphia: Temple University Press.

Brown, P., & Levinson, S. C. (1987). *Politeness: Some universals in language usage.* Cambridge: Cambridge University Press.

Bruder, G. (2003). Frontal and parietotemporal asymmetries in depressive disorders: Behavioral, electrophysiologic, and neuroimaging findings. In K. Hugdahl & R. Davidson (Eds.), *The asymmetrical brain* (pp. 719–742). Cambridge, MA: The MIT Press.

Brüne, M. (2004). Schizophrenia – an evolutionary enigma? *Neuroscience and Biobehavioral Reviews, 28*(1), 41–53.

Bruner, J. (1990). *Acts of meaning.* Cambridge, MA: Harvard University Press.

Bruner, J. (1995). Meaning and self in cultural perspective. In D. Bakhurst & C. Sypnowich (Eds.), *The social self* (pp. 18–29). London: Sage.

Bulbulia, J. (2006). Nature's medicine: Religiosity as an adaptation for health and cooperation. In P. McNamara (Ed.), *Where God and science meet: How brain and evolutionary studies alter our understanding of religion, Vol. 1: Evolution, genes, and the religious brain* (pp. 87–121). Westport, CT, and London: Praeger Publishers.

Bulbulia, J. (2009). Religiosity as mental time travel: cognitive adaptations for religious behavior. In J. Schloss & M. Murray (Eds.), *The believing primate:*

Scientific, philosophical and theological perspectives on the evolution of religion. New York: Oxford University Press.

Cabana, T., Jolicoeur, P., & Michaud, J. (1993). Prenatal and postnatal growth and allometry of stature, head circumference, and brain weight in Québec children. *American Journal of Human Biology, 5*, 93–99.

Cardeña, E. (1992). Trance and possession as dissociative disorders. *Transcultural Psychiatric Research Review, 29*, 283–297.

Carlsson, A., Waters, N., & Carlsson, M. (1999). Neurotransmitter interactions in schizophrenia – therapeutic implications. *Biological Psychiatry, 46*, 1388–1395.

Carrazana, E., DeToledo, J., Rivas-Vasquez, R., Rey, G., & Wheeler, S. (1999). Epilepsy and religious experiences: Voodoo possession. *Epilepsia, 40*, 239–241.

Carver, C. S., & Scheier, M. F. (1981). *Attention and self-regulation: A control theory approach to human behavior.* New York: Springer.

Castillo, R. J. (1994). Spirit possession in South Asia, dissociation or hysteria? Part 1: Theoretical background. *Culture, Medicine and Psychiatry, 18*, 1–21.

Cavalli-Sforza, L. L. (1998). The Chinese human genome diversity project. *Proceedings of the National Academy of Sciences of the United States of America, 95*(20), 11501–11503.

Chan, D., Fox, N. C., Jenkins, R., Scahill, R. I., Crum, W. R., & Rossor, M. N. (2001). Rates of global and regional cerebral atrophy in Alzheimer's disease and frontotemporal dementia. *Neurology, 57*, 1756–1763.

Churchland, P. S. (2002). Self-representation in nervous systems. *Science, 296*, 308–310.

Cirignotta, F., Todesco, C. V., & Lugaresi, E. (1980). Temporal lobe epilepsy with ecstatic seizures (so-called Dostoevsky epilepsy). *Epilepsia, 21*, 705–710.

Cloninger, C. R. (1994). *The Temperament and Character Inventory (TCI): A guide to its development and use.* St. Louis, MO: Centre for Psychobiology of Personality, Washington University.

Cohen, E. (2007). *The mind possessed: The cognition of spirit possession in an Afro-Brazilian religious tradition.* New York: Oxford University Press.

Coles, R. (1990). *The spiritual life of children.* Boston: Peter Davison.

Comings, D. E., Gonzales, N., Saucier, G., Johnson, J. P., & MacMurray, J. P. (2000). The DRD4 gene and the spiritual transcendence scale of the character temperament index. *Psychiatric Genetics 10*(4), 185–189.

Conway, M. A., & Pleydell-Pearce, C. W. (2000). The construction of autobiographical memories in the self-memory system. *Psychological Review, 107*(2), 261–288.

Cools, R., Stefanova, E., Barker, R. A., Robbins, T. W., & Owen, A. M. (2002). Dopaminergic modulation of high-level cognition in Parkinson's disease: The role of the prefrontal cortex revealed by PET. *Brain, 125*, 584–594.

Cooper, J. R., Bloom, F. E., & Roth, R. H. (Eds.). (2003). *The biochemical basis of neuropharmacology*. Oxford: Oxford University Press.

Craik, F. I. M., Moroz, T. M., & Moscovitch, M. (1999). In search of the self: A positron emission tomography study. *Psychological Science, 10*, 129–178.

Crow, T. (2008). The 'big bang' theory of the origin of psychosis and the faculty of language. *Schizophrenia Research, 102*, 31–52.

Crow, T. J. (1993). Sexual selection, Machiavellian intelligence, and the origins of psychosis. *Lancet, 342*, 594–598.

Crow, T. J. (2000). Sexual selection, timing and an X-Y homologous gene: Did *Homo sapiens* speciate on the Y chromosome? *Psycoloquy, 11*, 1–18.

Cummings, J. L., & Mega, M. S. (2003). *Neuropsychiatry and behavioral neuroscience*. New York: Oxford University Press.

d'Aquili, E., & Newberg, A. (1993). Religious and mystical states: A neuropsychological model. *Zygon, 28*(2), 177–200.

D'Onofrio, B. M., Eaves, L. J., Murrelle, L., Maes, H. H., & Spilka, B. (1999). Understanding biological and social influences on religious affiliation, attitudes, and behaviors: A behavior genetic perspective. *Journal of Personality, 67*(6), 953–984.

Dagenbach, D., & Carr, T. H. (Eds.). (1994). *Inhibitory processes in attention, memory, and language*. San Diego: Academic Press.

Damasio, A. R., & Anderson, S. W. (2003). The frontal lobes. In K. M. Heilman & E. Valenstein (Eds.), *Clinical neuropsychology* (4th ed., pp. 404–446). New York: Oxford University Press.

Damasio, A., R., Tranel, D., & Damasio, H. (1990). Individuals with sociopathic behavior caused by frontal damage fail to respond autonomically to social stimuli. *Behavioral Brain Research, 41*, 81–94.

Damasio, A. R., Tranel, D., & Damasio, H. (1991). Somatic markers and the guidance of behavior: Theory and preliminary testing. In H. S. Levin, H. M. Eisenberg, & A. L. Benton (Eds.), *Frontal lobe function and dysfunction* (pp. 217–229). New York: Oxford University Press.

David, N., Newen, A., & Vogeley, K. (2008). The "sense of agency" and its underlying cognitive and neural mechanisms. *Consciousness and Cognition, 17*(2), 523–534.

Davidson, D. (2001). *Essays on actions and events*. New York: Oxford University Press.

Davison, G. C., & Neale, J. M. (1994). *Abnormal psychology* (6th ed.). New York: John Wiley and Sons, Inc.

Davie, M. R. (1929). *The evolution of war: A study of its role in early society*. New Haven, CT: Yale University Press.

Daw, N., Kakade, S., & Dayan, P. (2002). Opponent interactions between serotonin and dopamine. *Neural Network, 15*(4–6), 603–616.

Dean, B. (2003). The cortical serotonin 2A receptor and the pathology of schizophrenia: a likely accomplice. *Journal of Neurochemistry, 85*(1), 1–13.

Dempster, F. N., & Brainerd, C. J. (1995). *Interference and inhibition in cognition*. New York: Academic Press.

Dennett, D. C. (1991). *Consciousness explained*. Boston: Little Brown.

DePalatis, R. S. (2006). An exploration of the different responses to a deliverance ministry procedure: Possession trance and dissociation in the Protestant Christian expulsion ritual setting. Unpublished doctoral dissertation. Capella University, Minneapolis, MN.

Devinsky, O. (2000). Right cerebral hemisphere dominance for a sense of corporeal and emotional self. *Epilepsy & Behavior, 1*, 60–73.

Devinsky, O., Feldman, E., Burrowes, K., & Bromfield, E. (1989). Autoscopic phenomena with seizures. *Archives of Neurology, 46*, 1080–1088.

Devinsky, O., & Lai, G. (2008). Spirituality and religion in epilepsy. *Epilepsy and Behavior, 12*(4), 636–643.

Dewhurst, K., & Beard, A. W. (1970). Sudden religious conversions in temporal lobe epilepsy. *The British Journal of Psychiatry: The Journal of Mental Science, 117*, 497–507.

DiYanni, C., & Kelemen, D. (2005). Time to get a new mountain? The role of function in children's conception of natural kinds. *Cognition, 97*, 327–335.

Donahue, M. L., & Benson, P. L. (1995). Religion and the well-being of adolescents. *Journal of Social Issues, 51*, 145–160.

Dostoevsky, F. M. (1972). *Notes from underground: The double* (J. Coulson, trans.). Harmondsworth: Penguin. (Original work published 1846.)

Du Bois, J. W. (1986). Self-evidence and ritual speech. In W. Chafe & J. Nichols (Eds.), *Evidentiality: The linguistic coding of epistemology* (pp. 313–336). Norwood, NJ: Ablex.

Dupras, T. L., Schwarcz, H. P., & Fairgrieve, S. I. (2001). Infant feeding and weaning practices in Roman Egypt. *American Journal of Physical Anthropology, 115*, 204–212.

Durkheim, É. (1954). *The elementary forms of the religious life* (2nd French ed.). Glencoe, IL: Free Press. (Original work published 1912.)

Durston, S., Hulshoff Pol, H. E., Casey, B. J., Giedd, J. N., Buitelaar, J .K., & van Engeland, H. (2001). Anatomical MRI of the developing human brain: What have we learned? *Journal of the American Academy of Child and Adolescent Psychiatry, 40,* 1012–1020.

Edwards-Lee, T., Miller, B. L., Benson, D. F, Cummings, J. L., Russell, G. L., Boone, K., et al. (1997). The temporal variant of frontotemporal dementia. *Brain, 120,* 1027–1040.

Egan, M. F., Goldberg, T. E., Kolachana, B. S., Callicott, J. H., Mazzanti, C. M., Straub, R. E., et al. (2001). Effect of COMT Val108/158 Met genotype on frontal lobe function and risk for schizophrenia. *Proceedings of the National Academy of Sciences of the United States of America, 98,* 6917–6922.

Eisen, J. L., Goodman, W. K., Keller, M. B., Warshaw, M. G., DeMarco, L. M., Luce. D. D., et al. (1999). Patterns of remission and relapse in obsessive-compulsive disorder: A 2-year prospective study. *Journal of Clinical Psychiatry, 60,* 346–351.

Eisenberg, N., & Harris, J. D. (1984). Social competence: A developmental perspective. *School Psychology Review, 13,* 267–277.

Elkin, A. P. (1964). *The Australian Aborigines.* Garden City, NY: Doubleday.

Elkind, D. (1970). The origins of religion in the child. *Review of Religious Research, 12,* 35–42.

Epictetus. (1909–1914). The golden sayings of Epictetus. (H. Crossley, Trans.). In C. W. Eliot (Ed.), *The Harvard Classics* (Vol. II, Part 2). New York: Collier.

Erikson, M. G. (2001, March). *Possible selves revisited: Self-narratives about the future.* Paper presented at the centenary annual conference of the British Psychological Society, Glasgow.

Estioko-Griffin, A. A. (1986). Daughters of the forest. *Natural History, 95*(5), 36–43.

Evans, E. M. (2000). The emergence of beliefs about the origin of species in school-age children. *Merrill Palmer Quarterly, 46,* 221–254.

Feinberg, T. E., & Keenan, J. P. (2005). Where in the brain is the self? *Consciousness and Cognition, 14*(4), 661–678.

Ferracuti, S., Sacco, R., & Lazzari, R. (1996). Dissociative trance disorder: Clinical and Rorschach findings in ten persons reporting demon possession and treated by exorcism. *Journal of Personality Assessment, 66*(3), 525–539.

Fink, G. R., Markowitsch, H. J., Reinkemeier, M., Bruckbauer, T., Kessler, J., & Heiss, W. D. (1996). Cerebral representation of one's own past: Neural networks involved in autobiographical memory. *Journal of Neuroscience, 16*(13), 4275–4282.

Finlay, B. L., & Darlington, R. B. (1995). Linked regularities in the development and evolution of mammalian brains. *Science, 268*(5217), 1578–1584.

Finlay, B. L., Darlington, R. B., & Nicastro, N. (2001). Developmental structure in brain evolution. *Behavioral and Brain Sciences, 24*(2), 263–278.

Firth, R. (2001). Tikopia dreams: Personal images of social relality. *Journal of the Polynesian Society, 100*(1), 7–29.

Flaherty, A. W. (2005). Frontotemporal and dopaminergic control of idea generation and creative drive. *Journal of Comparative Neurology, 493*, 147–153.

Flor-Henry, P., Tomer, R., Kumpala, I., Koles, Z. J., & Yeudall, L. T. (1990). Neurophysiological and neuropsychological study of two cases of multiple personality syndrome and comparison with chronic hysteria. *International Journal of Psychophysiology, 10*(2), 151–161.

Fontaine, D., Mattei, V., & Roberts, P. H. (2007). Obsessive-compulsive disorder and the frontal lobes. In B. L. Miller & J. L. Cummings (Eds.), *The human frontal lobes: Functions and disorders* (2nd ed., pp. 621–635). New York: The Guilford Press.

Foulkes, D. (1982). *Children's dreams.* New York: Wiley.

Foulkes, D. (1999). *Children's dreaming and the development of consciousness.* Cambridge, MA: Harvard University Press.

Foulkes, D., Petrik, J., & Scott, E. A. (1978). Analysis of children's dreams at ages 7–8 and 13–14. *Sleep Research, 7*, 175.

Fowler, J. W. (1991). Stages in faith consciousness. *New Directions for Child Development, 52*, 27–45.

Friedkin, W. (Director), & Blatty, W. P. (Producer and Writer). (1973). *The exorcist* [Motion picture]. United States: Warner Bros. Pictures.

Fukada, A., & Asato, N. (2004). Universal politeness theory: Application to the use of Japanese honorifics. *Journal of Pragmatics, 36*, 1991–2002.

Fuster, J. M. (2008). *The prefrontal cortex* (4th ed.). San Diego: Academic Press.

Gallagher, I. (2000). Philosophical conceptions of the self: Implications for cognitive science. *Trends in Cognitive Sciences, 4*, 14–21.

Gallagher, S. (2003). Self-narrative in schizophrenia. In T. Kircher & A. David (Eds.), *The self in neuroscience and psychiatry* (pp. 336–360). Cambridge: Cambridge University Press.

Gallup, G. G. (1970). Chimpanzees: Self recognition. *Science, 167*(3914), 86–87.

Galton, C. J., Gomez-Anson, B., Antoun, N., Scheltens, P., Patterson, K., Graves, M., et al. (2001). The temporal lobe rating scale: Application to Alzheimer's disease and frontotemporal dementia. *Journal of Neurology, Neurosurgery, and Psychiatry, 70*, 407–423.

Gashghaei, H. T., Hilgetag, C. C., & Barbas, H. (2007). Sequence of information processing for emotions based on the anatomical dialogue between prefrontal cortex and amygdale. *Neuroimage, 34*(3), 905–923.

Gastaut, H. (1954). *Epilepsies*. Springfield, IL: C. C. Thomas.

Gaw, A. C., Ding, Q.-S., Levine, R. E., & Gaw, H.-F. (1998). The clinical characteristics of possession disorder among 20 Chinese patients in the Hebei province of China. *Psychiatric Service, 49*, 360–365.

Geertz, A. W. (2008), Comparing prayer: On science, universals and the human condition. In W. Braun & R. T. McCutcheon (Eds.), *Introducing religion: Essays in honor of Jonathan Z. Smith* (pp. 113–139). London: Equinox.

Geschwind, N. (1979). Behavioural changes in temporal lobe epilepsy. *Psychological Medicine, 9*, 217–219.

Geschwind, N. (1983). Interictal behavioral changes in epilepsy. *Epilepsia, 24*(Suppl. 1), 523–530.

Giacomelli, S., Palmery, M., Romanelli, L., Cheng, C. Y., & Silvestrini, B. (1998). Lysergic acid diethylamide (LSD) is a partial agonist of D2 dopaminergic receptors and it potentiates dopamine-mediated prolactin secretion in lactotrophs in vitro. *Life Sciences, 63*(3), 215–222.

Giedd, J. N., Blumenthal, J., Jeffries, N. O., Castellanos, F. X., Liu, H., Zijdenbos, A., et al. (1999). Brain development during childhood and adolescence: A longitudinal MRI study. *Nature Neuroscience, 2*(10), 861–863.

Gillihan, S. J., & Farah, M. J. (2005). Is self special? A critical review of evidence from experimental psychology and cognitive neuroscience. *Psychological Bulletin, 131*(1), 76–97.

Girard, R. (1987). *Things hidden since the foundation of the world*. Stanford, CA: Stanford University Press.

Glicksohn, J. (2001). Temporal cognition and the phenomenology of time: A multiplicative function for apparent duration. *Consciousness and Cognition, 10*(1), 1–25.

Goberman, A., & Coelho, C. (2002), Acoustic analysis of Parkinsonian speech I: Speech characteristics and L-Dopa therapy. *Neurorehabilitation, 17*, 237–246.

Goldberg, G. (1987). From intent to action: Evolution and function of the premotor systems of the front lobe. In E. Perecman (Ed.), *The frontal lobes revisited* (pp. 273–306). New York: The IRBN Press.

Goldberg, G., Mayer, N. H., & Toglia, J. U. (1981). Medial frontal cortex infarction and the alien hand sign. *Archives of Neurology, 38*(11), 683–686.

Goldish, M. (Ed.). (2003). *Spirit possession in Judaism*. Detroit: Wayne State University Press.

Goldman, R. (1964). *Religious thinking from childhood to adolescence*. New York: Routledge.

Goldman-Rakic, P. (1987). Circuitry of primate prefrontal cortex and regulation of behavior by representational memory. In V. Plum (Ed.), *Higher cortical function. Handbook of physiology* (pp. 373–417). New York: American Physiological Society.

Graham, L. R. (1995). *Performing dreams: Discourses of immortality among the Xavante of Central Brazil*. Austin: University of Texas Press.

Granqvist, P. (2006). Religion as a by-product of evolved psychology: The case of attachment and implications for brain and religion. In P. McNamara (Ed.), *Where God and science meet: How brain and evolutionary studies alter our understanding of religion: Vol. 2: The neurology of religious experience* (pp. 105–150). Westport, CT and London: Praeger Publishers.

Grattan, L. M., Bloomer, R. H., Archambault, F. X., & Eslinger, P. J. (1994). Cognitive flexibility and empathy after frontal lobe lesion. *Neuropsychiatry, Neuropsychology, and Behavioral Neurology, 7*, 251–259.

Greenberg, D., Witztum, E., & Pisante, J. (1987). Scrupulosity: Religious attitudes and clinical presentations. *British Journal of Medical Psychology, 60*, 29–37.

Gregor, T. (1981). A content analysis of Mehinaku dreams. *Ethos, 9*(4), 258–275.

Gregor, T. A. (1981). "Far, far away my shadow wandered . . . ": The dream theories of the Mehinanku Indians of Brazil. *American Ethnologist, 8*(4), 709–720.

Haig, D. (2000). Genomic imprinting, sex-biased dispersal, and social behavior. *Annals of the New York Academy of Sciences, 907*,149–163.

Haig, D. (2002). *Genomic imprinting and kinship*. Piscataway, NJ: Rutgers University Press.

Haig, D. (2004). Evolutionary conflicts in pregnancy and calcium metabolism. *Placenta, 25*(Suppl. A), S10–S15.

Haig, D. (2006). Intrapersonal conflict. In M. Jones & A.C. Fabian (Eds.), *Conflict* (pp. 8–22). Cambridge: Cambridge University Press.

Haig, D., & Westoby, M. (1988). Inclusive fitness, seed resources and maternal care. In J. L. Doust (Ed.), *Plant reproductive ecology* (pp. 60–79). New York: Oxford University Press.

Hallam, C. (1980). The double as incomplete self: Toward a definition of *Doppelgänger*. In E. Crook (Ed.), *Fearful symmetry: Doubles and doubling in literature and film* (Papers from the fifth annual Florida state conference on literature and film, pp. 1–31). Tallahassee: University Presses of Florida.

Hamer, D. (2004). *The God gene: How faith is hardwired into our genes*. New York: Doubleday.

Harner, M. (1972). *The Jivaro, people of the sacred waterfalls*. Garden City, NY: Doubleday/Natural History Press.

Harris, E., & McNamara, P. (2008). Is religiousness a biocultural adaptation? In J. Bulbulia, R. Sosis, R. Genet, E. Harris, K. Wyman, & C. Genet (Eds.), *The evolution of religion: Studies, theories, and critiques* (pp. 69–75). Santa Margarita, CA: Collins Foundation Press.

Harris, S., Sheth, S. A., & Cohen, M. S. (2008). Functional neuroimaging of belief, disbelief, and uncertainty. *Annals of Neurology, 63,* 141–147.

Hartmann, H. (1958). *Ego psychology and the problem of adaption.* New York: International Universities Press.

Haznedar, M. M., Roversi, F., Pallanti, S., Baldini-Rossi, N., Schnur, D. B., Licalzi, E. M., et al. (2005). Fronto-thalamo-striatal gray and white matter volumes and anisotropy of their connections in bipolar spectrum illnesses. *Biological Psychiatry, 57*(7), 733–742.

Heinrichs, R. W. (1989). Frontal cerebral lesions and violent incidents in chronic neuropsychiatric patients. *Biological Psychiatry, 25,* 174–178.

Henninger, P. (1992). Conditional handedness: Handedness changes in multiple personality disordered subjects reflect shift in hemispheric dominance. *Consciousness and Cognition, 1*(3), 265–287.

Herzog, H., Lele, R. R., Kuwert, T., Langen, K. J., Kops, E. R., & Feinendegen, L. E. (1990). Changed pattern of regional glucose metabolism during yoga meditative relaxation. *Neuropsychobiology, 23,* 182–187.

Hewlett, S. A. (1991). *When the bough breaks: The cost of neglecting our children.* New York: Basic Books.

Hoffman, M. L. (2000). Empathy and moral development: Implications for caring and justice. Cambridge: Cambridge University Press.

Hogarty, G. E., & Flesher, S. (1999a). Developmental theory for a cognitive enhancement therapy of schizophrenia. *Schizophrenia Bulletin, 25,* 677–692.

Hogarty, G. E., & Flesher, S. (1999b). Practice principles of cognitive enhancement therapy for schizophrenia. *Schizophrenia Bulletin, 25,* 693–708.

Hollan, D. (2000). Culture and dissociation in Toraja. *Transcultural Psychiatry, 37*(4), 545–559.

Hollan, D. (2003). The cultural and intersubjective context of dream remembrance and reporting: Dreams, aging, and the anthropological encounter in Toraja, Indonesia. In R. I. Lohmann (Ed.), *Dream travelers: Sleep experiences and culture in the Western Pacific* (pp. 168–187). New York: Palgrave Macmillan.

Holloway, R. L. (1968). The evolution of the primate brain: Some aspects of quantitative relations. *Brain Research, 7,* 121–172.

Howden, J. C. (1872–1873). The religious sentiments in epileptics. *Journal of Mental Science, 18,* 491–497.

Hoyle, R. H., & Sherrill, M. R. (2006). Future orientation in the self-system: Possible selves, self-regulation, and behavior. *Journal of Personality, 74,* 1673–1696.

Hoyle, R. H., & Sowards, B. A. (1993). Self-monitoring and the regulation of social experience: A control-process model. *Journal of Social and Clinical Psychology, 12*, 280–306.

Hughes, J. R. (2005). The idiosyncratic aspects of the epilepsy of Fyodor Dostoevsky. *Epilepsy & Behavior, 7*, 531–538.

Huguelet, P., Mohr, S., Borras, L., Gilliéron, C., & Brandt, P. Y. (2006). Spirituality and religious practices among outpatients with schizophrenia and their clinicians. *Psychiatric Services, 57*(3), 366–372.

Humphrey, C., & Laidlaw, J. (1994). *Archetypal actions: A theory of ritual as a mode of action and the case of the Jain Puja.* Oxford: Clarendon Press.

Humphrey, N. K. (1983). *Consciousness regained.* New York: Oxford University Press.

Huttenlocher, P. R., & Dabholkar, A. S. (1997). Regional differences in synaptogenesis in human cerebral cortex. *Journal of Comparative Neurology, 387*(2), 167–178.

Hyde, K. E. (1990). *Religion in childhood and adolescence: A comprehensive review of the research.* Birmingham, AL: Religious Education Press.

Ide, S. (1989). Formal forms and discernment: Two neglected aspects of universals of linguistic politeness. *Multilingua, 8*(2/3), 223–248.

Iqbal, N., & van Praag, H. (1995). The role of serotonin in schizophrenia. *European Neuropsychopharmacology, 5*(Suppl. 1), 11–23.

James, H., Sr. (1866). *Substance and shadow.* Boston: Houghton, Osgood, and Co.

James, W. (1902/1928). *The varieties of religious experience.* London: Longmans, Green and Co. (Original work published 1908.)

Johnson, D. D. P. (2005). God's punishment and public goods. A test of the supernatural punishment hypothesis in 186 world cultures. *Human Nature, 16*(4), 410–446.

Joober, R., Gauthier, J., Lal, S., Bloom, D., Lalonde, P., Rouleau, G., et al. (2002). Catechol-*O*-methyltransferase Val-108/158-Met gene variants associated with performance on the Wisconsin Card Sorting Test. *Archives of General Psychiatry, 59*, 662–663.

Kakigi, R., Nakata, H., Inui, K., Hiroc, N., Natgata, O., Honda, M., et al. (2005). Intracerebral pain processing in a Yoga Master who claims not to feel pain during meditation. *European Journal of Pain, 9*, 581–589.

Kasai, K., Shenton, M. E., Salisbury, D. F., Hirayasu, Y., Lee, C. U., Ciszewski, A. A., et al. (2003). Progressive decrease of left superior temporal gyrus gray matter volume in patients with first-episode schizophrenia. *American Journal of Psychiatry, 160*(1), 156–164.

Kato, M. V., Shimizu, T., Nagayoshi, M., Kaneko, A., Sasaki, M. S., & Ikawa, Y. (1996). Genomic imprinting of the human serotonin-receptor (*HTR2*) gene involved in development of retinoblastoma. *American Journal of Human Genetics, 59*, 1084–1090.

Katz, R. (1984). *Boiling energy: Community healing among the Kalahuri Kung*. Cambridge, MA: Harvard University Press.

Keane, W. (1997). Religious language. *Annual Review of Anthropology, 26*, 47–71.

Keenan, J. P., Nelson, A., O'Connor, M., & Pascual-Leone, A. (2001). Self-recognition and the right hemisphere. *Nature, 409*, 305.

Keenan, J. P., Rubio, J., Racioppi, C., Johnson, A., & Barnacz, A. (2005). The right hemisphere and the dark side of consciousness. *Cortex, 41*(5), 695–704.

Keesing, R. M. (1982). *Kwaio religion: The living and the death in a Solomon Island Society*. New York: Columbia University Press.

Kelemen, D. (2004). Are children "intuitive theists"? *Psychological Science, 15*(5), 295–301.

Kelley, W. M., Macrae, C. N., Wyland, C. L., Caglar, S., Inati, S., & Heatherton, T. F. (2002). Finding the self? An event-related fMRI study. *Journal of Cognitive Neuroscience, 14*(5), 785–794.

Kerpelman, J. L., & Lamke, L. K. (1997). Anticipation of future identities: A control theory approach to identity development within the context of serious dating relationships. *Personal Relationships, 4*, 47–62.

Kierkegaard, S. (1980). *Sickness unto death* (Howard and Edna Hong, Trans.). Princeton, NJ: Princeton University Press.

Kircher, T., & David, A. (Eds.) (2003). *The self in neuroscience and psychiatry*. New York: Cambridge University Press.

Kirkpatrick, L. A. (1999). Toward an evolutionary psychology of religion and personality. *Journal of Personality, 67*(6), 921–952.

Kirkpatrick, L. A. (2005). *Attachment, evolution, and the psychology of religion*. New York: The Guilford Press.

Kjaer, T., Bertelsen, C., Picinni, P., Brooks, D., Alving, J., & Lou, H. C. (2002). Increased dopamine tone during meditation-induced change of consciousness. *Cognitive Brain Research, 13*(2), 255–259.

Knight, N., Sousa, P., Barrett, J. L., & Atran, S. (2004). Children's attributions of beliefs to humans and God: Cross cultural evidence. *Cognitive Science, 28*, 117–126.

Koenig, L. B., & Bouchard, Jr., T. J. (2006). Genetic and environmental influences on the traditional moral values triad – authoritarianism, conservatism, and religiousness – as assessed by quantitative behavior genetic methods. In

P. McNamara (Ed.), *Where God and science meet: How brain and evolutionary studies alter our understanding of religion: Vol. 1: Evolution, genes, and the religious brain* (pp. 31–60). Westport, CT, and London: Praeger Publishers.

Koenig, L. B., McGue, M., Krueger, R. F., Bouchard, T. J. (2005). Religiousness: Findings for retrospective and current religiousness ratings. *Journal of Personality, 73*(2), 471–488.

Koob, G. F. (1992). Drugs of abuse: Anatomy, pharmacology and trends of reward pathways. *Trends in Pharmacological Sciences, 13*, 177–184.

Kubicki, M., Shenton, M. E., Salisbury, D. F., Hirayasu, Y., Kasai, K., Kikinis, R., et al. (2002). Voxel-based morphometric analysis of gray matter in first episode schizophrenia. *NeuroImage, 17*(4), 1711–1719.

Kuroki, N., Shenton, M. E., Salisbury, D. F., Hirayasu, Y., Onitsuka, T., Ersner-Hershfield, H., et al. (2006). Middle and inferior temporal gyrus gray matter volume abnormalities in first-episode schizophrenia: An MRI study. *American Journal of Psychiatry, 163*(12), 2103–2110.

Lancaster, J. B., & Lancaster, C. S. (1983). Parental investment: The hominid adaptation. In D. J. Ortner (Ed.), *How humans adapt: A biocultural odyssey* (pp. 33–56). Washington, DC: Smithsonian Institution Press.

Lawson, E. T., & McCauley, R. N. (1990). *Rethinking religion: Connecting cognition and culture.* Cambridge: Cambridge University Press.

Lazar, S. W., Bush, G., Gollub, R. L., Fricchione, G. L., Khalsa, G., & Benson, H. (2000). Functional brain mapping of the relaxation response and meditation. *NeuroReport, 11*, 1581–1585.

LeDoux, J. (2002). *Synaptic self: How our brains become who we are.* New York: Viking Press.

Lehmann, D., Faber, P. L., Achermann, P., Jeanmonod, D., Gianotti, L. R. R., & Pizzagalli, D. (2001). Brain sources of EEG gamma frequency during volitionally meditation-induced, altered states of consciousness, and experience of the self. *Psychiatry Research: Neuroimaging Section, 108*, 111–121.

Lesser, I. M., & Chung, J. A. (2007). *Depression.* In B. L. Miller & J. L. Cummings (Eds.), *The human frontal lobes: Functions and disorders* (2nd ed., pp. 636–648). New York: The Guilford Press.

Levin, H. S., Culhane, K. A., Hartmann, J., Evankovich, K., Mattson, A. J., Harward, H., et al. (1991). Developmental changes in performance on tests of purported frontal lobe functioning. *Developmental Neuropsychology, 7*, 377–395.

Lewis, D. A., Cruz, D., Eggan, S., & Erickson, S. (2004). Postnatal development of prefrontal inhibitory circuits and the pathophysiology of cognitive dysfunction in schizophrenia. *Annals of the New York Academy of Sciences, 1021*, 64–76.

Lewis, I. M. (1971). *Ecstatic religion: A study of Shamanism and spirit possession.* New York: Penguin Books.

Lewis-Fernandez, R. (1992). The proposed DSM-IV trance and possession disorder category: Potential benefits and risks. *Transcultural Psychiatric Research Review, 29*, 301–317.

Lhermitte, F. (1986). Human autonomy and the frontal lobes. Part II: Patient behavior in complex and social situations: The "environmental dependency syndrome." *Annals of Neurology, 19*(4), 335–343.

Lichtenberg, P., Bachner-Melman, R., Gritsenko, I., & Ebstein, R. P. (2000). Exploratory association study between catechol-O-methyltransferase (COMT) high/low enzyme activity polymorphism and hypnotizability. *American Journal of Medical Genetics Part B: Neuropsychiatric Genetics, 96*(6), 771–774.

Liénard, P., & Boyer, P. (2006). Why ritualized behavior? Precaution systems and action parsing in developmental, pathological and cultural rituals. *Behavioral and Brain Sciences, 29*, 1–56.

Loevinger, J. (1976). *Ego development: Conceptions and theories.* San Francisco: Jossey-Bass.

Loevinger, J., Wessler, R., & Redmore, C. (1970). *Measuring ego development* (Vol. 2). *Scoring manual for women and girls.* San Francisco: Jossey-Bass.

Lohmann, R. I. (2003a). Dream travels and anthropology. In R. I. Lohmann (Ed.), *Dream travelers: Sleep experiences and culture in the Western Pacific* (pp. 1–17). New York: Palgrave Macmillan.

Lohmann, R. I. (2003b). Supernatural encounters of the Asabano in two traditions and three states of consciousness. In R. I. Lohmann (Ed.), *Dream travelers: Sleep experiences and culture in the Western Pacific* (pp. 188–210). New York: Palgrave Macmillan.

Lohmann, R. I. (Ed.). (2003c). *Dream travelers: Sleep experiences and culture in the Western Pacific.* New York: Palgrave Macmillan.

Lou, H. C., Kjaer, T. W., Friberg, L., Wildschiodtz, G., Holm, S., & Nowak, M. (1999). A 15O-H2O PET study of meditation and the resting state of normal consciousness. *Human Brain Mapping, 7*, 98–105.

Luciana, M., Conklin, H. M., Hooper, C. J., & Yarger, R. S. (2005). The development of nonverbal working memory and executive control processes in adolescents, *Child Development, 76*, 697–712.

Lukianowicz, N. (1958). Autoscopic phenomena. *A. M. A. Archives of Neurology and Psychiatry, 80*, 199–205.

Lutkehaus, N. C., & Roscoe, P. B. (1995). *Gender rituals: Female initiation in Melanesia.* New York: Routledge.

Lutz, A., Brefczynski-Lewis, J., Johnstone, T., & Davidson, R. J. (2008). Regulation of the neural circuitry of emotion by compassion meditation: Effects of meditative expertise. *PLoS ONE, 3*(3), 1–10.

Mace, R., Holden, C. J., & Shennan, S. (Eds.). (2006). *The evolution of cultural diversity: A phylogenetic approach.* Walnut Creek, CA: Left Coast Press.

Malhotra, A. K., Kestler, L. J., Mazzanti, C., Bates, J. A., Goldberg, T., & Goldman, D. (2002). A functional polymorphism in the COMT gene and performance on a test of prefrontal cognition. *American Journal of Psychiatry, 159*, 652–654.

Malinar, A., & Basu, H. (2008). Ecstasy. In J. Corrigan (Ed.), *The Oxford handbook of religion and emotion* (pp. 241–258). New York: Oxford.

Marino, L. (2006 November/December). The ape in the mirror: Exploring animal self awareness. *Best Friends Magazine,* 20–21.

Markus, H. (1977). Self-schemata and information about the self. *Journal of Personality and Social Psychology, 35*, 63–78.

Markus, H., & Kunda, Z. (1986). Stability and malleability of the self-concept. *Journal of Personality and Social Psychology, 54*, 858–866.

Markus, H., & Nurius, P. (1986). Possible selves. *American Psychologist, 41*, 954–969.

Markus, H., & Ruvolo, A. (1989). Possible selves: Personalized representations of goals. In L. A. Pervin (Ed.), *Goal concepts in personality and social psychology* (pp. 211–241). Hillsdale, NJ: Erlbaum.

Markus, H., & Wurf, E. (1987). The dynamic self-concept. *Annual Review of Psychology, 38*, 299–337.

Mataix-Cols, D., Rauch, S. L., Manzo, P. A., Jenike, M. A., & Baer, L. (1999). Use of factor-analyzed symptom dimensions to predict outcome with serotonin reuptake inhibitors and placebo in the treatment of obsessive-compulsive disorder. *American Journal of Psychiatry, 156*, 1409–1416.

Mayer, E. (1911). A case illustrating so-called demon possession. *Journal of Abnormal Psychology, 6*, 265–278.

McAdams, D. P. (1996). Personality, modernity, and the storied self: A contemporary framework for studying persons. *Psychological Inquiry, 7*, 295–321.

McAllister, T. W., & Price, T. R. P. (1987). Aspects of the behavior of psychiatric in-patients with frontal lobe damage: Some implications for diagnosis and treatment. *Comprehensive Psychiatry, 28*, 14–21.

McCauley, R. N., & Lawson, E. T. (2002). *Bringing ritual to mind: Psychological foundations of religious forms.* Cambridge: Cambridge University Press.

McClenon, J. (2006). The ritual healing theory: Therapeutic suggestion and the origin of religion. In P. McNamara (Ed.), *Where God and science meet: How brain and evolutionary studies alter our understanding of religion: Vol. 1: Evolution, genes, and the religious brain* (pp. 135–158). Westport, CT, and London: Praeger Publishers.

McCord, J. (1983). A forty year perspective on effects of child abuse and neglect. *Child Abuse and Neglect, 7,* 265–270.

McCullough, M. E., & Willoughby, B. L. B. (2009). Religion, self-regulation, and self-control: Associations, explanations, and implications. *Psychological Bulletin, 135,* 69–93.

McGinn, B. (1994). *Antichrist: Two thousand years of the human fascination with evil.* San Francisco: Harper Books.

McNamara, P. (2002). *The frontal lobes, social intelligence, and religious worship. Ideas for creative research in neurobiology.* The John Templeton Foundation, West Conshohocken, PA (pp. 50–59).

McNamara, P. (2004). Genomic imprinting and neurodevelopmental disorders of sleep. *Sleep and Hypnosis, 6*(2), 100–108.

McNamara, P., McLaren, D., Smith, D., Brown, A., & Stickgold, R. (2005). A "Jekyll and Hyde" within: Aggressive versus friendly social interactions in REM and NREM dreams. *Psychological Science, 16*(2), 130–136.

McNamara, P., von Harscher, H., Scioli, T., Krueger, M., Lawson, D., & Durso, R. (1995). The sense of self after brain damage: Evidence from aphasics and individuals with Parkinson's disease. *Journal of Cognitive Rehabilitation, November/December,* 16–23.

McNamara, P., & Wildman, W. J. (In preparation). On religious consciousness. *Journal of Consciousness Studies.*

Metzinger, T. (2003). *Being no one: The self-model theory of subjectivity.* Cambridge, MA: The MIT Press.

Metzinger, T. (2006). Conscious volition and mental representation: Towards a more fine-grained analysis. In N. Sebanz & W. Prinz (Eds.), *Disorders of volition.* Cambridge, MA: The MIT Press.

Migliorelli, R., Starkstein, S. E., Teson, A., de Quiros, G., Vazquez, S., Leiguarda, R., et al. (1993). SPECT findings in patients with primary mania. *Journal of Neuropsychiatry and Clinical Neurosciences, 5,* 379–383.

Millan, M. J., Lejeune, F., & Gobert, A. (2000). Reciprocal autoreceptor and heteroreceptor control of serotonergic, dopaminergic, and noradrenergic transmission in the frontal cortex: Relevance to the actions of antidepressant agents. *Journal of Psychopharmacology, 14*, 114–138.

Miller, B., Seeley, W. W., Mychack, P., Rosen, H. J., Mena, I., & Boone, K. (2001). Neuroanatomy of the self: Evidence from patients with frontotemporal dementia. *Neurology, 57*(1), 817–821.

Miller, B. L., & Cummings, J. L. (Eds.). (2007). *The human frontal lobes: Functions and disorders*. New York: The Guilford Press.

Miller, B. L., Ikonte, C., Ponton, M., Levy, M., Boone, K., Darby, A., et al. (1997). A study of the Lund-Manchester research criteria for frontotemporal dementia: Clinical and single photon emission CT correlations. *Neurology, 48*, 937–942.

Miller, K. (1987). *Doubles: Studies in literary history*. Oxford: Oxford University Press.

Mills, S., & Raine, A. (1994). Brain imaging and violence. *Journal of Offender Rehabilitation, 21*, 145–158.

Mohr, S., Brandt, P. Y., Borras, L., Gilliéron, C., & Huguelet, P. (2006). Toward an integration of spirituality and religiousness into the psychosocial dimension of schizophrenia. *American Journal of Psychiatry, 163*(11), 1952–1959.

Mumford, L. (1966). *The myth of the machine: Technics and human development*. New York: Harcourt Brace and World, Inc.

Mummery, C. J., Patterson, K., Wise, R. J. S., Vandenberghe, R., Price, C. J., & Hodges, J. R. (1999). Disrupted temporal lobe connections in semantic dementia. *Brain, 122*, 61–73.

Murdock, G. P. (1965). *Culture and society*. Pittsburgh, PA: University of Pittsburgh Press.

Murdock, G. P., & White, D. R. (1969). Standard cross-cultural sample. *Ethnology, 8*, 329–369.

Napier, D. A. (1986). *Masks, transformation, and paradox*. Berkeley: University of California Press.

National Center on Addiction and Substance Abuse (NCASA) (2001). *So help me God: Substance abuse, religion, and spirituality*. New York: Columbia University.

Nauta, W. J. (1962). Neural associations of the amygdaloid complex in the monkey. *Brain, 85*, 505–520.

Neary, D., Snowden, J. S., Gustafson, L., Passant, U., Stuss, D., Black, S., et al. (1998). Frontotemporal lobar degeneration: A consensus on clinical diagnostic criteria. *Neurology, 51*(6), 1546–1554.

Newberg, A., Alavi, A., Baime, M., Pourdehnad, M., Santanna, J., & d'Aquili, E. (2001). The measurement of regional cerebral blood flow during the complex cognitive task of meditation: A preliminary SPECT study. *Psychiatry Research, 106*, 113–122.

Newberg, A., Pourdehnad, M., Alavi, A., & d'Aquili, E. G. (2003). Cerebral blood flow during meditative prayer: Preliminary findings and methodological issues. *Perceptual Motor Skills, 97*, 625–630.

Newberg, A. B., Wintering, N. A., Morgan, D., & Waldman, M. R. (2006). The measurement of regional cerebral blood flow during glossolalia: A preliminary SPECT study. *Psychiatry Research: Neuroimaging, 148*, 67–71.

Ng, B.-Y. (2000). Phenomenology of trance states seen at a psychiatric hospital in Singapore: A cross-cultural perspective. *Transcultural Psychiatry, 37*(4), 560–579.

Ng, B.-Y., & Chan, Y.-H. (2004). Psychosocial stressors that precipitate dissociative trance disorder in Singapore. *Australian and New Zealand Journal of Psychiatry, 38*, 426–432.

Nichols, D. E. (2004). Hallucinogens. *Pharmacology and Therapeutics, 101*, 131–181.

Nichols, D. E., & Chemel, B. R. (2006). The neuropharmacology of religious experience: Hallucinogens and the experience of the divine. In P. McNamara (Ed.), *Where God and science meet: How brain and evolutionary studies alter our understanding of religion* (Vol. 3, pp. 1–33). Westport, CT, and London: Praeger Publishers.

Nichols, S., & Stich, S. (2000). A cognitive theory of pretense. *Cognition, 74*(2), 115–147.

Norman, C. C., & Aron, A. (2003). Aspects of possible self that predict motivation to achieve or avoid it. *Journal of Experimental Social Psychology, 39*, 500–507.

Northoff, G., & Bermpohl, F. (2004). Cortical midline structures and the self. *Trends in Cognitive Sciences, 8*, 102–110.

Nyberg, L., McIntosh, A. R., Cabeza, R., Nilsson, L. G., Houle, S., Habib, R., et al. (1996). Network analysis of positron emission tomography regional cerebral blood flow data: Ensemble inhibition during episodic memory retrieval. *Journal of Neuroscience, 16*(11), 3753–3759.

O'Brien, M. J., Darwent, J., & Lyman, R. L. (2001). Cladistics is useful for reconstructing archaeological phylogenies: Palaeoindian points from the Southeastern United States. *Journal of Archeological Science, 28*(10), 1115–1136.

O'Brien, M. J., & Lyman, R. L. (2000). *Applying evolutionary archaeology: A systematic approach*. London: Kluwer Academic/Plenum.

O'Brien, M. J., Lyman, R. L., Saab, Y., Saab, E., Darwent, J., & Glover, D. S. (2002). Two issues in archaeological phylogenetics: Taxon construction and outgroup selection. *Journal of Theoretical Biology, 215*(2), 133–150.

Oatley, K. (2007). Narrative modes of consciousness and selfhood. In P. D. Zelazo, M. Moscovitch, & E. Thompson (Eds.), *The Cambridge handbook of consciousness* (pp. 375–402). New York: Cambridge University Press.

Obeyesekere, G. (1977). Psychocultural exegesis of a case of spirit possession in Sri Lanka. In V. Crapanzano & V. Garrison (Eds.), *Case studies in spirit possession* (pp. 235–294). New York: John Wiley.

Oesterreich, T. K. (1966). *Possession: Demoniacal and other among primitive races, in antiquity, the middle ages, and modern times.* (D. Ibberson, Trans.). New Hyde Park, NY: University Books. (Original work published 1921.)

Ogata, A., & Miyakawa, T. (1998). Religious experiences in epileptic patients with a focus on ictus-related episodes. *Psychiatry and Clinical Neurosciences, 52,* 321–325.

Ongur, D., & Price, J. L. (2000). The organization of networks within the orbital and medial prefrontal cortex of rats, monkeys and humans. *Cerebral Cortex, 10,* 206–219.

Oscar-Berman, M., McNamara, P., & Freedman, M. (1991). Delayed-response tasks: Parallels between experimental ablation studies and findings in patients with frontal lesions. In H. S. Levin, H. M. Eisenberg, & A. L. Benton (Eds.), *Frontal lobe function and dysfunction* (pp. 230–255). New York: Oxford University Press.

Oser, F., & Reich, H. (1990a). Moral judgment, religious judgment, world view and logical thought: A review of their relationship. Part One. *British Journal of Religious Education, 12*(2), 94–101.

Oser, F., & Reich, H. (1990b). Moral judgment, religious judgment, world view and logical thought: A review of their relationship. Part Two. *British Journal of Religious Education, 12*(3), 172–181.

Ott, U., Reuter, M., Hennig, J., & Vaitl, D. (2005). Evidence for the common biological basis of the absorption trait, hallucinogen effects, and positive symptoms: Epistasis between 5-HT2A and COMT polymorphisms. *American Journal of Medical Genetics Part B, 137B,* 29–32.

Oyserman, D., Bybee, D., Terry, K., & Hart-Johnson, T. (2004). Possible selves as roadmaps. *Journal of Research in Personality, 38,* 130–149.

Pahnke, W. (1967). LSD and religious experience. Paper presented to a public symposium at Wesleyan University, March 1967. R. C. DeBold & R. C. Leaf (Eds.), LSD, man & society. http://www.druglibrary.org/schaffer/LSD/pahnke3.htm (accessed November 14, 2008).

Passingham, R. E. (1995). *The frontal lobes and voluntary action.* New York: Oxford University Press.

Paus, T., Collins, D. L., Evans, A. C., Leonard, G., Pike, B., & Zijdenbos, A. (2001). Maturation of white matter in the human brain: A review of magnetic resonance studies. *Brain Research Bulletin, 54,* 255–266.

Peck, M. S. (2005). *Glimpses of the devil: A psychiatrist's personal accounts of possession, exorcism, and redemption.* New York: Free Press.

Pekala, R. J. (1991). *The phenomenology of conscious inventory (PCI).* West Chester, PA: Mid-Atlantic Educational Institute. (Original work published 1982.)

Persinger, M. A. (1983). Religious and mystical experiences as artifacts of temporal lobe function: A general hypothesis. *Perceptual and Motor Skills, 57,* 1255–1262.

Persinger, M. A. (1987). *Neuropsychological bases of God beliefs.* New York: Praeger Publishers.

Polimeni, J., & Reiss, J. P. (2003). Evolutionary perspectives on schizophrenia. *Canadian Journal of Psychiatry, 48,* 34–39.

Propp, V. (1968). *Morphology of the folktale* (L. Scott, Trans.). Austin: University of Texas Press. (Original work published 1927.)

Puri, B. K., Lekh, S. K., Nijran, K. S., Bagary, M. S., & Richardson, A. J. (2001). SPECT neuroimaging in schizophrenia with religious delusions. *International Journal of Psychophysiology, 40,* 143–148.

Putnam, F. W. (1988). The switch process in multiple personality disorder and other state-change disorders. *Dissociation, 1*(1), 24–32.

Pyysiäinen, I. (2003). True fiction: Philosophy and psychology of religious belief. *Philosophical Psychology, 16*(1), 109–125.

Pyysiäinen, I. (2004). *Magic, miracles, and religion: A scientist's perspective.* Walnut Creek, CA: AltaMira Press.

Rabbit, P. (1997). Introduction: Methodologies and models in the study of executive function. In P. Rabbit (Ed.), *Methodology of frontal and executive function* (pp. 1–38). New York: Psychology Press.

Raine, A., Buchsbaum, M. S., Stanley, J., & Lottenberg, S. (1994). Selective reductions in prefrontal glucose metabolism in murderers. *Biological Psychiatry, 36,* 365–373.

Rakic, P. (1995). A small step for the cell, a giant leap for mankind: a hypothesis of neocortical expansion during evolution. *Trends in Neurosciences, 18*(9), 383–388.

Ramachandran, V. S., & Blakeslee, S. (1998). *Phantoms in the brain: Probing the mysteries of the human mind.* New York: William Morrow.

Ramachandran, V. S., Hirstein, W. S., Armel, K. C., Tecoma, E., & Iragui, V. (October 25–30, 1997). The neural basis of religious experience. New Orleans, LA: 27th Annual Meeting. *Society for Neuroscience Abstracts, 23,* 519.1.

Rankin, K. P. (2006). Social cognition in frontal injury. In B. L. Miller & J. L. Cummings (Eds.), *The human frontal lobes: Functions and disorders* (2nd ed., pp. 345–360). New York: The Guilford Press.

Rappaport, R. (1989). Ritual. In E. Barnouw (Ed.), *International encyclopedia of communications* (Vol. 3, pp. 467–472). New York: Oxford University Press.

Rappaport, R. A. (1999). *Ritual and religion in the making of humanity*. New York: Cambridge University Press.

Regnerus, M. D. (2007). *Forbidden fruit: Sex and religion in the lives of American teenagers*. New York: Oxford University Press.

Resnick, J., Stickgold, R., Rittenhouse, C., & Hobson, J. A. (1994). Self-representation and bizarreness in children's dream reports collected in the home setting. *Consciousness and Cognition, 3*, 30–45.

Ricoeur, P. (1984). *Time and narrative*. Vol. I. Chicago: University of Chicago Press.

Ricoeur, P. (1992). *Oneself as another* (K. Blamey, Trans.). Chicago: University of Chicago Press. (Original work published 1990.)

Rizzuto, A.-M. (1991). Religious development: A psychoanalytic point of view. In F. K. Oser & W. G. Scarlett (Eds.), *Religious development in childhood and adolescence* (pp. 47–60). San Francisco: Jossey-Bass.

Robbins, J. (2003). Dreaming and the defeat of charisma: Disconnecting dreams from leadership among the Urapmin of Papua New Guinea. In R. I. Lohmann (Ed.), *Dream travelers: Sleep experiences and culture in the Western Pacific* (pp. 18–41). New York: Palgrave Macmillan.

Roberts, J. K. A., & Guberman, A. (1989). Religion and epilepsy. *Psychiatric Journal of the University of Ottawa: Revue de psychiatrie de l'Universitie d'Ottawa, 14*(1), 282–286.

Rolls, E. T. (2004). The functions of the orbitofrontal cortex. *Brain and Cognition, 55*, 11–29.

Rosen, H. J., Perry, R. J., Murphy, J., Kramer, J. H., Mychack, P., Schuff, N., et al. (2002). Emotion comprehension in the temporal variant of frontotemporal dementia. *Brain, 125*(10), 2286–2295.

Rosengren, K., Johnson, C., & Harris, P. L. (2000). *Imagining the impossible: The development of magical, scientific, and religious thinking in contemporary society*. New York: Cambridge University Press.

Samango-Sprouse, C. (1999). Frontal lobe development in childhood. In B. L. Miller & J. L. Cummings (Eds.), *The human frontal lobes: Functions and disorders* (pp. 584–604). New York: The Guilford Press.

Sameroff, A. J., & Haith, M. M. (Eds.). (1996). *The five to seven year shift: The age of reason and responsibility*. Chicago: University of Chicago Press.

Saver, J. L., & Rabin, J. (1997). The neural substrates of religious experience. *Journal of Neuropsychiatry and Clinical Neurosciences, 9*(3), 498–510.

Savitz, J., Solms, M., Pietersen, E., Ramesar, R., & Flor-Henry, P. (2004). Dissociative identity disorder associated with mania and changes in handedness. *Cognitive and Behavioral Neurology, 17,* 233–237.

Schaefer, S. B., & Furst, P. T. (1997). *People of the Peyote: Huichol Indian history, religion, and survival.* Albuquerque, NM: University of New Mexico Press.

Schectman, M. (1996). *The constitution of selves.* Ithaca, NY: Cornell University Press.

Schjødt, U., Geertz, A., Stødkild-Jørgensen, H., & Roepstorff, A. (2009, forthcoming). Highly religious participants recruit areas of social cognition in personal prayer. *Social Cognitive and Affective Neuroscience.*

Schjødt, U., Stødkild-Jørgensen, H., Geertz, A. W., & Roepstorff, A. (2008). Rewarding prayers. *Neuroscience Letters, 443*(3), 165–168.

Schlegel, A., & Barry, H., III. (1991). *Adolescence: An anthropological inquiry.* New York: Free Press.

Schmeltzer, G. (2002). The effectiveness of a meditation group on the self-control of adolescent boys in a secure juvenile detention center. Unpublished doctoral dissertation, Northeastern University, Boston.

Schneider, A., & Domhoff, G. W. (1999). DreamBank. http://www.dreambank.net (accessed October 19, 2008).

Schnider, A., & Gutbrod, K. (1999). Traumatic brain injury. In B. L. Miller & J. L. Cummings (Eds.), *The human frontal lobes: Functions and disorders* (pp. 487–508). New York: The Guilford Press.

Scholem, G. (1941). *Major trends in Jewish mysticism.* Berlin: Schocken Books.

Schultz, W., Romo, R., Ljungberg, J., Mirenowicz, J., Hollerman, J., & Dickinson, A. (1995). Reward-related signals carried by dopamine neurons. In J. Houk, J. Davis, & D. Beiser (Eds.), *Models of information processing in the basal ganglia* (pp. 233–248). Cambridge, MA: The MIT Press.

Schweder, R. A. (1982). Beyond self-constructed knowledge: The study of culture and morality. *Merrill-Palmer Quarterly, 28,* 41–69.

Schweder, R. A., & LeVine, R. A. (1975). Dream concepts of Hausa children: A critique of the "Doctrine of Invariant Sequence" in cognitive development. *Ethos, 3*(2), 209–230.

Seaquist, C. (2006). Mind design and the capacity for ritual performance. In P. McNamara (Ed.), *Where God and science meet: How brain and evolutionary studies alter our understanding of religion: Vol. 2: The neurology of religious experience* (pp. 205–227). Westport, CT, and London: Praeger Publishers.

Sebanz, N., & Prinz, W. (Eds.). (2006). *Disorders of volition*. Cambridge, MA: The MIT Press.

Seeley, W. W., & Sturm, V. E. (2007). Self-representation and the frontal lobes. In B. L. Miller & J. L. Cummings (Eds.), *The human frontal lobes: Functions and disorders* (pp. 317–334). New York: The Guilford Press.

Sellen, D. W., & Smay, D. B. (2001). Relationship between subsistence and age at weaning in "preindustrial" societies. *Human Nature, 12*, 47–87.

Serafetinides, E. A. (1965). The EEG effects of LSD-25 in epileptic patients before and after temporal lobectomy. *Psychopharmacologia, 7*(6), 453–460.

Shallice, T., & Burgess, P. W. (1991) Higher-order cognitive impairments and frontal lobe lesions in man. In H. S. Levin, H. M. Eisenberg, & A. L. Benton (Eds.), *Frontal lobe function and dysfunction* (pp. 125–138). New York: Oxford University Press.

Shaw, R. (1992). Dreaming as accomplishment: Power, the individual and Temne divination. In M. C. Jedrej & R. Shaw (Eds.), *Dreaming, religion and society in Africa* (pp. 36–54). Leiden, The Netherlands: E. J. Brill.

Shennan, S. (2002). *Genes, memes and human history*. London: Thames & Hudson.

Shennan, S. J., & Wilkinson, J. R. (2001). Ceramic style change and neutral evolution: A case study from neolithic Europe. *American Antiquity, 66*, 577–593.

Shenton, M. A., Kikinis, R., Jolesz, F. A., Pollak, S. D., LeMay, M., Wible, C. G., et al. (1992). Abnormalities of the left temporal lobe and thought disorder in schizophrenia: A quantitative magnetic resonance imagery study. *The New England Journal of Medicine, 327*, 604–612.

Siddle, R., Haddock, G., Tarrier, N., & Garagher, E. B. (2002). Religious delusions in patients admitted to hospital with schizophrenia. *Social Psychiatry and Psychiatric Epidemiology, 37*(3), 130–138.

Skorecki, K., Selig, S., Blazer, S., Bradman, R., Bradman, N., Warburton, P. J., et al. (1997). Y chromosomes of Jewish priests. *Nature, 385*, 32.

Smith, C. (2003). Theorizing religious effects among American adolescents. *Journal for the Scientific Study of Religion, 42*, 17–30.

Smith, S., Arnett, P., & Newman, J. (1992). Neuropsychological differentiation of psychopathic and nonpsychopathic criminal offenders. *Personality and Individual Differences, 13*, 1233–1243.

Somer, E., & Saadon, M. (2000). Stambali: Dissociative possession and trance in a Tunisian healing dance. *Transcultural Psychiatry, 37*(4), 580–599.

Sorabji, R. (2006). *Ancient and modern insights about individuality, life and death*. Chicago: University of Chicago Press.

Sosis, R. (2006). Religious behaviors, badges, and bans: Signaling theory and the evolution of religion. In P. McNamara (Ed.), *Where God and science meet: How brain and evolutionary sciences alter our understanding of religion, Vol. I: Evolutionary approaches* (pp. 61–86). Westport, CT: Praeger Publishers.

Sowell, E. R., Thompson, P. M., Tessner, K. D., & Toga, A. W. (2001). Mapping continued brain growth and gray matter density reduction in dorsal frontal cortex: Inverse relationships during postadolescent brain maturation. *Journal of Neuroscience, 21*(22), 8819–8829.

Sperry, R. W. (1974). Lateral specialization in the surgically separated hemispheres. In F. O. Schmitt & F. G. Worden (Eds.), *The neurosciences: Third study program* (p. 5). Cambridge, MA: The MIT Press.

Spreng, R. N., Mar, R. A., & Kim, A. S. N. (2009). The common neural basis of autobiographical memory, prospection, navigation, theory of mind and the default mode: A quantitative meta-analysis. *Journal of Cognitive Neuroscience, 21*, 489–510.

Starkstein, S. E., & Merello, M. (2002). *Psychiatric and cognitive disorders in Parkinson's disease.* Cambridge: Cambridge University Press.

Starkstein, S. E., & Robinson, R. G. (1991). Dementia of depression in Parkinson's disease and stroke. *Journal of Nervous and Mental Disease, 179*(10), 593–601.

Starkstein, S. E., & Robinson, R. G. (1997). Mechanism of disinhibition after brain lesion. *Journal of Nervous and Mental Disease, 185*(2), 108–114.

Starkstein, S. E., & Robinson, R. G. (1999). Depression and frontal lobe disorders. In B. L. Miller and J. L. Cummings (Eds.), *The human frontal lobes: Functions and disorders* (pp. 537–546). New York: The Guilford Press.

Steadman, L. B., & Palmer, C. T. (2008). *The supernatural and natural selection: The evolution of religion.* Boulder, CO, and London: Paradigm Publishers.

Steketee, G., Quay, S., & White, K. (1991). Religion and guilt in OCD patients. *Journal of Anxiety Disorders, 5*, 359–367.

Sterelny, K. (2004). Externalism, epistemic artefacts and the extended mind. In R. Schantz (Ed.), *The externalist challenge. New studies on cognition and intentionality* (pp. 239–254). Berlin and New York: De Gruyter.

Stevens, A., & Price, J. (1996). *Evolutionary psychiatry: A new beginning.* London: Routledge.

Stigby, B., Rodenberg, J. C., & Moth, H. B. (1981). Electroencephalographic findings during mantra meditation (transcendental meditation). A controlled, quantitative study of experienced meditators. *Electroencephalography and Clinical Neurophysiology, 51*(4), 434–442.

Stout, D. (2002). Skill and cognition in stone tool production: An ethnographic case study from Irian Jaya. *Current Anthropology, 43*(5), 693–722.

Strauch, I. (2005). REM dreaming in the transition from late childhood to adolescence: A longitudinal study. *Dreaming, 15*, 155–169.

Suddath, R. L., Casanova, M. F., Goldberg, T. E., Daniel, D. G., Kelsoe, J. R., & Weinberger, D. R. (1989). Temporal lobe pathology in schizophrenia: A quantitative magnetic resonance imaging study. *American Journal of Psychiatry, 146*, 464–472.

Sviri, S. (2002). The self and its transformation in Sūfīsm. In D. Shulman & G. G. Stroumsa (Eds.), *Self and self-transformation in the history of religions* (pp. 195–215). New York: Oxford University Press.

Tambiah, S. (1979). A performative approach to ritual. *Proceedings of the British Academy, 65*, 113–169.

Tamminen, K. (1991). *Religious development in childhood and youth: An empirical study*. Helsinki: Suomalainen Tiedeakatemia.

Taupin, P., & Gage, F. H. (2002). Adult neurogenesis and neural stem cells of the central nervous system in mammals. *Journal of Neuroscience Research, 69*, 745–749.

Tebēcis, A. K. (1975). A controlled study of the EEG during transcendental meditation: Comparison with hypnosis. *Folia Psychiatrica et Neurologica Japonica, 29*(4), 305–313.

Tedlock, B. (Ed.). (1987). *Dreaming: Anthropological and psychological interpretations*. Cambridge: Cambridge University Press.

Tek, C., & Ulug, B. (2001). Religiosity and religious obsessions in obsessive-compulsive disorder. *Psychiatry Research, 104*(2), 99–108.

Todd, J., & Dewhurst, K. (1955). The double: Its psycho-pathology and psycho-physiology. *The Journal of Nervous and Mental Disease, 122*, 47–77.

Tomic, M., & Joksimovic, J. (2000). Psychomimetics moderately affect dopamine receptor binding in the rat brain. *Neurochemistry International, 36*(2), 137–142.

Tonkinson, R. (1974). *The Jigalong mob: Aboriginal victors of the desert crusade*. Menlo Park: Cummings.

Trimble, M., & Freeman, A. (2006). An investigation of religiosity and the Gastaut-Geschwind syndrome in patients with temporal lobe epilepsy. *Epilepsy and Behavior, 9*(3), 407–414.

Trimble, M. R. (2007). *The soul in the brain: The cerebral basis of language, art, and belief*. Baltimore, MD: Johns Hopkins Press.

Troster, A. I., & Woods, S. P. (2003). Neuropsychological aspects of Parkinson's disease and parkinsonian syndromes. In R. Pahwa, K. E. Lyons, & W. C. Koller (Eds.), *Handbook of Parkinson's disease* (pp. 127–157). New York: Dekker.

Tucker, D. M., Novelly, R. A., & Walker, P. J. (1987). Hyperreligiosity in temporal lobe epilepsy: Redefining the relationship. *The Journal of Nervous and Mental Disease, 175*(3), 181–184.

Tucker, D. M., & Williamson, P. A. (1984). Asymmetric neural control systems in human self-regulation. *Psychological Review, 91*(2), 185–215.

Tycko, B., & Morison, I. M. (2002). Physiological functions of imprinted genes. *Journal of Cellular Physiology, 192*(3), 245–258.

Tzu, C. (1965). *The way of Chuang Tzu* (Thomas Merton, Trans./Ed.). New York: New Directions Publishing Corporation.

Uddin, L. Q., Iacoboni, M., Lange, C., & Keenan, J. P. (2007). The self and social cognition: The role of cortical midline structures and mirror neurons. *Trends in Cognitive Sciences, 11*(4), 153–157.

Unger, S. M. (1965). The current status of psychotherapeutically-oriented LSD research in the United States. Unpublished paper read to the New York State Psychological Association on April 30, 1965. In LSD and religious experience. Paper presented to a public symposium at Wesleyan University, March 1967. In R. C. DeBold & R. C. Leaf (Eds.), *LSD, man & society*. http://www.druglibrary.org/schaffer/LSD/pahnke3.htm (accessed November 14, 2008).

Van de Castle, R. (1994). *Our dreaming mind*. New York: Ballantine Books.

van Der Hart, O., Witztum, E., & Friedman, B. (1993). From hysterical psychosis to reactive dissociative psychosis. *Journal of Traumatic Stress, 6*, 1–13.

Van Hoesen, G. W. (1981). The differential distribution, diversity and sprouting of cortical projections to the amygdale in the rhesus monkey. In Y. Ben-Ari (Ed.), *The amygdaloid complex: INSERM symposium no. 20* (pp. 77–90). New York: Elsevier/North Holland Biomedical Press.

Vogeley, K., & Fink, G. R. (2003). Neural correlates of first-person-perspective. *Trends in Cognitive Sciences, 7*, 38–42.

Vogeley, K., Kurthen, M., Falkai, P., & Maier, W. (1999). Essential functions of the human self model are implemented in the prefrontal cortex. *Conscious and Cognition, 8*(3), 343–363.

Vollenweider, F. X. (1998). Advances and pathophysiological models of hallucinogenic drug actions in humans: A preamble to schizophrenia research. *Pharmacopsychiatry, 31*(Suppl. 2), 92–103.

von Balthasar, H. (1997). *Tragedy under grace*. San Francisco: Ignatius Press.

Wang, P. N., & Miller, B. L. (2007). Clinical aspects of frontotemporal dementia. In B. Miller & J. Cummings (Eds.), *The human frontal lobes: Functions and disorders* (pp. 365–381). New York: The Guilford Press.

Ward, C. A., & Beaubrun, M. H. (1980). The psychodynamics of demon possession. *Journal for the Scientific Study of Religion, 19,* 201–207.

Waterlow, J. C., Ashworth, A., & Griffiths, M. (1980). Faltering in infant growth in less developed countries. *Lancet, 2,* 1176–1178.

Watson, P. J., Hood, R. W., Morris, R. J., & Hall, J. R. (1984). Empathy, religious orientation, and social desirability. *Journal of Psychology, 117,* 211–216.

Waxman, S. G., & Geschwind, N. (1975). The interictal behavior syndrome of temporal lobe epilepsy. *Archives of General Psychiatry, 32*(12), 1580–1586.

Weaver, A. J., Kline, A. E., Samford, J. A., Lucas, L. A., Larson, D. B., & Gorsuch, R. L. (1998). Is religion taboo in psychology? A systematic analysis of research on religion in seven major American Psychological Association journals: 1991–1994. *Journal of Psychology and Christianity, 17,* 220–232.

Weinberger, D. R. (1986). The pathogenesis of schizophrenia: A neurodevelopmental theory. In H. A. W. Nasrallah & D. R. Weinberger (Eds.), *The neurology of schizophrenia* (pp. 397–406). Amsterdam: Elsevier.

Werlen, I. (1984). *Ritual und sprache.* Tübingen: Gunter Narr.

Wheeler, M. A., Stuss, D. T., & Tulving, E. (1997). Toward a theory of episodic memory: The frontal lobes and autonoetic consciousness. *Psychological Bulletin, 121*(3), 331–354.

Whitehouse, H. (2002). Modes of religiosity: A cognitive explanation of the sociopolitical dynamics of religion. *Method and Theory in the Study of Religion, 14,* 293–315.

Whitehouse, H. (2004). *Modes of religiosity: A cognitive theory of religious transmission.* Walnut Creek, CA: AltaMira Press.

Whitty, M. (2002). Possible selves: An exploration of the utility of a narrative approach. *Identity: An International Journal of Theory and Research, 2,* 211–228.

Wildman, W., & McNamara, P. (2008). Challenges facing the neurological study of religious behavior, belief and experience. *Method and Theory in the Study of Religion, 20,* 212–242.

Wildman, W. J. (2002). Consciousness expanded. In S. Menon, A. Sinha, & B. V. Sreekantan (Eds.), *Science and metaphysics: A discussion on consciousness and genetics* (pp. 125–141). Bangalore: National Institute of Advanced Studies.

Wildman, W. J., & Brothers, L. A. (1999). A neuropsychological-semiotic model of religious experiences. In R. J. Russell, N. Murphy, T. C. Meyering, & M. Arbib (Eds.), *Neuroscience and the person* (pp. 347–418). Berkeley, CA: Center for Theology and the Natural Sciences.

Wilson, W. P. (1998). Religion and psychoses. In H. Koenig (Ed.), *Handbook of religion and mental health* (pp. 161–174). San Diego: Academic Press.

Winikoff, B., Durongdej, S., & Cerf, B. (1988). Infant feeding in Bangkok, Thailand. In B. Winikoff, M. A. Castle, & V. H. Laukaran (Eds.), *Feeding infants in four societies: Causes and consequences of mother's choices* (pp. 15–42). New York: Greenwood Press.

Winstanley, C. A., Theobald, D. E. H., Dalley, J. W., Cardinal, R. N., & Robbins, T. W. (2006). Double dissociation between serotonergic and dopaminergic modulation of medial prefrontal and orbitofrontal cortex during a test of impulsive choice. *Cerebral Cortex, 16*, 106–114.

Wise, R. A. (2005). Forebrain substrates of reward and motivation. *Journal of Comparative Neurology, 493*, 115–121.

Wise, R. A., & Bozarth, M. A. (1987). A psychomotor stimulant theory of addiction. *Psychological Review, 94*, 469–492.

Worden, R. (1998). The evolution of language from social intelligence. In J. R. Hurford, M. Studdert-Kennedy, & C. Knight (Eds.), *Approaches to the evolution of language: Social and cognitive bases* (pp. 148–169). Cambridge: Cambridge University Press.

Worthington, E. L., Kurusu, T. A., McCullough, M. E., & Sandage, S. J. (1996). Empirical research on religion and psychotherapeutic processes and outcomes: A 10-year review and research prospectus. *Psychological Bulletin, 119*(3), 448–487.

Wuerfel, J., Krishnamoorthy, E. S., Brown, R. C., Lemieux, L., Koepp, M., Tebartz van Elst, L., et al. (2004). Religiosity is associated with hippocampal but not amygdala volumes in patients with refractory epilepsy. *Journal of Neurology, Neurosurgery, and Psychiatry, 75*, 640–642.

Index

Aaron, the brother of Moses, 227
Abua tribal peoples. *See* possession,
    spirit possession; masking
    rituals and; sacredness of mask
    makers
Acheulean tradition. *See* ritual, tools
adolescence
  development of cognitive functions,
    243–244
  development of frontal and temporal
    lobes, 242
  religiosity, 242
agency. *See* Self, agency
  hyper-active agency detection device,
    194. *See also* God concepts
agent
  full strategic access, 194
  intellect, 24, 40–43
    and the executive Self, 41
  supernatural, 193. *See also* dream
    characteristics
akrasia, 22, 43, 74
Al-Balkhi, Shaqiq. *See* Islamic mystical
    practices
alien hand syndrome. *See* Self,
    breakdown of the exectuive
    Self
Al-Tirmidhi, Al-Hakim. *See* Islamic
    mystical practices
amygdala, 64

as part of the mesocortical system,
    157
connections of the, 127–128
disorders enhancing religious
    experience and, 106
glossolalia and, 125
hallucinogens and, 134
in neurochemistry of frontal lobes,
    141
meditation and, 126
neuroimaging of religion and, 108
regulation of emotion, 128
religious expression and, 127
role in frontotemporal dementia, 102
role in religiosity, 90, 94, 105, 127,
    233
role in Temporal Lobe Epilepsy (TLE),
    91, 93, 97
schizophrenia and, 96
ancestor worship, 226
Andalusia, 7
Andamanese. *See* possession, the
    double, immortal soul
Anneliese, Michel. *See The Exorcism of*
    Emily Rose
anterior cingulate, AC, 61
  supragenual part, SAC, 61
anterior temporal cortex, 60, 61
  executive role of the, 62. *See also*
    prefrontal cortex

32503094R00178

Made in the USA
San Bernardino, CA
07 April 2016